The Heart Will Find a Way

The Heart Will Find a Way

Stories of heartache, heartbreak and heartbalm

Edited by
Anjanette Fennell

with
Anne-marie Taplin and Megan Close Zavala

southern key
PRESS

Copyright © 2024 Southern Key Press

All rights reserved.

No part of this book may be reproduced in any form or by any electronic or mechanical means, including information storage and retrieval systems, without written permission from the author of the piece, except for the use of brief quotations in a book review. Any enquiries should be addressed to Southern Key Press at southernkeypress@gmail.com

Cover Design by Iqra Qutub

Interior Design by Brad Fennell

ISBN: 978-0-6455648-7-7 (print)

ISBN: 978-0-6455648-8-4 (ebook)

Contents

Introduction	xi
1. Heart (Beating its) Message *by Anjanette Fennell*	1
2. Wellspring *by Corinne Beinke*	6
3. Pippa's Legacy *by Sara Foster*	14
4. The Shearer *by Maura Pierlot*	20
5. Pull and Whoosh *by Anna Hayes*	26
6. The Living List *by Mercedes Mercier*	32
7. Death and the Art of Living *by Nina D Campbell*	39
8. Gertie Up at the Grand *by Athena Law*	45
9. Feathers Like Fingerprints *By Linda Brucesmith*	52
10. Howzat! *by Angelina Hurley*	61
11. Morning Rays *by Melissa A Kitchen*	69
12. Must Save the World Before Breakfast *by Daan Spijer*	74
13. Love the World, Again *by Catherine Edwards*	84
14. It's Been a Year *by Emma Grey*	89
15. Day 120 *by Raabia Qadir*	92
16. Esmerelda's Heartfelt Christmas *by Lisa Heidke*	98

17. Millefiori *by Amanda Beckett*	116
18. Losing Harry *By Anne-marie Taplin*	123
19. Songs of Yesterday's Tomorrows *by Samara Lo*	136
20. A Mother's Love Letter *by Anita East*	142
21. Delivery *by Andrea McMahon*	156
22. The Women in White *by Sky Harrison*	164
23. Not for This World *by Pat Saunders*	174
24. Sky Chase *by Nina Cullen*	185
25. Building Something New *by Ruth Morgan*	191
26. Sisters at Heart *by Juliet Madison*	198
27. Wallaby *by Vanessa Hardy*	206
28. Palimpsest *by RS Morgan*	213
29. Yiayia's Doesn Madder Policy *by Katherine Lykos*	220
30. A Winter's Warmth *by Darry Fraser*	226
31. Feeling My Way *by Monique Mulligan*	240
32. A Lesson in Loss *by Teena Raffa-Mulligan*	250
33. Facing Our Fears *by Zibby Owens*	256
34. The Moment I Knew (Again) *by Kylie Ladd*	261
35. How to Mend a Broken Heart *by Rachael Robertson*	264
36. Maurice *by Helen Auld*	271

37. Miss Tilly's Story *by AL Maze*	280
38. Burn *by Carolyn Dunn*	294
39. This Too Shall Pass *by Trisha Helbers*	300
40. Out on a Limb *by Mary Howley*	307
41. Honey *by Lisa Ireland*	315
About the Editors	323

Introduction

Sudden loss of family or friends is hard – maybe especially so if you feel as if you missed the chance to say what you wanted, to do what you wanted, to let them know how much you cared. When I lost one of my cousins a few years ago, it hit hard. Michael was two years younger than me and, at least based on everything I knew, healthy and full of life as a young father of two incredible sons. In addition to the grief I felt in his loss, I felt enormous fear and anxiety: if he could be gone so suddenly, any of us could. Thinking critically, of course, I already knew this, but now I was facing the truth of it more acutely. I resolved to live more consciously in the present moment, with intention.

Then days and months passed and my attention was pulled along by the daily routine and everyone else's needs. I tried to course correct with greater awareness, but time and time again, I fell back into one-day thinking, practical living and, honestly, subtly ignoring the internal whisper to *take action* on things that mattered to me.

The spark for this anthology was lit after a medical episode of my own shook me awake, knowing that I needed to move towards doing the things I truly valued. I invited others to share stories from their memory or imagination that highlighted both the light and shadow in life – these stories show our human journey from loss and heartbreak to hope and love.

I feel extremely passionate about sharing stories that connect, validate, challenge and honour, so I also wanted to give the project a tangible community benefit...supporting an organisation that is doing incredibly valuable work in the world: the Indigenous Literacy Foundation.

Acknowledgement of Country: I want to acknowledge the Awabakal people as the custodians of the lands and waters of the Newcastle region, on which much of the work of this project was completed. I pay respect to Elders past, present and emerging. I acknowledge and respect the Awabakal people's cultural, spiritual, physical and emotional connection with their land, waters and community.

Anjanette x

Chapter 1

Heart (Beating its) Message
by Anjanette Fennell

The beeping is distracting enough, but then the alarm goes off...

As my heart flops like a fish out of water, I'm consumed by conflicting thoughts – 'What if this doesn't stop?!' and 'Why is the nurse just standing there looking at the machines and making me listen to the incessant alarm?!' followed by 'You must control this, breathe slowly, stop freaking out, you're probably making it worse!'

The junior nurse just continues to look at the monitors before peeking her head out into the corridor.

My eyes have been desperately searching the walls for some sort of *anything* to flip the switch to feel positive or hopeful, but all I see are bold-type words like WARNING! or ALERT! or DISEASE! Pictures of needles or pain scales with their yellow-faced expressions, in case you can't come up with a number, but can identify with an emoji.

Although I'm in the safest place I could be, should anything go wrong, I feel more alone and vulnerable than I've felt in my entire life.

Every inhale sucks my disposable mask into my mouth and I wonder if they can see my fear. I can't tell, so I close my eyes - it makes me feel somehow less alone. Calling now for her supervisor as she watches the monitor, the young nurse is taking my pulse and saying something I can't pay attention to.

I keep my eyes closed and begin my next exhale, willing my heart to slow down and get back into rhythm. Surely it can't keep going like this!

But it doesn't obey my mind. I'm annoyed that I can't make it behave, even though I realise it's a totally ridiculous response. Suddenly my heart begins to resume its usual slow, steady, beautifully boring beat.

The senior nurse, who'd taken my blood a few hours earlier, looks down at me and asks, 'Are you alright, mate?'

That's when I lose it behind my mask. I can't speak; my throat constricts. I just shake my head, crying and squeak, 'I'm just tired.'

Truthfully, I was hoping the nurse might say something like, 'Oh, you just get yourself some electrolytes!' or 'Maybe up your potassium by eating an extra banana or two over the next few days!' but the bloodwork results showed that both were normal.

And my heart, well, was not.

'But it's definitely not just anxiety – something is definitely happening here,' she says.

Thanks – that part, I knew.

I've struggled with anxiety off and on for almost thirty years now. And while I believe we're all 'in progress', it's not been troublesome for quite a while. That said, I've felt the kind of heart racing, terrific pounding that you think might literally burst or, more appallingly, actually be audible to people nearby.

But with my anxiety, as personally mortifying as it was, I always felt the regular rhythm of it. My anxious heart felt more like a train gaining ever-increasing speed on the rails, barrelling faster and harder, not knowing when it might stop. These episodes were more like the train jumped the track, its wheels magically shifting from round to some sort of irregular shape with clunky edges – jarring, stilted then speeding up, then flipping to another set of tracks before slowing and again finding a regular pace.

Checking out of Emergency, I drive myself home and try to go to sleep. Sure, I'm still without answers or solutions, but they assured me it hadn't been a heart attack. I find myself laying in bed next to my husband in the sort of 3.00am quiet that causes ALL of the emotions to tumble out.

Silently crying on my side of the bed, I wonder what would happen if I died in the night.

My mind races with practical fears like, 'You haven't even finalised your will!' and 'Will B know what to put in P's lunch-box?' along with questions that felt like face slaps, 'Have I actually done what I've wanted in life?' and 'Have I wasted time just saying *Yes* and not being brave enough to leave a legacy more than beautiful kids and a half-arsed life?'

It is a heartbreaking (though not surprising) realisation that I haven't actually been living the life I'd told myself I wanted.

Sure, I've taken small steps, but always seem to back away from the edge – turning toward the safe, the known, the easy-but-not-my-life sorts of things.

The fact that my HEART is at the centre of this seems like one of the Universe's cute (read: uncannily symbolic) messages... *Listen to your heart.*

It's something I share with writers. All. The. Time.

But have I actually been doing it myself? It's time to own up: if I *have* been doing it at all, I've been phoning it in.

Two weeks later and I'm still on the path of discovery.

As I write this, I'm wearing a Holter monitor. I've had another ECG and more blood tests are scheduled. I recognise that I haven't got time to ease into change. My heart has shown me, undeniably, that I have to launch myself fully into the things that delight me – even as they feel scary.

My first delightfully scary thing is finally writing my second book. And, while I'm writing, my bigger, more delightfully scary thing is to *actually* start my publishing imprint. I know what I love and I've just wasted too much time telling myself stories about how I'm not ready or worthy of doing these things.

Most of us recognise we're not promised a specific amount of time. Yet, for so many (including myself), we take daily action as if we have *endless time.*

'Someone wants me to do XYZ (even if it means less time for my own project)? Sure. I'll just catch up on my thing next week/next month/sometime soon.'

Or, 'I'm not an expert at ABC which is part of this new direction I want to take, so I'd better research/take a course/interview the 'real' experts before I take the next step.'

A self-sabotage I've gotten quite accustomed to operating under sounds like, 'I don't want to let my clients/friends/family down', but my heart has just definitively jolted me awake.

I now realise I'm more afraid of letting *myself* down by leading a mediocre, risk-averse life that doesn't reflect the fullness of who I am. I could fail. I could fall on my face publicly. I could stuff things up. But if I died then, after trying, at least I would know I was going for something special – that I had been truly LIVING.

Waiting to be magically more confident isn't a 'plan' that's going to get me anywhere. But taking the imperfect action IS... even if I disappoint people who might wish I were doing something else.

I was reminded of a piece from Brené Brown's book *The Gifts of Imperfection* about the word 'courage'. In it she shares that the root of the word courage is 'cor', the Latin word for heart, and one of the word's earliest meanings was literally 'to speak one's mind by telling all one's heart.'

Ultimately, I'm grateful for the chance to still speak my mind by telling all of my heart. My heart knows and now my words (and actions) need to follow it up.

It's time. For me. And for YOU.

If there is a book you want to write...
If there is a career change you've dreamt of making...
If there is something you've always wanted to do...
Begin.

Anjanette Fennell is a literary agent, writing coach and podcaster who has been helping writers find their way to the page and publication for more than a decade. She happily reads more than she writes, but does let the muse take over now and again. Check out her writerly convos with authors at Writers Talking podcast.

Chapter 2

Wellspring

by Corinne Beinke

The car rolled onto the unsealed road, waking Ava from an uncomfortable sleep in the back seat. She opened her eyes just as the taxi pulled onto the gravel driveway in front of the small stone cottage. *A place that time forgot to touch*, Ava thought, as she pulled herself to her feet. As the driver handed Ava her bags, she noted the look he gave her. She'd become quite accustomed to this particular gaze–sympathetic eyes concealing shameful relief.

With the taxi out of sight, Ava let her eyes rest on the giant yew tree outside the cottage. Its trunk, woven like the braid that once hung over her right shoulder, was twice as wide as her outstretched arms. Its presence was steady and wise, the grandmother spirit she craved.

'I'm home' she whispered, her body softening with each breath. This weathered elder had known her since she was a child; she had seen her first steps, her first kiss. The memories of this land and those summers had remained imprinted on her heart and to simply reminisce had always been enough, until now. Everyone said she was crazy to be travelling in her condition, but dreams filled with chestnut trees, hidden copses and wide open fields spoke to her every night.

When she happened upon a book on medicinal weeds of the

British Isles and an old postcard from Cornwall, the synchronicities were too much to ignore. And the fact that the yew tree had been a symbol of death and resurrection to her Celtic ancestors only pulled at her roots more. *This is exactly where I'm meant to be.*

Ava reached into the backpack leaning against the gate and pulled out a small material bag. Inside was a collection of dried flowers, shells, stones and ribbons of cotton, linen and leather. She pulled out one of the cream-coloured threads and walked towards the immense yew tree. The largest of the branches created a web-like canopy that extended out wide before reaching back towards the ground. Ava placed her arm around one of the thick branches and let her clammy cheek rest upon its skin. With her eyes closed, she whispered into the arms of the elder and loosely tied the ribbon around its branch.

Now that her respect had been given and her prayers received, Ava collected her bags and walked towards the stone house doors.

The chair next to the fireplace still smelled of burning wood and the shadow of winter's long sleep seemed to linger on the dark beams of the ceiling. Ava pulled her feet out of the boots she'd been wearing since locking the doors to her inner-city apartment nearly thirty hours before. She stretched out her toes and let the thin column of light from the window warm her skin.

The journey had been hard, there was no denying that. But it had been over a decade since she'd even stepped on a plane, let alone crossed continents and time zones. Still, she sensed a spark of vitality returning to her body and the shedding of years of stagnation falling away.

Outside, the morning sun illuminated the path to the grove hidden beyond the apple trees. *I'm coming*, she spoke to the more-than-human world awaiting her arrival. A few late-season apples hung from the trees like forgotten baubles, clinging to the memory of festivities and joy.

Ava pulled out an intricately woven cross from the pocket of her long cotton skirt and hung it from one of the branches of the tree. She hadn't planned to arrive on the sacred day of Imbolc – a celebration of light, new life and the coming spring.

But she also didn't believe in accidents.

Ava's interest in the natural world began during her long months spent in and out of hospital beds. The concrete jungle she'd once loved suddenly felt suffocating and empty. Short escapes to wider places, wilder spaces, made her question the years she'd spent living and working in the intense flames of industry. The pace was all wrong. The intention, misguided. Ava wondered when her disenchantment began and when they had all become so separate.

It was then that the dreams had begun.

After multiple failed treatments she felt like a broken compass, endlessly spinning with no clear path forward and no way of going back. In this new, unheroic healing world, weeds were suddenly medicine and emotions were stored like wind-up toys waiting to jump out at any moment.

She began exploring how to make tinctures, oxymels and tea blends. It came so naturally to her, new yet somehow familiar. As her formulations became more complex she stopped using the books she'd collected and instead moved intuitively, combining her knowledge of herbal constitutions and a deeper sense of knowing–a remembering.

When her energy allowed, she would tend to her terrace garden, finding solace in the company of seeds and saplings. She learnt to decipher the whispers of the wild between her cool gentle fingers, knowing exactly what they needed to bloom into wholeness. She came to love the garden etched on the cracks of her hands, each a reminder of a morning well spent.

The call of a small wren at the entrance of the grove pulled Ava's attention from the apple tree. She brushed her finger across the moss-lined trunk, her light touch a morse code of gratitude. The wren flew into the small group of ancient trees ahead, leaving a clear path of dappled sunlight for Ava to follow.

Now that the trail was overgrown and lush with the first

growth of spring, stinging nettles stretched their serrated leaves and hairy stems across the path, making Ava smile at the memory of their first encounter. Nearby dock leaves had soothed the stinging lumps on her young legs, but the scars of their unapologetic sting had remained on her heart.

Ava looked at the long arms of nettles blocking her path. *Well, look at you taking up space.* 'I see you, old friend', she said out loud as she pinched the top of the leaves between her fingers, separating the long stems and walking further into the grove. Ava glanced back at the cluster of vital green medicine. The primordial weed had become an unexpected ally over recent months. The strong overnight infusions had flooded her body with nourishment, satiating a thirst she never knew she had.

The more she had read up on nettles, the more she had longed to meet and harvest their fresh leaves. The best she could do in the city was order dry herbs, shipped halfway across the world. Sufficient of course, but incomparable to the sacred act of wildcrafting on her homeland.

Ava stepped carefully along the path, unaware of the curtain of green closing in behind her. She watched as her toes disappeared beneath a pillow of chickweed, her bare feet pale and skeletal, kissing the beds of moss that lined the trail. Once, her feet had slid into sky-blue plimsolls and skipped over the tree roots in search of faeries high up in the trees.

She smiled at the memory as she bent down to pick a chickweed flower with tiny star-like eyes. Night lights for the fae. Ava twirled the flowers between her fingers as pages of folklore flicked through her mind.

The sudden sound of hurried footsteps made her fall to one side in search of a ghostly memory in the trees. But her eyes were only met with the yellow gaze of a crow, watching her from a high branch overhead. A wave of dizziness forced Ava to close her eyes and dig her fingers in the damp soil, anchoring herself in the moment of pain. *Is it time?* she spoke to the canopy of trees overhead.

The leaves seemed to blink in response, an eruption of movement speckling the ground with sunlight and the first falling seeds of spring. Ava sipped from the water bottle she'd brought in her bag and pulled herself up using the strong branch of a nearby tree; the exhaustion of the journey home was creeping into her waning body. She wrapped an arm around her waist and placed a shaking hand over her heart.

Tend to your body as you would your garden, she reminded herself before stepping back onto the path.

Up ahead a fallen oak tree was being eased into the afterlife with the help of the angels of the Earth. Falling apart can be beautiful too.

She looked at the mushrooms blooming on the body of the trunk. The way the fungi fed on the decomposing bark was poetic, miraculous even. A reminder of the aliveness beneath her feet. She climbed over the fallen tree, being careful not to disturb the moss that covered huge areas of the decaying trunk and set her eyes on a thicket of dark green at the edge of the grove.

As she approached, she noticed a cool change in temperature, the air suddenly damp on her skin. Brambles entwined with long stems of ivy concealed the edge of a stone structure next to the stump of an oak tree. Ava peered over the top, her breath caught in her chest as the images that had haunted her were suddenly there, sharp and alive.

She walked to the other side of the structure, where a row of lias stone encircled a hole in the earth. Ava placed her hands on the lichen covering the stones and peered into the darkness below. The ancient chalice seemed as though it were emerging from the earth. *Or perhaps returning to it*, Ava thought as she took in her surroundings.

The stone where she knelt was worn and misshapen, imprinted with the memory of a thousand knees. The air felt thick and heavy, and the shadows of whispered prayers seemed to linger in the branches of the encircling trees. She reached into her bag and found her pouch of offerings. Beneath the shells and dried flowers, she found the hairpin she'd kept for this very moment. She bent the metal between her fingers, brought it to her lips and leant over the opening of the well.

The dark water cast shapes around her silhouette, disguising her sunken eyes and pallid skin. Ava dropped the pin into the well and watched as the ripples erased the edges of her face. She watched until her shape disappeared. Until she soaked into the rocks and became a part of them. One with them.

A gust of wind allowed a column of light to penetrate the thick canopy above, and the glow on the water suddenly revealed an altered reflection; suddenly she had hair like feathers, the colour of dusk, and her eyes were painted with a single strip of black.

Two crows hovered above her shoulders, their harrowing gaze focused on her eyes in the water. Ava turned abruptly but there was nothing to see, only the silence and stillness of the invisible. She looked back into the dark water just as the grove was enveloped by the shadow of trees once more.

Ava crawled back to the oak tree stump, never taking her eyes off the opening in the grove floor. Slumping between its exposed roots, she felt as though the base of the tree was pressing into her back and moulding its skin into the curves of her body. She pressed her head more firmly into its peeling bark. The fear and confusion at what she'd just seen was disorientating, so she let her eyes track the surrounding trees, moving her neck slowly and deliberately in an attempt to settle her agitated nerves.

Ava stopped when the wren landed in front of a silvery bush of mugwort nearby, its onyx eyes fixed on hers for just a moment. She reached out and let her cupped hand glide up the plant's long angular stem and cotton-like leaves. She tried to regain a sense of calm by breathing in their familiar musky smell, but her attention was drawn to something glinting in the soil. A tiny face in a premature grave of rotten leaves. Ava blew off the soil and stroked her thumb across the cool, smooth figure of a bear. Her bear.

She pulled herself back to the tree stump, still clutching the pendant in her hands, and curled up between its roots. 'I remember', she whispered as the elders leaned their branches in closer, shrouding the grove into darkness.

Ava gasped when the ghost of a girl she once knew suddenly appeared from the well, her easy laughter filling the silence of the grove as she swung threaded conkers from a string. Pearl-like droplets started to slide from Ava's eyes, blurring her vision and tickling her ears as they slid from her cheek to the ground. Her body shook with emotion as she imagined inhabiting the skin of this fearless girl whose voice once roared with truth and fury.

The girl who could smell danger and dance with the wolves and witches of her dreams. She'd left that body the morning she ran from the grove, shedding her skin as he tugged at her soft edges. She left and she swore she would never return. Heavy tears began to fall as Ava reached out an arm, 'I'm sorry,' she keened, 'I'm sorry I left you.'

She clawed her fingers into the earth and imagined pulling back the parts of herself she'd squashed and tamed, her jagged edges smoothed into someone acceptable, someone safe, someone whole.

The taste of soil on her lips focused her waning energy back to the girl, who appeared closer now, her hair suddenly dark and feather-like, her eyes as green as nettles against the black strip across her eyes.

Bending down close she wiped a single tear from Ava's cheek just as two crows landed on the stump above Ava's head. She took hold of her hand and leaned in close, her breathless incantation carried on the wind, sending a flurry of birds out of their high branches and into the fields beyond the grove.

Ava let out a slow exhalation as her body settled more deeply into the crevices of the ground. The weight of her grief and shame melted into the welcoming arms of the Earth, her steady inhale so willing and ready to receive it all. She let the more-than-human world midwife her into new realms of being, knowing that a wellspring of life would soon emerge in her place.

Corinne Beinke was born in the UK and lives on Australia's Sunshine Coast with her young family. She has published works of non-fiction with *Epic-Unlimited* and *Slow Journal* and also enjoys writing short stories and poetry. Through her writing, Corinne tries to inspire hope, slow living and the importance of connection to the natural world.

Chapter 3

Pippa's Legacy

by Sara Foster

In 2021, a friend of mine suddenly got very sick, very fast. Pippa was a reserved woman, whom I'd gotten to know because our children were drawn together and had fast become inseparable. My daughter sat between her two young girls in age: seven to their six and nine. We called them 'the triplets' and soon they spent half the time at my house, and half at hers.

Pippa had been suffering for a while with debilitating symptoms, which no doctor could quite pin down. Her forearms were strapped up because she was finding it painful to use her hands. She couldn't sleep. Her body ached. She was exhausted, and she was lonely – a single mum without much backup on hand, with a complex family background. She was also emotionally restless. Struggling to keep pace with the girls' growth, wanting to deepen her connection with her grown-up sons, fearful for their futures and still processing multiple traumas of her own.

She told me some of this in a heart-to-heart at our local café, during the brief period when she really started opening up to me. I knew she was asking for help, but I also knew she didn't want me to immediately overwhelm her with books and resources. First and foremost, she just needed someone to listen.

We didn't get much chance to talk further. A few weeks later,

Pippa called me one evening at nine-thirty, extremely distressed. A lab technician had phoned her and told her to go straight to the hospital; something was very wrong with her blood test results. I went and collected her girls and took them to my house for the night. Then I drove Pippa to the Emergency Department, and she put me down as her next of kin.

Between that night in early December, and the day she died, on the second of April 2022, Pippa was hardly out of hospital.

She had leukemia–the worst kind, AML, with only a fourteen percent survival rate. Her girls were shuffled between me and another close friend until their Nanna could get here from New Zealand in the last few weeks of Pip's life (Covid restrictions caused a lot of hurdles). I took care of Pippa's two shell-shocked children as best I could when I had them, and every minute my heart ached so hard for them, and for my own child too, who thought of Pippa as her second mum.

It felt as though we were all sleepwalking, while carrying on with the daily routine of life for the kids' sakes. I spent a lot of time on the phone to the hospital, trying to get updates, wanting to make sure Pippa was being looked after, but for weeks I hardly saw her, because she didn't want visitors while she was sick, and we were always terrified of her catching Covid. Every plan to see her became a military operation–the doctors insisting we meet outside, at a distance, fully masked up–and ended up causing Pippa so much distress she would back out. She just wanted to cuddle her babies, not endure the torture of waving at them in full PPE. So instead she spent those last few months with only masked-up nurses for company. I know from little notes she wrote that her dreams were simple things: getting back to her children, going home to have a nice bath, some spaghetti bolognese and a glass of red wine.

And then, Covid didn't matter any more. The doctors told us there was nothing they could do, and Pippa had only days left. In that last week she went from having hardly any visitors to barely being alone, although the hospital's Covid restrictions caused extra agonies as we had to fight to get people in to see her.

Pippa was gravely ill, a husk of her former self, with sallow skin, and numerous tubes invading her body to help it function. She could barely open her chapped lips to take in sips of water. She wasn't being given food any more, but incredibly, she still insisted on chemo. Forty-eight hours before she died I watched her swallow those poisonous pills that were supposed to heal her, because she was still determined to do everything she could to get home to her children. Even though she moaned in pain each time she moved, and was barely conscious, she made sure she took those pills. And one of the few things she managed to murmur to me was an apology, for 'all the trouble'.

That was Pippa. Reserved, quiet, but oh so kind. Thinking of others and not wanting anyone to have to go out of their way for her. Surely, if there was anything fair about life, such a beautiful soul shouldn't suffer this way. But there was nothing fair about what I witnessed in her final days.

And after she'd gone, the loss and the injustice of it was torment. I was plagued by the last images I had of her in that hospital bed; the terrible vulnerability and brutality of it all. I kept going because I knew how much she would want me to be strong for her kids, but life felt chaotic, senseless and pointless. Ridiculous even. Here we were trying to find purpose in our days, when *that* could happen to someone you loved.

And yet, right after she died, there was a sense of her being around us. The night she died, the fire alarm went off at her home and they had trouble shutting it down–which felt to me like a metaphor for the anger, frustration and agony Pippa would have felt at being permanently separated from her kids.

We held a beach memorial in a spot that didn't allow dogs, but a little terrier made a beeline for us and didn't want to leave. Only when its owner called it back did we realise the pup's name was 'Pippa'. And Pippa's favourite AC-DC tunes came on all the time, interrupting playlists that they weren't a part of. I was noticing a lot of these things, along with the other friend who had cared for Pippa's children, but of course we were. Didn't it simply show how much we longed for her to still be here?

Of course we were looking for her everywhere, and picking up on any signal we could find that she was with us. I heard more than one sceptical commentator dismiss these occurrences as *coincidence*, and I was wary too. I've always been fascinated by belief systems and the things people decide are 'signs', and I suspect that if you look for a sign to back up your thinking, you'll usually find one. I've known more than one person suffering from addiction who became obsessed with signs, using them to fall deeper into their own traps. So I've never been entirely convinced that the signs the grieving and the desperate so readily cling to aren't just random occurrences that back up what you most want to believe.

In the month after she died, we packed up Pippa's house, and got her children ready to go to their new lives in New Zealand with their Nanna. My family already had a holiday booked the week before Nanna and the girls were due to leave, so we went away, somewhat unwillingly, not keen to give up more time together before they were gone. But we needed rest too, and the chance to get a different perspective on things. While we were there, I slept deeply. And one night, I had one of the most vivid dreams I've ever had in my life. It was all about Pippa.

To begin with, we were at her wedding. She was getting married and I was her bridesmaid. We were dancing together, and we were *so, so happy*. Over a year later, I can still remember that feeling of elation. We were dancing to a Feargal Sharkey song, an artist I had barely thought of since I was a kid–and in the dream I knew it was him singing, but not the name of the song.

After we danced, we went outside to walk up a hill to the place Pippa would get married, but suddenly there were protesters on either side of us. They wore old-fashioned clothes and carried placards, and it was something to do with Ireland. Pippa turned to me and said, 'I felt like Micah Fitzgerald.' I had no idea what she was talking about.

Finally, we reached the top of the hill and Pippa stood next to the man she was going to marry. His name was Herbert Whittle. I only knew that much, and then the dream began to dissolve, but I woke up with those three names imprinted on my mind.

Feargal Sharkey. Micah Fitzgerald. Herbert Whittle.

I have never before or since woken from a dream with a list of names! And I'm terrible at remembering names in general, so I quickly wrote down the entire dream before I could forget it. And then I went to research the names on Google.

The song I'd loved as a child was Feargal Sharkey's 'A Good Heart (these days is hard to find)'. It was perfect for the moment. A sweet message from my friend saying thanks for all I'd done.

The Irish-related name, Micah Fitzgerald, was confusing. Nothing matched as I thought this was a girl's name. But then I found Michael Fitzgerald – the first high-ranking IRA officer to die on hunger strike. The Irish placards and protestors made sense, alluding to the awful realisation I'd had that final day in the hospital, when I saw the sign 'nil by mouth' and understood that they'd stopped feeding her in the days before she died. *She's starving to death*, I'd thought in horror. As had Michael Fitzgerald. Not Micah, as I thought I heard in the dream. *Michael.*

And the last name: Herbert Whittle. I put that one into Google not expecting much at all, but to my surprise I found @herbertwhittle is the Instagram handle of a fellow Western Australian writer called Karen Whittle-Herbert. And the last thing she'd read and put on her feed: my own book: *The Hush*. She'd given it eleven out of ten.

Three random names, containing three messages that all clearly meant something to me.

Thank you for being a friend in tough times.
You saw what I went through.
You're doing what you're meant to be doing. Just. Keep. Going.

Each time I tell this true story (and I haven't told it publicly before), I wonder what people will make of it. Proof of the afterlife? Or just bereaved Sara gone kooky, finding messages in her dreams. However, it doesn't really matter what the consensus is, because this dream wasn't meant for anyone but me.

And when I woke up, I felt comforted and at peace. And I also knew in my heart that this was Pippa saying not just thank you, but *goodbye*. I've never dreamt of her again.

Pippa's death changed me.

She taught me about sacrifice and presence. About how so many of the things we deem important really don't matter at all. I thought I would have to live with so much pain after my friend died, and I still miss her and sometimes feel confronted by everything I saw and what she went through. However, eighteen months later, thanks to her generous and determined spirit whilst alive, and the incredible dream I had after she died, it's only love that I'm feeling as I write this.

So much love. That's what Pippa made sure she left me with, in the end.

Sara Foster writes fiction with strong female contemporary characters. *The Hush* (2021), is a thriller now optioned for television. Her publishing history includes the novella, *The Deceit* and six psychological suspense novels: *You Don't Know Me* (also a drama podcast), *The Hidden Hours* (optioned for TV), *All That is Lost Between Us*, *Shallow Breath*, *Beneath the Shadows* and *Come Back to Me*. Sara completed her PhD in 2023. Her new novel will be published in 2024.

Chapter 4

The Shearer

by Maura Pierlot

The mother of all hangovers hits me, a jolt of lightning right between the eyes. My usual wake-up call. Then the stifling heat. It's gripping me by the throat, searing me inside out. The kind of heat that makes you pray for a quick death.

Mustering all my strength, I blink once, twice, willing a blurry world to focus. My fingers rub the pillowcase, searching for her split-ends. They used to tickle my nose but I wouldn't even brush them away this time.

'Wake up, ya lazy bludger,' she jokes, one knee nudging me out of bed, the other trapping me close. Her auburn curls spill over my shoulder and smell like rosemary. 'C'mon, the sooner you go, the sooner you'll be back.'

That was Sue when she was happy… in the beginning.

I spy my grubby jeans and drag them close, fumbling in the pockets for the foil pack. *You better stay off the grog or you'll be checking out of this world early, just like your ol' man*, the doctor told me last year. Or something like that–I wasn't listening much. I pop out two aspirins, one for my heart, the other for my head, and coax them to the back of my throat with the last drops of Jack. The doc didn't tell me that part.

My feet are like old friends, once attached, now strangers, but

I manage to find them, quickly testing their loyalty until my joints protest. Never expected my bones to declare war at thirty-eight, but that's what shearing does to you.

'When are you back?' she asks me with a weary smile, but two weeks seems too long to say aloud. 'Before you know it,' I lean in to whisper, closing the door to her day with a kiss.

That was Sue, not long after we married, when the light started to dim.

Yesterday I cracked two hundred–gnarly wethers, every bloody one of them. That's five hundred dollars clear in my hand, thank you very much. Ol' man Jenkins, a sorry excuse for a contractor, was over the moon. *Every shed needs a gun shearer*, he told me when we downed tools. *Keeps the other fellas honest.* I felt good about myself for the first time in ages, until I found out he told Robbo the same thing, even though he barely topped one hundred and sixty. That's cos Jenkins is a pivoter, always keeping us on our toes, and a mean son of a bitch.

I massage my temples, waiting for the tablets to kick in. I don't remember much about last night, except Robbo swiping my keys, getting all high 'n mighty on me when we got booted from the pub.

'You're so blind you can't even find your goddamn ute, let alone drive it,' he insisted.

Funny, cos I reckon he was more pissed than me – kept thrusting the bottle of Bundaberg my way, his jabs sharp, like a crazed boxer.

'Bloody oath, Robbo, you offering me a swig or trying to crack me over the head with it?' I hollered, ducking and weaving.

He stepped off the kerb, eyes locked on my ute. 'There's the beast!'

In the streetlight's eerie glow, the old heap looked radioactive, paint the colour of a tennis ball. When Robbo was done dodging imaginary traffic, he made his way across the road to take the wheel. I caught the Bundy on the full and raised the bottle skyward because at 2.00am, everything's worth celebrating.

'To the Green Ghost!' I cried out. That was Sue's name for it. Said my ute was always appearing without warning, then vanishing just as quick.

'Sure you're not just passing through?' she asks me with a faraway look in her eye. 'Gotta follow the work, Suzie Q, but ya know I'm coming back,' I tell her, just like I did the last time, and the time before that, when she needed reminding.

That was Sue, ten years after we married, when the shadows grew long.

There's no wind but the screen door bangs against the frame, thanks to a missing hinge. I kick it open and step outside to a heat so intense, it lacerates the air. Camellias lay crushed under the ute's back end, a fragrant red carpet to see me off. Looks like Robbo mowed down the whole bed but, knowing Jenkins, I'll somehow cop the blame.

I throw my gear in the tray then crank the engine, stunned the keys are there. There's no sign of Robbo in the side mirror. Damn fool, I nearly ran him over last time, and don't know how I'd ever explain that to his missus. Must've shot off early. He's a tough ol' bloke, getting up before the crack of dawn, though knowing Robbo, he didn't sleep as it interferes with his drink and all.

The Green Ghost chugs over the brow of the hill and down the long drive, spitting gravel the whole way. I palm a left at the front gate, letting my eyes wander for one last look at the stack of concrete blocks Jenkins calls home. He's so proud of his little shitbox, like it's some bloody castle. Not sure what he does with all the coin he makes off us. Must be a punter.

Just you wait, Suzie Q! One day, I'm gonna give up this game and buy us a nice big house near the coast. You can pop your easel on the verandah and paint the ocean,' I promise her. She crams her favourite daisies, the purple-tipped ones, in a skinny vase. *'I'd like that,'* she says like she means it, but her voice is far away.

That was Sue, feeling her way in the dark.

Two hundred kilometres tick over in no time – two hundred kays of nothing but ash-coloured sky, dirt road and scrub. I stick my head out the window, hoping the rush of air revives me, but cop a fly in the mouth instead. Fiddling with the rear-view mirror is a waste of time – the back windscreen's still coated with bird shit and thick dust. Sue would call it *burnt sienna*. That's artist-speak for *red-brown*. The front's not much better, thanks to a nasty crack on the windscreen that's moving all over the place, like Robbo last night. The radio lights up and I punch all the buttons. There's nothing but static – a dull drone then a deafening roar, violent waves crashing against cliffs.

'You and me, we're salty, not sweet,' she says on our last drive to the coast, when the sliver of deep blue reveals itself in the distance. 'Your sweat, my tears, the ocean. It's meant to be healing, salt, but I reckon it just makes the pain worse.'

That was Sue, trying to find her way ashore.

The road's my home now. I travel from shed to shed, hoping new horizons will help me forget, but the memories follow. I clutch the wheel of the Green Ghost like a lover who wants to take me places, if only I'd listen, if only I could work out what she needs. I look after her, fill her up when she's low, talk to her. I take real good care of her. But I can feel her pulling away. She's buckling under me, shuddering. She's breaking down and I'm losing my grip.

The lamp is hanging off the night table but the globe's still flickering. Empty medicine bottles litter the floor. Her arm dangles over the edge of the bed, fingers curled as if trying to grasp something, her lips parted ever so slightly.

That was Sue, two years ago, when she surrendered to the darkness.

I see a sign that says *$1 lunch* and wonder if someone forgot the zero but pull over anyway for a feed and diesel. The second I step out, the blowies attack. One's buzzing right in front of my nose, the bugger following me all the way to the front door. The mat has no guts to it, but I find a small patch to scrape off my boots and step inside.

The place looks deserted, and I figure it's closed until I see a slight figure huddled in a corner booth. She's twirling her hair around her finger, nose in a book but I can't make out the title. She's about thirty, maybe thirty-five – hard to tell. The paperback's so worn the pages are jutting out everywhere. She pokes them back in, real frustrated, then bangs it a few times on the table, like the dealer at that casino where Robbo and I lost our shirts and then some.

I order a flat white and sit a few tables away. She stares at me as if that's an odd thing to do. Or maybe she's smirking. I can't read her, and don't know why I'm even trying.

My coffee arrives with the local rag and a sigh from the waitress, who seems tired for eight am and two customers. I turn to the back page, my eyes drifting over the cricket score to the woman in the booth.

She looks over at me and smiles. I smile back, even though I don't want to. I feel a burning sensation in the pit of my stomach. It's not a pain, more of an ache, but a different one – real raw. My head's telling my body to relax but I find myself standing. I grab my mug and head over to her.

She's leaning forward over a bowl of steaming hot chips, inhaling blissfully, like she's sniffing some rare flower. Her hair's the colour of straw and just as messy. A curl pops out from behind her ear, and she tames it with a clip. Then she blizzards the chips with salt, bringing the first handful to her lips.

I clear my throat, swallowing my intention halfway. She smiles so wide that a few chips break free. When our eyes meet, she blushes, still chewing and smiling, like it's no big deal.

'Name's Michael,' I tell her, raising my steaming mug like I'm about to toast her, 'but everyone calls me Mick.'

'Daisy,' she mumbles, leaning in with her shoulder. A simple nod summons me to join her.

I park my coffee too eagerly to take back and grasp her hand with my thick mitt. I expect her skin to be soft, delicate, like her name, but it's rough – cracked, even. We shake hands longer than we should, our calluses rubbing against each other like sandpaper, smoothing away all the dead skin.

Maura Pierlot is an award-winning author, playwright and filmmaker based in Canberra. *Fragments*, her acclaimed play, book and web series, is now a feature-length film touring festivals. Maura's picture books include *Alphabetter – A Better You and Me, from A to Z* (Affirm Press, 2024) and *What Will You Make Today?* (Storytorch Press, 2023). She runs The Book Bench Project in Canberra and holds a PhD in philosophy.

Chapter 5

Pull and Whoosh

by Anna Hayes

It was about as cold as a winter's day could get at the pier, but Curtis didn't alter his daily routine. It had served him well for decades and he wasn't about to tempt fate now. He was, however, beginning to feel more self-conscious.

With every early morning stroll he took to that particular spot on the pier, he felt extra eyes on him. Frowns of confusion and consternation, probably wondering what home he had escaped from and why someone hadn't stopped him, given his current state.

Yes, his wetsuit was sagging slightly in certain places. And yes, his white legs with knees knobbly and knocking together in the merciless temperature had been starved of sunlight for some time.

But he was still as fit as a drover's dog, his mind as sharp as a barber's blade, and all the sceptical looks in the world weren't going to stop him from doing what he loved. And, despite the looks, no one had actually ever tried to stop him on what he referred to as his daily pilgrimage.

He smiled at people as he walked past but not because he wanted to reassure them of the soundness of his mind. Well, maybe there was a little bit of that, but it was mostly because a smile would generally elicit one of two favourable outcomes.

Either people would smile back and carry on with their day, or they would say hello and maybe ask where he was off to; marvel at his robustness when he told them.

But it had been weeks since anyone had stopped to talk, everyone scurrying about their day-to-day lives, watching for where their 'oodle' dog did its business, or talking on phones they didn't even hold to their ear anymore–tunnel vision, as cold if not colder than the Antarctic wind flying up to meet them.

He used to have all sorts of interesting conversations on the pier, from the windswept American tourists who hadn't known about Melbourne's unforgiving winter to the Irish immigrant, lonesome and wondering about his place in the world.

But everyone was busy now–unapproachable. Even sitting on a bench, looking out at the water, many people managed to give off a 'do not disturb' vibe.

As he walked, Curtis thought about his mother. It was the regular reverie; when he was by the sea, he thought of her, and how she had taught him to swim right at this very pier.

The salt water burned his eyes but he recovered quickly, peeling them open to get his bearings.

'Raymond, you have to learn to open your eyes! You can't swim blind if your boat sinks, you'll end up in a shark's jaws!'

Raymond... he had always been indifferent to the name, preferred to go by Curtis and, luckily, found himself in fraternities where surnames were frequently preferred.

'Curtis, over here! Pass it to me!'

'Curtis, excellent work on the Henson merger–you'll be up for my job next!'

Curtis had never enjoyed boats–sinking or otherwise. He could have taken up sailing if he had wanted, and it would certainly have fit in with his work colleagues. But something about boating made him uncomfortable. It was that idea that one could somehow master the ocean, that you could best its power by owning a bigger boat or a more expensive one. He'd always felt that swimming was a more noble, more reverential way of enjoying the sea.

Religious, if you liked, but Curtis had never really been the spiritual type: *Ocean, I am in your hands; forgive me for this trespass, have mercy on my soul.*

He supposed it was like his daily baptism.

He was almost at the sweet spot–the part of the pier where you could jump in, still with care, but without fear of death or dismemberment. Curtis never underestimated the dangers–there had been accidents here over the years, some with tragic outcomes.

But he knew these waters, knew the geography of their underlying terrain–the shelves and dips–learned over years and decades, etched into his memory since he was a child.

His father had been a reluctant swimmer; his mother, the first cousin of a dolphin. Even in a choppy sea, she could glide effortlessly through the swells and waves, ducking instinctively at the right times, moving almost as if she were part of the water itself.

'Mum, I'm stuck!'

Both parents saw the dilemma. Mr Curtis was about to dive in but his wife stopped him with a hand on his chest and a firm 'no'–her teaching voice unleashed.

'You're in a rip, Raymond,' she said calmly, walking along the pier, keeping level with him as he struggled against the unending fight.

'What does that mean?' he yelled, his wind-milling arms starting to tire.

'Stop swimming,' she said firmly.

'What?' Curtis was alarmed.

'Just stop swimming, let it carry you out. You're nearly at the end of it. I can see it from here.'

Curtis's eyes darted frantically around; he was frightened, but followed his mother's advice, laying back and concentrating on keeping his head above the surface. The water pulled him out, like his mother had when teaching him backstroke and he had been afraid to float on his back.

'That's good, you're nearly out, well done.'

Curtis prided himself on his memory but of all the big days in his life – and there were many–that was the day he recalled more vividly than any other. He remembered that feeling of stillness when he reached the end of the rip, a moment of suspension before the *whoosh* of the next wave.

The pull and the whoosh–that was how he'd labelled the currents as a ten-year-old.

That was how he still labelled them.

'Ok, swim to the beach. Watch out for darker water; those are the rips,' Mrs Curtis said, turning on the pier to walk alongside him. It was as if she had an invisible lead on him, giving him space but ultimately close enough in case of emergency.

'How can I see the colour of the water from down here?' Curtis had grumbled as he switched from front crawl to breast-stroke, working all of his muscles just as she had instructed him.

'You'll learn. With time.'

And he had learned. He'd found himself in many rips over the years–both in water and on land. He still felt a thin sliver of panic when it happened but manoeuvring them felt like second nature now. He had learned to flow with the pull, surge with the whoosh.

He stopped walking, glad that the pier was quieter this far down. He looked out at the water–dark grey and choppy, angry and provocative. Overcast days made it harder to spot the rips–the sun had a way of illuminating the dangers, though it seemed quite clear today.

But no, there was one. He squinted to see the telltale darker water, a thin channel about fifty metres away. He applauded the rip's deceptive nature, its ability to hide in plain sight–a deadly foe lying in wait in an already uncompromising host.

His mother had died suddenly the year he'd started secondary school. Her doctor was never able to give any explanation other than a heart attack. She had been fit, active, free of contributing vices like alcohol or cigarettes. None of those things meant anything to Curtis at the time, but age and wisdom brought the revelation that sometimes things couldn't be explained. Though he tried, through various methods, for years afterwards.

Although Curtis was a man of habit, today he found himself deviating. He looked outward, instead of to the shore; traced the channel of the rip and wondered to himself: where might he end up? How far would he get in these temperatures, just floating along with the current? King Island? Tasmania? With some huge will of superhuman resilience, could he make it to Antarctica? Just in time to watch the ice caps melt and the penguins marching?

The thought intrigued him–how many times, over the decades, had he thought about just floating away from everything? All the stress and strife, the money concerns, the wedding guest list, the fight with the tradie who just wouldn't listen, the fight with the boss who later became his employee, the health scares and resultant issues, the loss, the pain, the heartache...

A ghost of movement drew his attention to the horizon–some small flicker in his peripheral vision. His eyesight wasn't what it used to be, even though he had never needed glasses. And while his imagination was inclined to ramble, he was quite sure that the disruption in the distance had been a dolphin, leaping from the water.

Curtis cast one last look at the rip in the distance – he couldn't see where it ended but that was ok–it had to stop somewhere.

He braced his knees, steeled himself for the cold, and jumped.

Anna Hayes is a media professional, writer and editor, originally from Wexford, Ireland. She has been published in Irish literary journal, *The Blue Nib*, and in Melbourne Writers Group anthology *Secrets and Lies*. Anna's story, 'Orphan' placed joint second in the 2022 Odyssey House Short Story Competition. She is currently working on her first novel between head injuries on hockey pitches, grumbling about writer's block and exchanging procrastination for prevarication.

Chapter 6

The Living List

by Mercedes Mercier

My heart pounds in my chest, so fast that it's making me dizzy. My eyes are clenched shut, but it doesn't help. I still know what lies in front of me, what I have to face.

There's a tap on my shoulder and I jump. The barest hint of a laugh close to my left ear, torn away by the wind.

'You gonna open your eyes?' the man's voice is deep, amused. His body presses against mine; his chest hard against my back. I can smell him: sweat barely covered by an acrid deodorant. My stomach churns. I long to break free of him, to run, to be anywhere but here, but I can't. I'm trapped.

'Come on,' he says. 'You can't get all the way up here and not have a look.'

Oh god. He's right. I take a deep, shuddering breath and crack my eyes open. I can see the ground, thousands of feet below. Fifteen thousand, to be precise.

I moan. 'Why am I doing this again?'

'Because you almost died,' he reminds me. Ray, I remember suddenly, my panic easing slightly to allow a sliver of rational thought. That's the instructor's name. Ray.

'And this is on your Living List.'

I clench my hands tighter around the straps across my chest.

The material cuts into my palms, stinging, reminding me that I'm alive.

Ray's right. That's why I'm here; why I chose to spend a random summer weekend testing the limits of my fear.

My story had come spilling out to him a couple of hours ago, while he was fitting my harness. I'd been trying to cover my nerves as the perfectly good plane that I'd decided to throw myself out of taxied towards the open hangar.

My Living List. The list I'd created for myself to celebrate the fact that, eighteen months ago, I very nearly hadn't been.

The first sign that something was wrong wasn't a sudden burst of agony… it was innocuous back pain. More of an ache, really, like I'd slept in the wrong position. Or lifted a weight the wrong way at the gym. It was easy to dismiss, to ignore. A painkiller took care of it. At first.

But over the following days, the pain kept building. And then it started to spread. Soon, my stomach was hurting. It wasn't anything I hadn't got used to feeling each month, but it didn't fall in my regular cycle.

A few more days and the niggling aching had turned into full-blown pain. Nothing I was doing could ease it; painkillers wouldn't even touch the sides of the raging beast that had set up camp inside of me.

And then, one evening, my mother cracked open the bathroom door as I sat in the bath, staring down at my swollen belly.

'Sweetheart, how are you?'

Her eyes widened as she caught sight of me, head hanging over my engorged belly. I looked like I was eight months pregnant, but I wasn't.

'I'm taking you to the hospital. Now.'

Her voice brooked no argument, not that I had the energy to argue. She rushed over and wrapped me in a towel, yelling at my dad to get dressed and to the car.

Life over the next hour came in snatches. It felt like minutes later that I was being wheeled from the hospital waiting room to the operating theatre. I had no idea what was going on. Someone had put a needle in my arm that pushed dye through my veins while I lay in a metal tube. The dye had felt hot and uncomfortable, but was nothing compared to the grinding, tearing pain in my stomach. In the next instant, it seemed, I was back in my room, with the CT scan finished. A doctor walked briskly in, giving my parents a brief smile before turning his attention to me.

'We need to operate right now,' he told me. He was calm, but there was a suppressed energy in him that was contagious.

'What's happening?' Mum asked from the seat next to my bed. She hadn't left her position since I'd been taken to the ward, not even to go to the toilet.

'She's got a burst appendix. I don't know how bad it is until I get in there, but judging by the look of her, we haven't got too long.'

'God,' my dad muttered, then, seeing my face, reached over and took my hand. 'You'll be alright, sweetheart. You're in the right place.'

He squeezed my fingers. I barely felt it. I closed my eyes as I was wheeled from the room. The next time I opened them I was in a corridor, all alone. Sterile white walls surrounded me, an insipid painting of a vase of flowers was the only thing of interest in my vicinity. I tried to distract myself by counting the petals, but it didn't work.

A blanket, freshly warmed, was wrapped around me. But no matter how warm it was, my body wouldn't stop shaking. Was I going to die? Was I living the last moments of my life in this bland corridor, with disinfectant stinging my nostrils, separated from my family?

It felt like both seconds and days before a nurse appeared and wheeled me into a world of metallic coldness. Everything in the operating theatre was silver. A huge round disc hung over me, the countless lights inside blindingly bright. A couple of nurses, gowned and masked, stood on my left. I recognised the doctor's steely blue eyes above his own mask, his cap hiding his closely shorn grey hair.

They all stared down at me, lying cold and vulnerable in the spotlights. I was the star of a show that I didn't want to be part of.

'Just a little prick,' the nurse murmured, and I felt the splinter-pain of the needle sliding into my vein.

Within seconds the edges of my vision were darkening, the room sliding out of focus. The sudden lack of control over my own body ignited a deep, primitive fear, and I fought the blackness with everything I had. I thrashed and gasped, adrenaline warring with the anaesthetic in my bloodstream. A nurse on my left held onto my forearm tightly.

'I can't...' I started, staring into the eyes of the masked doctor, but it was like someone had snuck up behind me and knocked me over the head. Everything went black.

'Are you awake?'

I couldn't make sense of the words. I had no idea where I was, or what had happened. I cracked my eyes open. Everything was blurry. I blinked a few times, and my vision solidified into a man standing at my bedside. The doctor.

'You're in recovery,' he told me. 'Things were pretty bad in there. Infection had spread throughout your stomach, and your body had almost gone into sepsis. Thankfully I could clear it all out and you're going to be just fine.'

He smiled his gentle smile. 'But I estimate you were less than twenty-four hours away from death.'

I just nodded, fatigue dragging the edges of my awareness away. This time, the slip into unconsciousness felt gentle, like a relief.

The next time I woke up, I was back on the ward, in my room. Mum was sitting in the same seat, her upper body sprawled onto my bed, sound asleep.

I stared at her dark hair, the doctor's words circling my brain.

I'd almost died. I'd come within hours of passing away. The thought was so foreign, so terrifying, that my mind shied away from it. I was nineteen years old, and I'd almost died? As quietly as I could, I eased the blankets off of me, pulling my blue gown to the side.

There it was. A twenty-centimetre scar running vertically from my belly button down to my pelvis, covered in white tape. Evidence that another human being had cut my body open to save my life. Tears started rolling down my cheeks and my throat ached with the raw pain of holding back my sobs. My body jolted as they tried to escape my lips.

I slowly calmed down, my snuffles easing. Mum was still sound asleep. I knew in time I would go through all the emotions over this experience. I'd be furious that it happened to me. I'd be depressed that my previously smooth, flat teenage stomach was marred by an ugly red line, forever reminding me of what I went through. But, finally, I'd accept this as part of my life journey.

I glanced at the bedside table next to me. A pad of paper, emblazoned with the hospital logo, sat next to a pen. I pulled them closer, the IV painkiller keeping my body's reaction to being cut open and sewn back up at bay. I wrote three words.

My Living List.

What are things that I've been wanting to do, but hadn't got around to? I asked myself. Things I wouldn't have been able to experience if I'd died last night.

The first one was easy: live overseas.

I'd wanted to move to London for years, but had decided that going to uni was a safer path. I wrote it down. What else?

I'd been wanting to volunteer with animals, but had never made the time between studying, working part-time and socialising. I wrote that down too. I tapped the pen against my teeth. Grey light was edging the blinds over the window; dawn wasn't far away. Suddenly, I felt inexplicably exhausted.

Fighting to keep my eyes open for a few more seconds, I

scrawled down my last goal before my body pulled me back into sleep: go sky-diving.

And today, jumping out of this plane over a southern Adelaide beach, is the first item I'm going to be able to tick off my Living List.

'This is the stupidest idea I've ever had.' I pitch my voice loud, so Ray can hear every word. 'I almost die, so to celebrate, I do something that could get me killed? Smart. Very smart.'

He chuckles, his breath tickling my ear. 'You've got this, mate. You can do it.'

I straighten my shoulders; they press against his solid, comforting chest. 'You're right. I can do this.'

'You ready?'

'Yeah.' My voice catches, barely audible over the rushing wind. I clear my throat. 'I'm ready.'

'Good. We'll go on one, okay?'

'Three...'

He rocks our joined bodies back and forth, back and forth. The sky gets closer, then further away, closer, then further. I haul in a breath that feels snatched from the wind. My pulse thunders in my ears.

'Two...'

I picture myself falling, air pressing against my face and the ground rushing up... then the parachute snatching us from freefall. I picture our slow descent from the sky, the whole earth stretched out in front of us. Exhilaration roaring through my body.

'One...'

I grin.

We jump.

Mercedes Mercier writes crime stories with twisting plots and relatable characters, and also works in Australia's criminal justice system. After a brush with death, Mercedes now throws herself into life – she has lived overseas, achieved a black belt in karate, skydived, and volunteered with animals. She loves to read, travel, try new restaurants, and listen to true crime podcasts. Mercedes lives in Adelaide surrounded by nature, with her partner and her dog.

Chapter 7

Death and the Art of Living

by Nina D Campbell

'It's cancer.'

My mother's words hang in the air between us as I perch on the edge of her hospital bed. She was admitted two days ago for exploratory surgery; respiratory issues from a flu she just couldn't shake. Her warm hand finds mine and she squeezes it. Tight. Then tighter. Her lips tremble as she tries to smile.

'I need you to be brave. Don't cry, you have to go back to work.'

Death sits behind me but we haven't been introduced. A shiver chases her chilly finger as it traces a slow path down my spine.

I open my mouth to speak but nothing comes out. My mind whirls like a fairground ride. Thoughts fly here and there, darting around my mother's words, but never quite landing.

'It's too late–no treatment–not long...'

None of these words fit in the life I have planned. A life with two parents to guide me as I stretch into adult life. Death's hands wind around my lungs, crushing the air out of them. I don't know how, but I find my way out of that ward and into the lift. When it clunks to a stop on the ground floor, I keep falling.

Stumbling towards a blurry entrance, my knees soften and my

stomach churns. The wall is cold beneath my palm as I steady myself. Relief trickles through me when I see the toilet door. It closes with a soft thud and I'm alone. At last. Away from the eyes of so many strangers. Eyes that catch mine and slide away as if they can see the gaping wound growing inside me.

With no reason to continue the charade, I collapse onto a closed toilet seat as tears explode. These aren't quiet tears - torn from down deep, they come as great guttural sobs, accompanied by other noises that are barely human. Phlegm clogs my throat and bubbles from my nostrils. I tug on the toilet paper in a feeble attempt to mop up the mess and flush it away.

My grief shatters. It embeds itself in my skin and in the cubicle walls, like tiny splinters of glass. I feel Her presence again. She's beside me, Her hand resting on my shoulder.

'You'll have your mother for six weeks.'

Her voice is soft and sad and certain, and I want Her to be wrong. I want the tests to be wrong. The doctors to be wrong.

It's Tuesday.

Six Mondays later I sit beside my mother's lifeless body. I take her cold hand in mine, press my lips to her palm and place it against my cheek. No more words of wisdom. No more mother's hugs.

Exactly six weeks from diagnosis to death.

In the aftermath of my mother's death, I struggle to right the sinking ship of self. Emotions crash over me and through me like a tsunami. Waves of physical pain that sweep me sideways, tilt the world and dump me, gasping for breath beneath a roiling ocean of confusion.

When the waters recede, things aren't much better. The world left in their wake is broken and disjointed–a dangerous place where vibrant, living, breathing souls can be snatched away without warning, without making any sense in the story of my life.

Even as I struggle to stuff emotions down deep into the dark recesses of my awareness, I cannot ignore the terrible truth that people die. Parents die. My mother's mortality begs a bigger question–one that cannot be ignored.

Am I walking a knife edge between birth and death? Could a sudden slip pitch me back into the black abyss of un-beingness?

Questions tumble around inside me as I walk, wraith-like through the world. In the weeks and months that follow my mother's death I walk a lot–almost constantly–whenever I'm awake. My body processes pain and loss on a cellular level as I move, as my mind struggles to right itself.

Up on a misty mountain, one dark and frosty morning, I find I am no longer walking alone. Although the path is empty, I feel an undeniable presence. Death with her icy chill, walks silently beside me.

She casts no shadow, displaces no air molecules. Her presence is felt with a sense not numbered amongst the usual five. My mind swirls with uncertainty, with fear. What does it mean? Has she come for me?

But somewhere in the midst of this madness, everything stops. Falls silent. Suddenly. No more words. No more thoughts. Just me and the mist and the presence of Death.

When I return to the house, something has changed. The bricks are brighter, the bare branches of oak trees seem almost sinister and the smell of morning dew is overpowering. I feel no connection with this place.

I'm surprised that my key slides easily into the lock and turns. My senses remain heightened as I walk down the hall to the bathroom and splash water on my face. Far from earthing me, the icy water feels like a thousand tiny razor blades slicing through my skin.

The face in the mirror is unfamiliar. I look deep into her eyes and I'm falling, sinking into the inky blackness of her irises as the sound of my breath echoes off shiny white tiles. I step back and slide down the wall to sit at its base. My head falls and the room spins. Vertigo. Above me the ceiling ripples. The floor falls away.

I am stillness at the centre of a spinning vortex. The only sound I hear is the rasp of my breath and the thud of my heart. *Lub dub. Lub dub. Lub dub.* I focus on the rhythmic sound. On the feeling of air filling my lungs and falling away. My heart. My breath. This moment.

It takes a while for the world to stop whirling, for the waves of emotion to stop battering my shores.

Eventually, I pull myself up from the floor and make a cup of tea. The cup warms my hands; the sensation is pleasant. Around me the intensity of sound, colour and smell begins to fade.

Breaths become deeper. My body becomes my own again and settles in the house I call home.

My mother is gone. But life has not. As life gently reasserts itself around me, I dust off the ashes of my grief for a time and sit in silence. Just me, and the cup, and the tea. My pulse thrums in the quiet and thoughts begin to stir.

What is Death? Why do we die? Is there some meaning beyond the biological imperative for renewal? Must the old die and decay simply to make way for the new?

Standing outside myself for a moment, I see that Death has stripped me bare, undone the ties that bound me to my meaning. Death has left me naked to face undeniable truths that I had thought too terrible to comprehend.

In our youth-focused, wellness-obsessed, social-media-curated lives, dying is taboo. A topic to be shunned, a truth to be evaded. Death in our culture is *failure*.

We cling to life as if dying was optional, anointing doctors as high priests and priestesses to worship at the altar of medical science. While these are noble professions and we celebrate the discoveries that extend or increase the quality of our lives, still Death will find us all in Her time.

If there is a meaning in Death it is denied to the living. We can only guess at what lies beyond that last breath. While Faith is a comfort to many, many more will walk on without it.

The unknowable number of our days must be filled with something. Once we know Death, once we accept the finite nature of our lives in more than abstract terms, it changes everything.

For some it becomes a driving force, a power that propels them to succeed. To others it's a burden, a fear that binds them to the past. Some speak of a newfound clarity, while others find the world darker.

Death has changed me too.

My mother's voice was the first I heard from deep within her womb. Her embrace was my protection, providing comfort, security and love. Her wisdom, often unwanted, proved invaluable as I ventured out into the world.

She was far from perfect, but she was perfectly mine.

Now her voice is silent and her embrace is gone. The world has moved beyond her wisdom leaving me to define my own. Death has taught me what it is to truly miss someone, to feel their absence as an absolute rather than a transient truth.

And in doing so, Death has taught me a deeper truth. For knowing what I would miss has shown me what to embrace. Not grand gestures nor crowning successes–for me it is the mundane moments that I treasure most.

The sound of my partner's breath as he slips into sleep. The weight of my dog as she leans against me on the couch. The smile that spreads over a friend's face when we meet.

Death has shown me what is precious, what is important. Death has taught me how to live.

Nina D. Campbell is the author of *Daughters of Eve*, shortlisted for the Danger Awards and long-listed for the Davitt Awards in 2023. Nina studied theatre and literature at university before working as a professional writer across the community and public sectors. A midlife health challenge changed her priorities, and she now writes fiction full time, with a focus on stories about strong women.

Chapter 8

Gertie Up at the Grand
by Athena Law

He finds himself outside the old corner pub again. A leisurely stroll yesterday to rediscover the town of his childhood had led him past the imposing building and now here he is once more, standing on the sunbaked footpath, staring up at the pub. Family commitments complete, he was supposed to be preparing for his long, solitary drive home, yet an odd longing had compelled him back. Uncharacteristically, he ignored his carefully planned schedule.

Clearly long-shuttered, the pub's leadlight windows are filmed with dust and neglect. Impressive once, three storeys high with deep verandahs fringed with ornate ironwork, it now has the distinct, solitary feel of being utterly forgotten about. *You and me both*, he muses, running a hand along the grimy stonework of the windowsill.

It's the sort of country town where the main street is a slow parade of utes bearing hay and cattle dogs, farmers driving with tanned forearms resting along their opened windows. The sort of town where dressing for a night out means tucking a checked shirt into your cleanest jeans and shining up your RM Williams boots. Back in the day, that night out would have brought you here, to the Grand Hotel. It was the last of its kind, and now the other establishments were all the same–loud music, jangling pokies and deep-fried food on the menu.

Standing here, he can recognise the odd feeling again. It's a fluttering inside, a nostalgia for days gone by, an emotional reaching for a simpler time, with a tremor of hopefulness that it could be like that again. Hopefulness he hasn't felt for a long time. *I could rescue it*, he thinks, tracing his finger along the lines of the soft lead between the pink and green glass until it reaches the edge of a faded 'For Sale' sign. *It could be grand once more.*

Before another conscious thought can form, he strides down the footpath and into the real estate office to enquire, purposefully ignoring the butterflies in his belly.

'The old pub?'

The agent hasn't bothered getting up from behind his desk and is shaking his head in disbelief, 'Mate, what would you be wanting to go and do a thing like that for?'

He is at a loss how to respond, not knowing rightly himself.

'Well, I'll tell you one thing for free, I'm not stepping foot into that joint again. Things aren't right, if you get my gist. How about you just grab the keys–' He tossed the set across to him. 'Take your time, when you're done, stick them under the doormat, I'll get them in the morning. And good luck to you.'

There is no hesitating now. The walk back to the corner is decisive, eager. The largest key turns smoothly in the timber front door, which opens with barely a creak. Inside, the bright January morning sunshine filters softly through the coloured glass and decades of dust creating an almost magical haze.

He moves from room to room, around the dark forms of old tables and stacks of chairs, using the torch app on his phone when he needs to. If it wasn't for the stacks of fabric-draped furniture and stale air scented faintly with nicotine and beer it could be as if the pub had just closed yesterday. Everything looks as if it's still here, ready to use at a moment's notice; the original light fittings hang silently, tall silver ashtrays stand to attention, though long-dead plants droop in large pots, withered and brown.

He hesitates at the bottom of a steep timber staircase, a rusted tin sign tacked to the wall proclaiming: GUESTS ONLY and in smaller lettering underneath: NO ACCESS TO THIS STAIRWAY BEFORE 10AM. He checks the time automatically and laughs to himself. It's after ten but he thinks he may delay a visit upstairs to another day, he'll need a stronger torch for that.

He is back in the front bar again. A long timber bench runs the length of the room, a tarnished metal footrail protruding from the base all the way along. On the wall behind the bar are shelves of bottles and, above them, are dozens and dozens of hats. Mainly Akubras, a few of them felt or straw, all of them well-worn, sweat-stained or ripped, with small tags attached to the brims.

The hats have a fine lamina of dust, in fact everything in the room does, but he notices that the timber bar itself is catching the light and appears to be shinier than everything else. He moves towards it, extends his arm, runs his finger disbelievingly along the top–spotless.

'Tsk, tsk!'

His hand is swatted away from the gleaming surface with what seems to be a rag.

'Clean as a whistle my bar–when they call me Dirty Gertie it's as a joke of course. No fingerprints if you please!'

He steps back, gaping, then remembers his manners.

'My apologies, I thought the place was vacant, I had the key, he gave me the key–'

He hears himself stammering and stops, trying to gather his thoughts. She briskly buffs his fingerprints from the polished surface then tucks the rag away in her apron pocket.

'You're nothing but welcome, lad. It's a hot day, why don't you pull up a stool and have a cold one on me?'

It isn't a suggestion, he can tell. He retrieves a stool from the leaning pile against the side wall and places it carefully in front of the bar, sitting down slowly and taking in the woman across from him.

Standing not much more than five feet tall, she has greying hair gathered up high, a long-sleeved navy blouse tucked into a long navy skirt, a crisp white apron tied around her waist, and a quizzical expression on her face.

'New in town, are you? I never forget a face.'

Before he has a chance to answer, she continues. 'That's what the constable down the road always says - you need to know who someone is, then go see Gertie up at the Grand, she'll soon have it sorted, lickety-split.'

It really is a warm day. Sweat is gathering at the nape of his neck. He looks across at the business side of the bar but can't see the promised cold beer in evidence. Discreetly pats his phone where it's nestled in his jeans pocket, and momentarily considers stepping out to phone the agent, to ask why he hadn't warned him of someone still being in residence here.

'You'll want to know about the hats, everyone does on their first visit. The very day I opened this hotel it began–with this one right here,' She deftly flips a stockman's hat off a hook, seemingly in pride of place above the till.

'It were my husband's hat, bless his soul. My Albert passed just a month before this place was finished being built, only thirty-five he was. I had the thought to pop this here, so he could watch over me. Ah, listen to me going on, so sentimental!' She strokes the worn hat fondly and then places it back on its hook.

'And then not long after, my best regulars started putting their old hats up when it was time for a new one, or people just passing through who found it a bit of fun. Sometimes blokes who'd had a few too many sherbets just left them behind here by accident. That tidy dark brown one up there–it's from the mayor, he's signed the brim you know. And that round straw one, Donny Davies brought me back from the Orient, very exotic.'

He silently debates whether to correct her on appropriate place-naming, and ponders if he should clarify to which country she is referring, however Gertie has already moved on.

'That one up the top row with the ripped brim, that were

Jack Wilson's. He courted me for a while, well when I say a while, it was probably two years in all, but he kept going out droving and then coming back. I was younger then, and I thought I might have it in me to marry again. That was just before Christmas, and I was going to say yes when he came back.'

Gertie takes a deep breath in through her nose, she pulls the rag back out of her apron pocket and begins to polish the already-immaculate bar, her face turned away from him.

'He was kicked in the head by a horse on Christmas Eve. He never came back. So, he never knew my answer. They were kind enough to bring me his hat though.'

She uses the soft cloth to dab at her eyes, and when she looks back at him he can see the lines that grief, worry and hard work have etched upon her face.

'Are you wondering why it's right up the top? I know you must be. I kept carrying that darned thing around with me, but there was still work to be done. I had people to meet, new people like you. And my regulars, oh they needed me I can tell you. They still need me.'

He can't help himself. He gestures around the shuttered, dusty room.

'I noticed that your pub seems to be all closed up now? Might it be time to retire?' He asks as gently as possible.

'Oh son, you don't know the half of it. These old bones are tired, I am so very tired. But I must stay on, I'm the only one that remembers.'

She turns to the wall of hats, leans heavily back against the bar and stares upwards.

'I can tell you every name, every story. Their tipple of choice, the names of their kids, the names of their best dogs. Who went off to fight, who didn't return. Who they loved, who they shouldn't have loved, how they lived, how they died. I am the only one that remembers them, and so I must stay.'

He is getting warm again. The air is stale and close and he's beginning to feel a little light-headed.

'Listen to me prattle on! And now I see we're all out of beer, what poor hospitality. It's not usually me doing all the talking, Gertie up at the Grand is a listener for the ages, that's what they say. Now, if I can't offer you a frothy then let me give you this.'

She produces a tan-coloured Akubra from behind the bar and offers it to him.

'This was going to be Jack's Christmas present. I think it's only right you should have it. I'll have to be shutting now, but will you be back to see me soon?'

'I hope so,' he says, and stands up, hat clasped in both hands. He politely stacks the stool back against the wall and when he turns back to promise to return, Gertie is gone.

He calls out a farewell anyway and with a last look at the extraordinary wall of hats, carefully shuts and locks the heavy front door behind him. He slips the keys under the mat as promised and slowly walks the few metres to his car.

He turns the Akubra around, it's heavy and good quality, faded on the top but a richer tan colour underneath. As he raises his head to settle the hat into place, he sees the plaque above the front door of the pub. ESTABLISHED 1913, Proprietors Albert & Gertrude George.

He finds himself in the doorway of the real estate agency yet again. The agent gets out of his chair this time, eyebrows raised.

'Draw up the paperwork, please,' he is saying before he can even think it through.

'It's time for the Grand to have a new publican. Something tells me I have a lot of people to meet, and more hats to gather.'

The butterflies flickering in his belly intensify. The hopefulness hasn't left him after all.

Athena Law lives and writes in the lush Queensland hinterland. One of her stories was shortlisted for the Scarlet Stiletto award, and others have been published by the Australian Writers Centre and *The Ekphrastic Review*. An expert-level procrastinator, she has avoided completing her first novel by attempting to train her ragdoll cats to be more affectionate, listening to writing podcasts and baking her way through her grandmother's recipe book.

Chapter 9

Feathers Like Fingerprints
By Linda Brucesmith

Thelma Street hill pulled everything away from the house. Balls escaped and had to be chased before they bounced into the carpark of the supermarket...down there.

Running was a scary business because downhill falls dropped further and hit the ground harder.

On blazing February days we left the school bus at the far side of the supermarket, adjusted school bags over our shoulders, then trudged in sweaty silence up the hill.

The hill shaped everything.

Forty years pass before my return to Thelma Street on a soft summer's evening. I pull up in a new car before the old house and gaze at the verandah that looks out over Brisbane City. The sparrow's feather I have with me–deep brown and speckled with black – curls around my forefinger. I stroke it with my thumb.

The house seems smaller. Once, the verandah was so high– such a glamorous addition to the lounge room where adults gathered around a well-stocked bar and danced to scratchy 1930s tunes my father played on his reel-to-reel sound system.

Up the drive, the garages under the house opened to a flight of stairs. At the top was a landing. More steps led down to the front door on one side, up to the living area on the other. A hall stand finished with a large mirror, hat and coat hooks stood against the wall of the landing. Arriving home each afternoon, we'd dumped our school gloves and hats there before climbing the final set of stairs to my mother's pink and white meringues, jam-filled donuts and iced milkshakes.

I remember.

My father was a doctor. During the week, he worked in the city. After hours and on weekends he saw patients in a space tucked under the lounge room and verandah. The surgery was a place where he burned things off people's skin and wrote prescriptions at the Cutler desk his father had used in the same way.

People said my father was *devilishly handsome.* At the time, I understood them to mean his movie-star looks made him somehow naughty. Much later, I looked at a black and white photograph of him as he was in the late 1950s when my parents first met–moustache, dinner suit, and a look that *expected* admiration – and understood what devilish really meant.

He wore hats. They hung with our school hats on the hall stand. My panama was trimmed with an apple green and navy blue band; his fedoras with bands of shining fabric and feathers on one side. The panama was regularly squashed. The fedoras weren't.

Over the years, he swept us off to school in a series of larger-than-life cars – a powder-blue DeSoto, a black Cadillac, two Buicks. Each day I sat in the slippery leather front seat next to him, my sister in the back, his hat for the day on my lap.

One morning, he passed me a hat I hadn't seen before. I was dazzled by the feather tucked into the band, all iridescent green and shot through with a flash of golden yellow and – I saw as I held it up–two delicately fine bands of red.

My father asked if I liked it.

'Oh, yes,' I said.

Not the hat so much, but the feather. The feathers in his other hats were brown and speckled with black and pretty enough, but this!

My sister wriggled forward to inspect the feather with me.

Feathers, my father told us, *are like fingerprints. No two people have the same fingerprints, no two birds have the same feathers marked in the same way.* He smiled.

My sister inspected her hands. I stroked the only green feather of its kind with my one-of-a-kind finger.

That summer, the green-feathered hat travelled with us daily. I studied it, smoothed its brightness with my thumb as we drove down Thelma Street, into the buzz of peak hour traffic. I gave it up reluctantly when we arrived at our school gates, left the car to climb another hill to the junior school cloak room, then attended lessons at wooden desks with wrought iron legs and tops that lifted.

I sat in the front row while the rest of the class was rotated, because I couldn't read the blackboard from anywhere else.

Eventually, my father exchanged one of the Buicks for a green Ford GT with a vast bonnet and a broad black racing stripe. Soon after, we started including passengers in the runs to school – stopping first for schoolmates, Vicky and Kerry, then again to collect someone who worked with Dad, called Margaret.

While we squeezed into the back seat with our bags and books on our laps, Margaret took over the front seat, and care of the green-feathered hat.

My mother was a dancer. In Nazi Germany she performed at the Hamburg State Opera for the Germans, then for the Americans. In a persistently bombed city, her coffee merchant father frayed her nerves by tuning his radio to the BBC then opening the second-floor windows of his study wide; the announcer's voice drifted, crisp and British, to the street below.

Later, she ignored air raid sirens to hunt rubbled streets for food with her best friend, another dancer. 'People *looked* at Charlotte; I was too sweet.'

She met the doctor after the war at Hamburg's *Zillertal* beerhouse – an ornate, wood panelled place frequented by ships' officers and their wives. She was with her sister and her sister's husband. He was with his mother on a world tour. The attraction was magnetic.

Within months she had boarded a ship, made the six-week voyage for a country she knew nothing about, arriving in the heat of Queensland and my father. Without a word of English, she acquired the translated works of Goethe, Schiller and Hesse, then read and re-read them with the help of an English-German dictionary. This, she felt, would prepare her for the profound conversations she expected to enjoy in her new home.

Before long, she was struck by Australians' capacity to talk endlessly about the weather, the German equivalent of talking about nothing.

Years later, she was still working to make sense of things.

There was Brisbane's sensuality–its flame-red poincianas and perfumed frangipanis, black-eyed possums and warbling magpies, diamond light and electrical storms. There were mosquitoes to slap at, flies to brush away and breezy Queenslander-style homes to settle into. There were the local ladies who tut-tutted over her not wearing a hat to church; when they did, she stopped attending altogether.

Around the time the Ford took up residence in the garage– dwarfing my mother's Volkswagen – a crust settled over her softness. My mother resurrected the cigarettes she had given up in Europe. Each night after dinner she put us in front of television then disappeared outside to smoke and think.

Knowing how much my father disapproved of smoking, worried he might appear, surprise and chastise her, I would follow her out and sit in the darkness beside her.

One evening, when the cicadas were loud and the stars white, she contemplated me through a tendril of smoke. My father had called her *alien*, she said. I didn't know what that meant.

She told me stories of criticisms used like razor blades on skin–an adult world I didn't understand or, in truth, want to know about. Night after night, I listened.

When we heard the Ford pull in I worried at her anxiety as she stubbed out her cigarette and threw it, no *pushed* it, into the garden. I watched her flee to the shower where she would try– never quite successfully – to wash the smoke away.

Hurriedly, she would urge us to my father as he poured wine, then she would vanish to warm his dinner. There at the bar I would conjure bright, artificial things to say before she reappeared and we disappeared, relieved to get away, to bed.

Each morning, we continued to punctuate our drives into the city by stopping first for Vicki and Kerry – who waited at the end of their driveway–and then for Margaret, who would be standing at her cottage's front gate.

One morning when Margaret wasn't there, my father glanced at her open front door then told me to run in, hurry things along.

I didn't want to. There was a brittle space between the car and Margaret's home I had no interest in breaking through. Margaret's familiarity with us as she slid into the front seat each day made me feel sulky and grim.

I felt sulky now as I marched up the path, up the steps and across her verandah. I knocked bad-temperedly and the sound bounced off the wood-panelled walls inside. I peered through the door into a hallway hung with native art. On a small table beside Margaret's handbag sat a hat just like my father's.

Without thinking I stepped in, picked it up. Tucked into the band was an iridescent green feather shot through with yellow and two delicately fine bands of red.

At that moment Margaret appeared, glanced at the hat, smiled broadly, swept it from me and put it back on the table. She placed one hand firmly on my back and ushered me out. While she chattered about how silly, how *sorry* she was for keeping us waiting, I felt something important had ended. A tightness in my temples said it must be made to start again.

Quietly, I slipped into the back seat next to my sister who looked at Margaret's back then made a *bleaggh* face, eyes dancing. When she saw my expression, she stopped.

That night, my father came home early. We were sitting at the dinner table. I was watching through the servery window as my mother filled our plates when we heard the car pull in. I saw her stop, listening like a cat.

By the time my father made his way into the dining room, my mother had set his meal on the table. He swung in, smiling and jovial. My sister looked up at him, asked what was cooking, good looking and giggled as she picked up her fork.

My father kissed the top of her head, hugged my mother. He disappeared, returned with a bottle of wine and two glasses. My mother regarded him thoughtfully, then smiled.

With that, the world inched back into place. Watching my father flirt with my mother and seeing her glow, I cuddled into my dressing gown, breathed the aromas of warm food. Thinking to make things perfect, I opened my mouth to point out the one small thing that still needed fixing.

'You left your hat at Margaret's,' I said to my father.

'No sweetheart, my hat's in the car,' he said. So handsome.

'The one with the feather,' I looked at him.

'That's right,' he said.

'The fingerprint feather,' I explained.

'Yes, Lou. That's right.'

My mother was staring at me.

I was panicked by the shift I felt happening. Still, I knew I was right. This morning the hat had been where it wasn't supposed to be.

I started again. 'When I went into Margaret's this morning your hat was in the hallway. You must have left it there.'

My father's knife and fork hovered over his plate.

'No, love. I didn't leave my hat at Margaret's. It's in the car. Eat up.'

His reaction–part warning, part dismissal–confused me. He was quite clearly wrong and his pretending otherwise was infuriating.

'Your hat wasn't in the car this morning. It was on Margaret's table. I saw it when I went in to get her. She took it away from me and pushed me out the door...' My words tumbled out.

Now my mother was on her feet. My father slammed his hand on the table. I kept on. Surely they weren't thinking I was lying? That was too much. I glared at my father...

'...she sat in the front seat and said stupid things to you like she always does,' I said loudly.

My mother left the room. I heard her footsteps hurrying down the stairs, the garage door opening, a silence, a slamming of the Ford's heavy door. Then she reappeared, holding my father's hat. She turned it carefully, so I could see the feather.

'You see?' she said.

'You see?' my father echoed, tiredly.

I looked from his hard face to her pale one, bewildered by the heaviness in the room. My sister stared at me in wonder. I burst into tears, the only escape I could find.

'Time for bed, I think,' my mother said.

I went to my father. He put his arms around me, squeezed me tight.

'I'll put your hat away,' I said.

'Good girl,' he said.

'Good night *Süsse,* my sweetheart,' said my mother.

I picked up the hat. My mother gazed at my father hopelessly. I took the hat down the stairs to the landing and stood there with it, stroking the little feather with my thumb, marvelling at its unique loveliness, just like a fingerprint.

One of a kind.

It must be true, Daddy. You told me so.

My parents separated soon after.

I sit in my car, stare up at the old house on this soft summer's evening and wait. The light changes. As the space between then and now disappears, I hear again the Ford as it pulls past me. I see the young doctor as he comes home early. I watch as he pauses after getting out of the car, rests his forehead briefly on the car roof, squares his shoulders, picks up his bag, arranges his face into a smile.

I step onto the street. In the shimmering moments between sunset and dark, I hurry across the road, up the drive and move silently behind my father. He is young. Oh, so young.

There, at the top of the stairs, is the reel-to-reel sound system where my father told my sister, when she asked what he did, that he was a song-and-dance man. There is the fireplace where my mother warmed our pyjamas on cold August nights. There, behind me through the open curtains are the verandah and the lights of Brisbane.

When we reach the dining room, I step back against the window. There we are. Two girls, fresh and pink-cheeked. My sister asks our father what's cooking. He kisses her, smiles at our mother and hugs her. He disappears, returns with wine and two glasses, pours. There I am, bubbling with the thrill of his early arrival, opening my mouth to speak.

I stare at the child I was, communing with her. She shivers a little, frowns. Her father glances at her.

'Yes, Lou?'

'I...' she considers me, regards him. 'I can't see the blackboard except from the front row and everyone else can,' she says.

I smile. Her parents are united in concern.

'Will I have to wear glasses?' Lou asks. Her sister twinkles across the table. Her father quashes her with a look.

'You might, darling, but let's get you tested first. For now, it's bedtime.'

Lou goes to him, squeezes him tight. Her sister follows, ready for bed. When they are gone, my mother and father sit quietly together.

Leaving them there, I find my way down the stairs, pause by the hats on the hall stand. I turn away from the formal entry, take the steps to the garage, peer into the passenger seat of the big Ford. I see the hat. Carefully, quietly, I open the car door, take it out. I stroke the feather tucked into the hatband with my thumb, admire its bright green and yellow, its two delicately fine bands of red.

I take the hat inside with me. I climb to the landing. Before I place it on the hall stand with our school hats, I remove the little feather and its distracting brilliance and replace it with the simple brown sparrow's feather I have brought with me.

Softly, I open the front door, slip through, pull it shut while time falls forward. Tomorrow, I will visit the home my parents later built by the beach, where there are no hills at all.

Linda Brucesmith writes speculative and literary fiction. Her work has appeared in *The Big Issue*, Melbourne Books' Award Winning Australian Writing 2014, and The Fiction Desk's 2013 *New Ghost Stories* anthology (London). She won the Fellowship of Australian Writers' Mornington Peninsula Prize 2013, was shortlisted for the 2013 KSP Speculative Fiction Awards and the 2013 Aeon Awards (Ireland), and highly commended in the 2012 Fellowship of Australian Writers National Literary Awards.

Chapter 10

Howzat!

by Angelina Hurley

Dad was always in the garage painting, while in the background, the crackling sound of a transistor radio was joined by the loud snoring of Spencer, our Labrador-Great Dane cross. I stood blurry-eyed at the garage door, watching Dad create his art. Bold, broad, multi-coloured brush strokes danced alongside each other while others crashed and then blended together. The subject became clearer once he stood back from his easel – a portrait of Dad's childhood hero, Eddie Gilbert. A hero to my father and to our community, the Aboriginal cricketer is famous for outing the legendary Donald Bradman for a duck. Bradman himself acknowledged Gilbert as one of the fastest bowlers he had ever encountered. Drawings, sketches, newspaper clippings, photos and paintings of Uncle Eddie Gilbert lined the garage.

While Dad was painting, Mum, an early riser, would glide by our bedrooms and say, 'Come on, you kids. Get up. Get Ready.' I had been instructed to go and collect Dad from the garage. Mum had been up for ages, cleaning the house and making breakfast, wielding a congested old vacuum cleaner into our bedrooms to make sure we got up.

Motionless, Dad stood for ages looking at his work, sizing up the painting, when I broke the silence. 'Dad, Breakfast is ready.'

'Yeah, yeah,' he replied without moving.

'Today's the day, my brother,' I heard him say as I headed back up to the house.

On Christmas Day 1980, eleven months earlier, it wasn't the usual humidity-drenched morning that woke my parents. It was the high-pitched screams of excitement from my brother and me echoing down the hallway of our house in East Brisbane.

'I've got a big present,' my brother, Ngulang, announced.

'I've got two,' I screeched.

We threw ourselves at the feet of that Christmas tree, a tree that was traditionally 'found' a few days before Christmas in the bush, by my Dad with the help of one of our Uncles or an older cousin. Propped up in a bucket of dirt in the corner of the room, it was lovingly decorated by my mother, with wrapped presents perfectly arranged underneath. Presents that were unceremoniously uncovered in seconds by us kids.

Christmas was announced by the frenzy of wrapping paper being flung into the air, and Spencer's barks as he helped by catching the paper and ripping it to pieces all over the lounge room. Ignoring the mess she would have to clean up, and the destruction of the wrapping paper she hoped to reuse, Mum always greeted us with a smile and a hug. Her heart filled with joy at her children's happiness.

'Merry Christmas, baby,' she'd say.

Dad was excited for a different reason. 'What did you get?' he'd ask, as if he didn't know.

Second to being a visual artist, my father's favourite pastime was being a sports fanatic. For six months of the year, our family would be inundated by football and for the other six by cricket. Dad's obsession leaked into every part of our lives. Wherever he could, Dad would include his love of sport. So, it was no surprise that after unveiling our Christmas presents, my brother and I stared at each other bemused. Like any other twelve and thirteen-year-old at the time, we'd spent months hoping and wishing for the latest trending items.

For my brother, it was a skateboard, and for me, a 1980s metallic-blue Walkman. Dad would always buy us the presents we wanted, but he would also buy us what he wanted too. He was so excited to give my brother his new cricket bat and me my new cricket ball.

'What am I gonna do with this?' I asked.

'Ronnie!' Mum rolled her eyes.

'What?! We can all play together,' he said. 'It'll be deadly.'

Dad had a knack for talking my brother and me into playing cricket in the backyard. We didn't last long on that sweltering thirty-five-degree Brisbane summer day. Even Spencer's enthusiasm waned at having to retrieve a ball that Dad would smash across neighbouring backyards. Reprieve only arrived at the sound of my mother calling us in to eat. Mum's bemusement was yet to come.

Just as she instructed me to set the table, Dad brought out yet another of his fantastic gifts. Mum's eyes widened, impressed by the huge box it came in. What was supposed to be the sewing machine she had been hinting at for years turned out, in fact, to be the cricket-themed board game *Test Match*. Another thing my sports-fanatic father wanted.

The look of disappointment on Mum's face was too much for Dad to bear. It didn't take long for him to produce the impressively wrapped present she really wanted. He wasn't about to let anything get in the way of the pending indulgent three-course Master Chef Christmas lunch she was famous for preparing every year. It was only after the bloating and rumbling of stomachs had subsided, that we participated in the family fun of manoeuvring a set of figurines around a green felt cricket field in a game of Test Match. Boxing Day, 1980, the cricket theme would carry on.

Our old Queenslander sat regally on a mound alongside many

others that lined Vulture Street back then. We had a great view of the river and the city from our lounge room, free from the encroaching development of high-rise apartment blocks, and often hung out the sliding stained-glass windows, peacefully absorbing the panorama of inner-city suburbia. The Gabba, the famous Woolloongabba Stadium, venue for all the major matches, was just up the road from where we lived. The only thing that would interrupt the serenity was, you guessed it, cricket season.

Two sounds resonate from my childhood, one is cheering crowds. All summer celebrations rang from the stadium. The buoyant roars of the fans after a six was struck floated through the air across the whole neighbourhood. The other sound is the sports commentary that came from my Dad's art studio in the backyard garage, where he worked. The blare of obnoxious discourse from the transistor radio that he was glued to all summer long. It hurt my ears, hence my necessary request for a Walkman at Christmas.

The new year, 1981, had kicked in before we knew it. It was the year two synchronous events took place. Dad's passion for sports went beyond just being a fan to playing it, too. If Dad wasn't painting, he'd be playing cricket. He'd play every weekend.

My brother and I would often get conned into playing cricket in the backyard with Dad. *One cent per ball*, he'd say, the promise to pay kept us playing all afternoon. We don't remember ever getting paid.

That November, trials were taking place for members of local cricket teams to compete for selections into the state team. We were dragged to game after game that summer in the lead-up. We were super grateful for our Christmas presents during the long days when Dad played with his local team on the weekends. The Walkman entertained me through Dad's drawn-out matches, and the skateboard kept my brother busy zipping around the park, while my mother, under the cover of a shady tree, only stopped crocheting to wave at Dad when he bowled someone out.

'Howzaaaaaaat!' you'd hear him scream across the field.

Saturday, 28 November 1981, the day Dad told his portrait of Uncle Eddie Gilbert, was 'the day'. It was a slow, traffic-congested drive to the park where Dad played cricket and where the trials were being held that weekend. People were everywhere. We couldn't figure out why. Dad's games had never been that popular, but that day, Dad was convinced he would be a contender and make the state team.

I thought all those people couldn't all be going to Dad's trials. I was right. An historic event was also taking place that day, the test match between Australia and Pakistan at the Gabba. Crowds were lining the streets, the buzz contagious, and spilling over to the park where Dad's team was playing. What was usually a boring, drawn-out day for us was filled with excitement and anticipation. We watched all the teams sweat in the blazing sun. We watched Dad play inning after inning. We clapped and cheered for every four he made to the boundary and every six he smashed beyond it. We jumped at every catch he took and bowled wickets that ended an opponent's run.

'He's out!' we yelled from the sideline.

At the top of the pitch, Dad stood staunch in his crisp, clean whites, meticulously prepared by Mum. He stood out – a tall Aboriginal man invoking the spirit of his hero, Uncle Eddie Gilbert. He'd stare for what seemed like ages, making the opposition wait before delivering a fastball. Batter after batter threw a tantrum after being bowled by Dad or being quickly caught out.

Dad's skill didn't go unnoticed by the judges, and nor did they by us as we watched for a reaction. We thought Dad was a shoo-in, but the stern faces of three white cricket officials judging the competition gave nothing away. There was a familiar sense of extreme conservatism, the kind that governed our state and our lives in Joh Bjelke-Petersen's corrupt conservative Queensland at the time. As if reenacting the closing of a parliamentary meeting, with an air of English aristocracy and arrogance, the sour-faced judges rose from their perches and left the viewing box.

The day came to a close. Player after player greeted Dad, congratulating him with a pat on the back. Even opposition players came over to shake his hand. One of the cricket officials appeared and posted a long list of the final selections on the noticeboard. Our family was nervous but confident. Dad had bowled his heart out that day. He took more wickets than any other player. He was a clear choice for selection. The crowd gathered around the notice dispersed to leave Dad standing alone.

'What happened?' asked Mum.

As he turned, the expression on his face was a composed combination of anger and disappointment. 'Go get the car,' he said as he walked away.

'The racist bastards,' said my Uncle, who'd accompanied us to the game.

As the crowd roared out of the Gabba stadium, we circled the block a few times in our old green Chrysler VF Valiant, but we couldn't find Dad.

'Can you see your father?' asked Mum, craning around to us kids in the back.

We were scanning the streets for ages when we noticed a small crowd of excited fans gathered around a cricket player on the corner. We slowed down in anticipation of possibly seeing a member of the Pakistani cricket team. As we turned the corner, the mystery celebrity was revealed.

'Is that ya bloody father?' asked Mum.

We found out later that signing autographs was common for Dad. After cricket practice on the weekend, dressed in his full cricket whites, he would frequently stand on that corner near the Gabba stadium signing autographs. An Aboriginal cricketer? Really? It was easier and highly amusing to Dad to just let everyone believe that he was either an Indian or Pakistani player. He'd stand there for ages with his fans.

Belting the car horn, Mum slowed down. 'Ronnie! Get in the car!' she yelled.

Flashing a Cheshire-cat smile, Dad clocked us with an enthusiastic wave before two security guards appeared to interrupt the autograph-signing session. A frenzied and animated discussion followed before they whisked him away. What was going on? Was he being arrested?

Mum swiftly pulled the car over to the curb, and we all jumped out. Dad's small crowd waving photos, T-shirts and pens rushed towards the stadium gates, where they'd taken Dad. The security guards quickly shut and locked the gates in front of us. Dad didn't seem to be bothered. Looking back at us, he gave another wave and was ushered toward the cricket field.

'Ronnie!' Mum yelled after him, worried.

Forever seemed to pass as we waited outside those gates in silence. We tried to get the staff's attention, but they ignored us.

'Do you know him?' a fan asked my brother.

'Yeah, he's my dad,' he said.

'Oh my God! Can I have your autograph too?' she asked.

Mum clipped my brother across the back of his head as he too started signing autographs.

'What?' he said, looking up at her with a grin just as cheeky as Dad's.

A cricket player resembling Dad started walking onto the field.

'There he is!' screeched a fan.

As we stretched our necks to try to get a glimpse, the cheering of forty thousand cricket fans greeted him, and the raucous sound shook the Gabba's foundations. Suddenly, silence took over, but just for a moment until the distant sound of running feet and a cricket ball colliding with a set of wickets had the crowd in an uproar.

'HOWZAT!!!!!!!!!!' yelled forty thousand people.

My brother looked up at me. 'Was that Dad?'

Was it? Or was it mistaken identity? That's something we'd

never know for sure. Just like the crowd that gathered around him on the corner, Dad let our imaginations run free. From then on, this event would be known via the family Aboriginal Murri grapevine as the day Dad got selected to bowl for the Pakistani Cricket Team. Regardless of our disinterest in and dislike for cricket, my family holds this memory close to our hearts.

To this day, I can't help but giggle at the devoted fans' acquisition of cricketing memorabilia signed, *Love Ron xoxo*.

Angelina Hurley is a Brisbane writer across multiple genres from the Gooreng Gooreng and Mununjali nations on her father's side, and Birriah and Gamilaraay nations on her mother's side. Her father is renowned Aboriginal visual artist, Ron Hurley. Angelina's writing debuted with the 2009 short film, *Aunty Maggie and the Womba Wakgun*. She was awarded the 2011 American-Australian Fulbright Indigenous Scholar and is undertaking her PhD at Griffith University, focused on Aboriginal humour.

Chapter 11

Morning Rays

by Melissa A Kitchen

It was early dawn on the first Monday morning of my school vacation, and I was floating somewhere between slumber and being awake when I found myself awed by the streaks of brilliant sunlight shining through the windows.

The light of the rays reminded me of an idyllic painting that had hung in my grandmother's living room. I had lost myself in that country scene many times as a young child, exploring each sheep, shrub, tree and fence. Green meadows and flowers covered the hillside, and the baby blue sky and the white fluffy clouds were alight with golden highlights; this was how she pictured Heaven must look.

In these early morning hours, it felt as if those same rays were shining through the windows of my living room, bringing me a feeling of peace that I had never experienced before.

Just last evening, I – a senior in high school–had hung out with friends in the basement of my family's split-level ranch. We watched videos of a dance that our band had performed for at our local high school. We had a great time reviewing and critiquing each song from the performance, and doing this was a way to keep that night alive for us.

I knew when I left for college in the fall these performances would be few and far between...if I would even be able to continue with the band at all. While I was ready and excited for my next steps at music school, I also knew in my heart that everything was changing. I was a year older than the other members of the band – my best friends, my teammates, my family for the last six years – and I would be the first to leave this tight-knit group that had grown up together.

I was grateful that I was even able to be there for the performance; I had originally been scheduled that week to be on my senior class trip to London. But outside circumstances had intervened–a *force majeure*, whatever the term–and the political climate was not safe for young travelers at this time. That December in 1985, five American citizens were killed in simultaneous terrorist attacks at the airports in Rome and Vienna. Libya was blamed, and the US ordered expanded sanctions. Then on 24 March 1986, US and Libyan forces clashed in the Gulf of Sidra.

From the very beginning of these clashes, I decided that I did not want to go on the trip. My closest friends were still all in, adamant about continuing with the trip as long as there was a trip to go on. I felt silly about my discomfort; my mother said she appreciated my decision though.

At the time, I didn't feel that traveling under unfriendly circumstances would be worth it. I had been to Spain on a previous school trip during my sophomore year, and I still have wonderful memories of interacting freely with locals. Now, I didn't think that any of those experiences would have been possible.

Eventually, on 5 April, terrorists bombed a West Berlin dance hall known to be frequented by US servicemen. One of these men and a Turkish woman were killed, and more than two hundred people were wounded. This was the final straw, and the tour group officially canceled the trip and returned all deposits and payments received.

On 14 April, less than a week from our original departure date, the United States struck back, with dramatic airstrikes against Tripoli and Benghazi. I was relieved to be home, safe and sound, watching videos, snacking on Ruffles potato chips and laughing at outtakes from the concert with my bandmates. I was grateful for this extra time with them, my people.

We were on the third replay of the recording, singing along to our own performance of the Motels' 'Only The Lonely' when we were interrupted by the doorbell. As I got up to answer it, I was surprised that my parents' friends, Mr and Mrs M, had already entered and were calling out to me. They found us in the basement.

I was confused as to why they had come over. My parents were out to dinner with friends–had they double-booked their night? Or maybe they were there to pick up my best friend, their daughter?

'My parents aren't here,' I said.

'Yes, we know,' Mrs. M said. She glanced timorously at Mr M. 'That's not why we are here, honey. We are actually here because your dad gave us a call.'

She looked around, noticing that my brother and sister had entered the room. 'Your father called to tell us they had to bring your mom to the hospital; she collapsed after dinner. He's with her now. We don't have a lot of information, but wanted to be with you guys while we waited for an update, or for them to return.'

What were they saying? My mother was thirty seven and healthy–never sick, aside from occasional headaches. Our gregarious group was now totally silent, broken by cautious murmurs or positive wishes.

'She'll be okay,' my friends said. 'We'll get good news soon.'

Several hours later, my father returned and joined us in the basement. His face was swollen from tears, and wracked from the strain of the stressful evening. At first, he was unable to speak, then he gathered us together.

'I don't have an actual update,' he said quietly as our family embraced. 'They're saying your mother had a cranial aneurysm, kind of like a time bomb that has been ticking unnoticed and that just decided to burst. We don't know what the outcome will be... we need to pray for a miracle. We can do that, right?'

He looked at us all for confirmation, and the four of us collapsed together into tears. Gradually, my friends left, offering words of support and encouragement. My father, sister, brother and I eventually snuggled up in different parts of the living room, comforting each other and awaiting the news of our miracle.

I could not imagine how this would have felt if I'd been continents away in London. I now knew the reason my trip was canceled and plans were changed: heaven had intervened. No one could sleep, but the room became silent as we reluctantly took turns dozing.

It was here that, somewhere between slumber and wakefulness, I found myself in awe of the streaks of brilliant sunlight shining through the windows. The light reminded me of the idyllic painting in my grandmother's living room.

I felt my attention guiding me towards the top of the entryway stairs, and then down to the front door. Even the three small windows in the door had bursts of golden light, the kind of rays that mesmerised me as a young child with their dancing dust particles.

I noticed a figure at the landing, in front of the door. I tried to make out the shape, but the light was so brilliant that all I could see was the outline. As I tried to focus my vision, out of the light I saw that the figure was my mother.

She was smiling up at me with her sparkling blue eyes and

crooked smile. I wanted to run to meet her, but I was frozen in place.

'Don't worry,' she said in a calm, loving tone. 'You're alright. You'll be alright. I will always be with you. I love you.'

I tried to respond, but the form seemed to dissipate into the morning light. I was back in the living room, the only one awake.

I would learn later that morning that my mother had passed away peacefully at the exact same time as my vision.

So it is, all these years later, that I reflect on my experience and see how it has been an anchor throughout my life. As an adolescent graduating high school without my mother, a young adult also losing my father, a young wife getting married without either of my parents, and eventually as a mother facing breast cancer and the fear that I, too, might leave my own children behind.

I have always found strength in my mother's words:

I am alright.

I will be alright.

She is always with me...and I am loved.

Since losing her parents at a young age, Melissa Kitchen has focused on preserving her past – building the bridge between generations for her children through documenting family stories. Author of *Bridging Your Past and Future: The Top 10 items to include when documenting your personal history* and host of the *Preserve Your Past* podcast, Melissa uses her talents as a teacher, counsellor, writer, and coach to help others do the same.

Chapter 12

Must Save the World Before Breakfast

by Daan Spijer

Trevor rolled over as the alarm sounded. He looked at the time and contemplated it before hitting the 'stop' button. Two hours before dawn. He let his head sink back onto the pillow. Why was he waking so early? He thought hard and then remembered – he'd promised the old man at the café he would join him at five o'clock to help him save the world. He groaned and then slowly rolled himself off the bed.

As he showered, he mused on how his unthinking responses to people's remarks sometimes landed him in things he really would rather avoid. This was an example.

He thought back to the day before. He'd been sitting in a local café with a cup of coffee, enjoying the fact that he'd been able to leave work early for a change. The owner of the place had quipped about some people taking it easy, instead of doing something important with their lives.

Trevor had responded with, 'Oh, I have. I've already saved the world today.'

'That's nothing, mate,' came the quick reply. 'I did that before breakfast.'

'What do you mean?'

'I get up early every morning to save the world before breakfast. You know, fix up the mess while most people are still in bed.'

Trevor didn't know how to take this. 'You're joking, right?'

'No mate. Every morning before breakfast.'

When he went to pay for his coffee, Trevor joked, 'Want some help?'

'With what?' the owner asked.

'Saving the world.'

The owner considered Trevor, then nodded. 'Right you are then. Five o'clock tomorrow morning, here.'

'You're *not* joking, are you?'

'No mate, I'm not joking. Important work to be done'

The owner gave Trevor his change and called after him as he made for the door, 'See you in the morning then.'

Trevor gave a thumbs-up sign as he left.

Now, as Trevor dressed warmly, he was having second thoughts. Not about getting up and out so early (this would be an adventure), but about the old man – whether he was off his tree and, maybe, even dangerous.

He arrived outside the café ten minutes early. It was too cold to stand still, so he walked up and down and repeatedly slapped his arms around his shoulders. He kept looking at his watch – had he been taken for a ride? Then at five o'clock on the dot, the old man came through the front door, carrying two steaming cups of coffee.

'Thought you might need waking up and warming up,' the old man said as he handed Trevor one of the cups. 'In fact, I doubted you would show.'

'Always up for a challenge,' Trevor replied. 'What tasks have you got lined up today?'

'Just the one,' was the reply. 'Come, we'll take my car. It's 'round the back.'

They drove for almost an hour along the bay and into the city. The only conversation was an exchange of names. The old man said his name was Ronald, but that some people called him

Batman, because of the large, black coat he often wore. 'Call me Ron,' he offered.

Ron pulled up and parked in a 'No Standing' zone outside the main railway station on the edge of the city. It was still dark and the cold air hit Trevor as he stepped out of the car.

From the back of the car Ron called, 'Here, give me a hand.'

Trevor joined him and saw two huge cooking pots in the boot. 'You take one, I'll take the other,' Ron told him, as he lifted one pot out and started carrying it into the station concourse. Trevor followed with the second. Damn, it was heavy! And it was uncomfortably warm against his leg.

'What's in them?' he called to Ron's back.

'Soup,' Ron called back over his shoulder.

Inside, there was a large gathering of dishevelled people. Many wore coats; some had scarves or beanies or both. Their breaths were clearly visible in the cold air, even under the concourse roof.

As Trevor and Ron proceeded with the heavy pots, the people in the crowd moved to make a path for them. At the far end stood a row of trestle tables on which were portable gas cookers, piles of bowls and spoons and mountains of bread rolls.

'Morning Batman,' called an old man, as Ron lifted his pot onto a cooker. 'You've brought Robin with you today.'

There was laughter from those who heard this. Ron smiled. 'Yeh. Saving the world is hard work on my own.' There was more laughter.

Someone called out, 'When are you going to bring Batgirl?'

'When she turns up,' Ron responded.

Other people arrived with more pots and soon the hungry assembly was tucking into bowls of steaming soup and fresh bread.

'Who are these people?' Trevor asked quietly as he ladled soup into bowls.

'Ask *them*,' Ron said.

'I can't do that!'

'Yes you can.'

Trevor felt self-conscious and it showed.

Ron grinned and addressed a teenage girl standing close by. 'Hey Amy, tell Robin here where you spent the night.'

The girl shrugged and pointed over her shoulder. 'In the doorway of the church out there.'

Trevor felt shocked. 'But you can't be more than fifteen. How come you don't have a home?'

The girl shrugged again. 'I'm twelve and me mum kicked me and my brother out when her new boyfriend moved in.'

Trevor didn't know how to respond. He looked at Ron and raised his eyebrows in a question. Ron inclined his head towards the crowd. 'All of them live out on the streets or in derelict buildings.'

Trevor looked out at this gathering of society's neglected and rejected, but didn't have much time to dwell on his thoughts – there were empty bowls to deal with and bowls to fill for those who wanted seconds.

Trevor's belly rumbled. 'Have some yourself,' Ron said as he handed Trevor a bowl of steaming soup. Trevor took it with a smile and a thank you. He already felt warm from the work and from the growing feeling that he was doing something worthwhile. He watched people who had come in on the first trains glance awkwardly towards the homeless eating their one 'good' meal of the day. Some of them looked affronted at this invasion of their world.

As people finished eating, most brought their spoons and empty bowls back. Some voiced thanks; others indicated their appreciation with a nod or a wave; some simply walked off.

'Do you come here every morning?' Trevor asked Ron.

'Yep. Every morning, no matter what the weather or the season. It's easier in the summer, though.'

Some of those who had been fed hung around to help carry things back to cars and to collect bowls and spoons which had been left lying around the station concourse. One old man grumbled loudly, 'Some people have no dignity,' as he picked up a broken bowl and a mess of bread pieces.

Trevor noticed that one of those clearing up was a woman of about his age – mid-twenties. He had noticed her earlier, because her clothes seemed in better condition than most. She caught Trevor looking at her and half smiled, before turning away. He asked Ron if he knew the woman.

'No, mate. Saw her for the first time last week. Don't know who she is. Why d'you ask?'

'I don't know. She looks vaguely familiar.' When he looked up again, he saw the woman walking off towards the street.

As the last of the soup kitchen was packed up and removed, the concourse was increasingly taken over by commuters, most of whom had no idea of what had been happening there for the past hour. It was as if the normal world had reclaimed its territory.

When Trevor and Ron returned to the car for the last time, there was a parking attendant standing nearby. Trevor expected a parking ticket, but the attendant spoke to Ron like a friend. 'Morning Batman.'

'Morning Rachmoon,' Ron replied. 'Thanks again for looking after us.'

Rachmoon raised his hand. 'No problem. Always happy to help you people.'

Trevor smiled at this obvious bending of the rules. The circle was wider than he realised.

As they drove back along the bay, Trevor asked Ron how long he had been doing this.

'Oh, I've been saving the world for years.' He thought for a while. 'Must be about four years now. I started after I opened the café.'

'Why?'

'I had to come through the city real early one morning and saw stuff being carried into the station, so I stopped and found out what was going on. I said I could help out with soup. The others are all from various restaurants. The rolls are donated by a couple of bakeries. It's all organised by one of the Rotary clubs.'

Back at the café, the place was abuzz with people tucking into eggs and sausages and bacon and fresh bread and coffee and juice.

'Hungry?'

Trevor nodded.

'What'll it be?'

'Scrambled eggs'd be great, thanks.'

Ron called out to one of the staff, 'Usual for me and scrambled eggs for Robin here. And...' He looked at Trevor. 'Coffee?'

'Long black, please.'

Trevor felt good. He looked at Ron, who was leaning back in his chair with a pleased look on his face. 'Do you want help again tomorrow?'

'Sure Robin. I'd enjoy the help... and the company.' He winked.

Trevor smiled. 'I can't wait to tell people at work how I helped save the world before breakfast.'

'Oh, you haven't done that yet, mate. You've only just started your apprenticeship.'

Next morning Trevor let himself in through the back door and helped load the car. He happily sipped his coffee as they drove into the city.

As he was filling bowls of soup, he noticed the better dressed woman again. She was standing on her own, leaning against a pillar. Ron noticed him looking.

'Go talk to her. We'll be alright here.'

'No, it's okay,' Trevor said, blushing.

'Go on, mate. Take yourself a bowl of soup. I know you're dying to.' Ron handed him a full bowl and gave him a friendly push.

Trevor felt self-conscious but tried to look nonchalant as he sauntered over to where the woman stood. 'Hi,' was all he managed.

She looked up, was about to say something but took a bite of her bread roll instead.

'I'm sorry,' Trevor ventured. 'I know this sounds stupid, but I think I know you from somewhere.'

'Maybe. You were here yesterday, right?'

'Yes. But I mean before that.' He studied her as she went back to eating. Then it hit him. 'Heidelberg Heights Secondary, right?'

She looked up, with a puzzled expression on her face.

'We were in French together, at school. My name's Trevor. Trevor Amorie.' He waited, holding his breath.

The woman studied him for a moment. 'Yes. I remember you. You used to piss the teacher off with your lame jokes.'

Trevor nodded, remembering how he used to try and cover his difficulty with the language by making fun of it. 'You're Julie, aren't you? You used to be really good.'

She nodded but didn't say any more.

'What happened? I mean, how come you're here?'

She looked up and tears glistened in her eyes.

'Sorry,' he said. 'I don't mean to pry.' He didn't know what else to say. Then he had a thought and pulled out his wallet. The woman looked shocked. 'No, no,' he assured her. 'I'm just going to give you my card from work.' He handed her a card and she looked at it and put it in her coat pocket.

'Please ring. I'd like to talk some more. When you feel like it. Please do,' he added.

She nodded and walked to the trestles to return her bowl and spoon. Then she left.

On the drive back with Ron, Trevor was quiet, deep in thought. He couldn't imagine why Julie would be out on the streets. Ron didn't say anything, or ask about Trevor's interest in the woman.

The next two mornings, Julie didn't come to the station for breakfast. Trevor worried that he had frightened her off. Then on the fifth morning of his helping Ron she was there again. Trevor nodded to her in acknowledgement, and left it at that.

Later that morning, at work, the receptionist buzzed him and said there was a woman on the line claiming to be calling on a private matter. Trevor's heart skipped a beat as he said he'd take the call.

'Hullo, Ron Amorie here.'

There was silence for some time, then a hesitant voice. 'Hi... I... I'd like to talk... but ... I... but not on the phone.'

Trevor arranged to meet Julie after work. He suggested a café in Fitzroy, near where she was sheltering in a disused warehouse. Next morning he drove to Ron's café half an hour early, knowing that Ron would be in the kitchen.

'Good morning Robin,' Ron said in surprise, when Trevor let himself in. 'Saving the world has become more urgent, has it?'

'Actually...' Trevor hesitated.

Ron stopped and looked intently at Trevor. 'Out with it, lad. What's on your mind?'

'Well, you see... Remember that woman at the station a couple of days ago? The one I told you I know from school?'

Ron nodded. 'Yes?'

'Can we give her a lift into town?'

'From where?'

'Eh, well... from here,' Trevor blurted out.

Ron studied him. 'What have you done, mate?'

'It's not like that, Ron.'

Ron raised his eyebrows.

'Honest Ron, she slept on the couch. I told her I might be able to help her find a job.' He stopped and looked at Ron, who was looking worried.

'It doesn't work like that, mate. You can't go taking them *all* home, you know.'

'I don't intend to. But I've heard an actress say recently that she can't save the whole world at once but that she'd save the world one child at a time. And this is someone I went to school with and I think I can help her before she sinks down to where most of the others are. There's still a good chance for her.'

Ron shook his head. 'Could be dangerous, you know, getting personally involved.'

Trevor grew angry. 'It's all well and good for you, saving the whole world each morning. But what about really saving one person? Why's that wrong? What are you afraid of? I don't...'

Ron held his hand up and Trevor stopped his outburst. 'You may be right, mate. I shouldn't judge. By all means bring her along.'

'Ta, Ron.' Trevor took a breath. 'You'll understand when you talk to her, none of it's her fault.' He went out through the back door to fetch Julie.

On the drive along the bay, Julie talked haltingly with Ron. She explained that she'd been married and had a two-year-old son. Her husband and son were killed in a car crash. She had no siblings and no family – her parents had both died some years before. Her husband's family would have nothing to do with her after the crash, blaming her. She'd become depressed, started taking drugs, lost her job and was kicked out of the rented flat.

After breakfast at the station, Julie helped clear up. Ron invited her back to his café for a 'better breakfast'. As the three of them tucked into their eggs, Ron was more thoughtful than Trevor had seen him before.

'Maybe I've been wrong,' Ron offered, looking at Trevor, then at Julie. 'Maybe I've been hiding, hoping not to get personally involved.'

The other two said nothing as Ron went back to eating. Then Ron looked at them again. 'Maybe the world can't be saved before breakfast. Maybe it takes all day.'

Trevor and Julie still said nothing. Ron looked at Julie. 'I need another waitress here, for the afternoon shift.' He took a sip of his coffee. 'Would you like the job?'

Julie's mouth fell open. She looked at Trevor, who smiled back and gave a nod in Ron's direction. Julie looked back at Ron. 'That... that would be great. I mean... yes please.' She smiled.

'Well,' Ron said. 'We must all try and save the world before dinner.'

Daan Spijer writes poetry, short stories, essays and plays, many of which have won awards. His work has appeared in several journals and anthologies, and he is a former editor of *The Australian Writer* and of a medical journal. Many of his short plays have been performed. Daan is a lawyer, mediator and a keen photographer. He lives with his wife and groodle in Mount Eliza on the Mornington Peninsula, Australia.

Chapter 13

Love the World, Again

by Catherine Edwards

The sky is bruised blue and grey in anticipation of the coming rain. A few lonely raindrops hit the window. An almost lazy rumble bounds through the house. My daughters come flying down the corridor and throw themselves on the couch, tucking their heads in under my arms. A streak of lightning ignites the whole sky.

I rub the girls' backs and listen as the storm approaches. At first, it is a distant drumming, drop after drop, and then it starts to run towards us and it sounds like a thousand tiny rocks hitting the glass. Thunder and lightning call to each other, filling the house with noise and sharp light. My daughters whimper and refuse to look, nestling deeper into the couch.

I want them to look out the window and see the leaves changing colour and turning slick under the water. I want them to see how the young trees dance in the wind. I want them to see the grass deepen to emerald green and the tiny white flowers hidden amongst the blades raise their heads in defiance. I want them to see those tiny flowers resist the storm and last through it.

I grew up in the country. In a place where rain was always welcome and when it came it was never gentle. It never drizzled or wept. It arrived in a flood. The soil gulped it down and rewarded us with meaty tomatoes and heady basil. Often it didn't rain and we relied on tanks and trucks. We drank powdered milk made with tank water that tasted like chalk and coated our tongues in white paste.

My childhood was spent outside in the weather. Autumn breezed in on southerly winds, chilling the mornings and keeping us tucked in our beds for longer. In deep winter, the fog was so thick you could scoop it with a spoon. Spring was a riot of colour and promise. And summer was when our limbs grew long and gangly and our skin shone with too much sun. Twilight was our favourite time when the sun dipped below the horizon and the sky turned pink. Cricket bats were bought out and we played until the mosquitos won. My childhood was one season following the other. One good thing after the last good thing.

Here and now, the rain settles into a persistent but gentle patter and my girls unhook themselves from my protection and shoot off back to their room to their books and games. The storm is already forgotten.

Lightning flickers in the distance and I strain to hear the thunder murmur. The thick humid air that has coated our skin during the day and rested heavy on us at night, has been washed away. I crack the window open an inch and the cool, clean air skips over my face. I breathe deeply. It is in these moments that I am learning to look for the good things and love the world again.

Another summer, years ago, we sat on the beach with our tiny girls, building sandcastles and dripping ice cream down our chins. The heat pressed down onto our skin and into our bones. The water rippled and shimmered. The girls were slick with sunscreen and gritty sand found its way into the creases in their thighs and arms.

Mid-afternoon, the wind arrived with a rage and determination that sent umbrellas windmilling down the beach and flinging towels into the ocean. We gathered our things and ran to the car, the sand whipping against our legs and stinging. Everyone ran to get off the beach. Not only had the wind changed, but something in our collective understanding had been piqued. Something was happening.

Back at our campground, the news was passed from tent to tent. Bushfires. Racing through the country. We made calculations, we debated. We talked to fellow campers, some of whom were already half-packed, their tents flapping about as they ripped the pegs from the ground.

We didn't want to drive and we didn't want to stay. We moved into a recently vacated cabin and watched the news. That night the sky glowed orange.

When we left the next day we travelled north towards my family in the country. The roads were blocked and we were turned away. We skirted the city and tried another way, only to be turned back again. It seemed like the whole world was on fire.

My family were lucky ones, they were safe. But the feeling of the furious wind speeding down the beach and driving us away has stuck with me over the years. I have cowered at the news and muted social media. I have bunkered down and made my world small in the hope that the furious wind will not find me or my family again.

But my girls ask questions and I am forced to look at the world again.

The world is a swirling mess of climate change and political unrest and war and heartache. Like the humid air we have lived with all summer, the chaos of the world hangs heavy over me and threatens to topple me. The effort of believing in better things, for more humanity, for more peace, is too much. It is easy to not look, and keep myself and my life small. I want to protect my girls from the furious wind and the reality of the world.

But at school, the girls are learning about asylum seekers and refugees, about climate action and Doctors Without Borders. It is a sanitised version but it is true and real. They run home with plans to collect their well-worn toys and books to donate to kids in need. They raid the pantry for cans of soup and bags of lentils to take for the school food drive. They beg me for coins for 'free-dress days' to fundraise for charities I've never heard of. They run from issue to issue with open hearts and open hands. They lap up the chance to help. They are not scared of the world.

The school takes them on an excursion to the Immigration Museum and I trudge along as a parent helper. Hand in hand the kids walk through rooms of stories. In one room an enormous wishing tree floats down from the ceiling. Hundreds of hand-scrawled notes of hopes and dreams hang off it. The notes flutter with the combined breath of thirty children. With chubby fingers wrapped around crayons and hushed whisperings, the girls write, 'love' and 'peace' on scraps of paper. With reverence, they peg them to the wishing tree and run to the next room to see what's next.

The next room is filled with walls of text and black-and-white photos. Cabinets display artefacts from the gold rush era and cooking tools bought over on boats and backs. The girls colour in pictures of maps and flags. They hear stories about First Australians and New Australians. These stories become part of their understanding of the world: that there is room for everyone. There is a time for gentleness and a time for fighting. There is a time to speak up and time to sit quietly and learn.

The hamster wheel of my mind tries to catch up with them and their fierce understanding of the world. They dance and play, they learn and act. Somehow they have found the balance.

And the shock of realisation leaves me breathless: maybe it was never meant to be me leading and teaching them. Maybe it was always meant to be them leading me towards hope and love. Perhaps this is how I start to nudge back into the world and see it clearly again. They don't see the chaos and failure, they see opportunity and life. I have forgotten the very ground I stand on and the beauty of small moments. I have forgotten that chaos can beget hope. My girls are showing me the way.

So I start small. I start by going back to the basics. Appreciating the smell of coffee brewing first thing in the morning. The feel of my daughter's hands in mine. Books and walks.

Mopping the floor until it shines. Poetry and tea. Texting a friend to share a recipe. The sun streaming through the windows in the early morning. Cake and laughter. Small and insignificant things that capture all that is good.

Watching the girls has taught me to slow down and take a moment to see what they do. The rainbow in the oily puddle in the middle of the road.

There are parts of this chaotic world that are hard to look at and I have hidden away from them. And in doing that I've also missed the goodness and joy and lightness that is waiting to be found. The one good thing that follows the last good thing. But my girls pay attention to the earth, the sky, to others and each other, and point the way ahead for me.

When I look at my girls and their wide-open hearts and hands, the readiness to step towards rather than turn away, that is when I see the world clearly. And when the storm clears and the cool air comes, and the tiny white flowers resist and thrive despite the storm, this is when I love the world again.

Catherine Edwards writes and dreams on the land of the Wurundjeri people (Melbourne, Australia). Her poems and creative non-fiction have been seen her shortlisted for the Ada Cambridge Biographical Prose Award, longlisted for the Big Issue Fiction Award, featured in the *Grieve* anthology and published locally. Catherine's love of nature is often present in her work. She is currently working on her first novel.

Chapter 14

It's Been a Year

by Emma Grey

One year living with his absence as an enormous, conspicuous, ever-present backdrop behind our 'show must go on' performance.

One year with a physical ache in my chest.

One year with unused shaving gear on his side of our bathroom vanity. A year with his jeans slung over a chair in our bedroom — his glasses up-turned on his desk.

One year of pulling into a driveway beside his car, being tricked sometimes into thinking he must be home.

A year of unlocking the front door of the house where we had our wedding reception. The house where we blended and extended our family. The house he died in. The home that held us through our happiest and saddest and scariest moments, making me love it and hate it and feel both trapped and safe within its walls.

One year of working on my laptop in the family room, just to feel closer to his study. One year of looking up, expecting to see him. Wanting to see him. Fearing I would.

One year of carrying all the things I always carried, plus all the things he did. One year of carrying double the load, plus a whole lot of things neither of us ever had to carry, the weight of which at times is almost unbearable.

One year of slowly learning to live without the lights on, learning to trust the darkness not to take people away.

One year of relentless decision-making. Of finding counsellors and moving schools and spending tens of thousands of dollars untangling the mess a person leaves when they step out of life, unprepared.

A year of worrying where we'll end up. How we'll make it through. A year of fumbling for the light. Finding it. Feeling the sun and the breeze on my skin again. Feeling guilty about it.

I couldn't imagine making it through this far. 'This time next year' felt an impossible ask when 'this time in an hour' was hard enough. How would we survive, this broken? We couldn't breathe. We couldn't stand. A simple trip to the supermarket was overwhelming. All this light. This noise. These people. These products he'd never need again. He'd never need anything, *ever again*. He would never *be* again.

I read somewhere that a widow's only task in the twelve months after her husband dies is to keep herself alive. Fleetingly, but deeply, I've wished I was at the end of my life. I've wanted to join him.

People said grief would come in waves. But there are no waves at first, when you're under the surface, drowning.

That first wave, when it does hit, hits *hard*.

You've ventured further from the beach than you realised. You think you're stronger than the rip until it drags you out and people have to save you again. You're rescued, you try to swim, you're dumped again, splattered on the sand, choking on it. You stagger to your feet and enter the water again, because you have to.

Repeat. Repeat, repeat, repeat.

This has been the worst and most expansive year of my life. At any moment it might all be taken away. Everything is brighter and more precious. Life is bigger. The world is smaller. People are closer. There's an urgency and a depth to life that I never could have understood without this. I've never let go of so much or taken on more.

In the twelve months since Jeff died, I've travelled more than forty thousand kilometres. I've wandered the streets of New York with millions of other people, alone. I've written hundreds of thousands of words. I've had a book published, received deals to publish two more and have a further two in mind. I've started rehearsing our musical. I've spent hours in interviews on radio and conquered a fear of appearing on TV. I've campaigned for heart health. I've won two awards. The kids have had graduations and formals and first loves and new schools and new jobs...

At every single step, I've turned to tell him, and he hasn't been there. *He keeps not being here.*

On the weekend, I watched parts of the *Titanic* movie with our son, who is currently fascinated with the ship. I didn't cry when Jack died. I cried at the sight of elderly Rose's framed photographs of all the adventures she went on to have in her life without him.

That's the very hardest part. The heart must go on.

Emma Grey is the author of six books, including *The Last Love Note,* YA novels *Unrequited* and *Tilly Maguire and the Royal Wedding Mess,* non-fiction title, *I Don't Have Time* (co-authored with Audrey Thomas) and the parenting memoir *Wits' End Before Breakfast! Confessions of a Working Mum.* She lives near Canberra, where her world centres on her family, writing, photography and endlessly chasing the Aurora Australis.

Chapter 15

Day 120

by Raabia Qadir

She stood with her back to the crowd and sipped her green tea, as the sweet smell of pot permeated the air and the party continued behind her. Here she was now, frail before forty.

The laughter and music in the background seemed to dim. Finally, she was beginning to see a window open up—it was somewhere over there, past the trees and the house with winking lights nestled amongst them.

It had taken over four months and a change of place to finally feel like there was a portal somewhere. When her doctor had said it would take one hundred and twenty days for the internal healing to be complete, she knew he had meant that it would take that long for the stitches and patches they had placed inside her body to become part of her. But even though her flesh had stopped gaping and oozing two months ago, she felt as if her soul had also been ripped open, and it remained unhealed.

What she would have given for this party's laughter one hundred and twenty days ago! How far away that hospital room felt. After all, time creates distance.

Back then, there had been white walls, the hum of the machines, and tubes pushing liquid medicines in through her veins and collecting fluids from her stomach and body cavity—then she had been *a thing*. True, they had always treated her like a person...but just as a person who had to be kept alive. There had been no pulsating joy in that room, no laughter, no passion, no reason to live.

Her kids, her husband, her parents, her aunt and even one of her dearest friends had come every day; they sat by her and tried to talk to her. They had kept her alive. She was aware that her doctor knew that she had given up. Those last two days in hospital she had done a lot of soul searching and had not come up with any regrets, so she had decided that she was ready to go. That's why the doctor had come in and said, 'You have to go home now.'

How that sentence had scared her. One hundred and twenty days ago, five days after three surgeries, she had to go home because he wasn't going to allow her to fade. That day was the one she counted from, not the day she was cut open and patched up.

She hadn't wanted to go home. There was always work to be done at home: things to be arranged and organized, projects to hand in, phone calls to be answered. She didn't have time to fade away at home; she would have to live because she couldn't seem to leave anything undone.

Kids would need their clothes sorted, their homework checked, and their Lego pieces found. Even if the grandparents took over the main jobs like mealtimes and school runs, there simply wouldn't be time to die. But, after staying in the hospital for eight dismal days, home she came.

It didn't make much difference for the next two months as she went in again and again to get new stitches and bandages. At times she ran her hands over the tape and thread holding the shell of her together, wondering why her life force didn't leak out. She could count on one hand the friends and relatives who sent well wishes. It was sad, she supposed, because the one thing she prided herself on was making connections and retaining relationships, and there she was, barely able to make it to the bathroom, and hardly anyone cared.

Mentally she shook her head at herself. All day she had been riding hard on the adults and children.

There was a loud burst of laughter behind her as the crowd mellowed into their seats and started a second joint. She turned and ran her eyes over the group, making sure nobody needed anything. She couldn't seem to help it, because she couldn't stand chaos; she had to organize things for everyone.

Not one of them had made it to her bedside, even to offer empty words of reassurance or help in any way. No babysitting duties shared, no meals arranged, no spirits lifted. She checked herself…was she sore about it? Was she angry?

Perhaps she was stupid, really. To plan, arrange and cajole a lot of people whom she was angry with to hang out together. However, she had always been this kind of stupid, unable to hold onto her anger, wanting to move on, wanting to build something. She hadn't learned; not even standing at the threshold of death had changed her. That was just sad, she decided.

People always talk about how being close to death, having their lives flash in front of their eyes, changes them. Some then grab onto life with both hands, some strive to improve themselves, and some find their drive or purpose. Yet here she was, still the same–no stronger, wiser or kinder–and still looking for stories to escape into, though now the stories just didn't come.

Even if someone gave her a scene, she couldn't complete it; the voices in her head had gone silent. What if the voices were angry with her for wanting to die? Her death would have left them voiceless as well, after all, untold stories are a crime, like lies by omission.

Was her anger one of those stories?

Despite knowing of her surgeries, people had still called her, asking for help, and even with no real will to live, she had helped. Why? Why had she done that?

Perhaps it was because she had been taught not to shirk her obligations; to die when someone wanted a shoulder to cry on was unacceptable. Did the mind make those decisions? Or did the soul come pre-programmed? She wasn't sure the mind had any real control at all. It probably wasn't about what she had learned; rather, it was a problem with her instincts.

She was low on self-preservation and high on service.

Perhaps that was it: if everyone has a calling, hers was to be of service. People go on and on about how the universe is love and how one must live in love, but for her it was service. Perhaps service itself was her version of love.

It wasn't like she was a doormat. To organise a bunch of adults and kids, for example, one needs to be fairly authoritative, and even argumentative, when toddlers are involved! Things don't get done otherwise.

As she looked over at the softly giggling, mellowed-out adults snuggling into their chairs, she knew she wasn't angry. As she shrugged and looked back out towards the darkened mountainside, she knew she was not a bit disappointed, either.

She had learned early on that people could only do what they were capable of doing, expecting any more was useless. She didn't look for reciprocity in her relationships; despite the capitalist ideal of being able to commodify service, service was without strings. There was no need for reciprocity, no obligation.

There was a song that she loved, and roughly translated, the verse went like this:

Count me among the lovers, but don't reward me for my devotion.

She wanted to be counted among the lovers, yet not being praised for it seemed appropriate; as if the service, her version of love, would be sullied by gratitude. Perhaps that's why all true lovers who become the subject of lore and legend are considered crazy; they don't conform to societal expectations and they do things that only make sense to them.

For her it had begun sometime between the age of thirteen

and sixteen, when she had decided she wouldn't wear the mantle of societal expectations, and so had begun a lifelong view from the outside.

Apparently, if you don't conform to what society expects, you certainly aren't part of it. And there began the struggle to constantly justify the lack of reciprocity. She couldn't reciprocate because society expected it, nor could she give up who she was because social expectations preached 'tit for tat'. She didn't want the gratitude, and she didn't want to be acknowledged for it; she just wanted to be seen.

This is who she was and what fed her soul, and she wanted it to be okay to be this way, being who she was, even if that meant giving of herself without asking for something in return.

The light blinking in that far-away window on the mountainside winked out. The stories weren't coming just yet; she would have to go and sit in the real world, sit without being seen.

The silence in her soul said no one inside was talking to her, either. She walked back to the group, where she was offered the joint once more. They laughed again softly, telling her it would help her unwind.

She wondered if it would bring the stories back, but then she shook her head: if she couldn't fit dying into her schedule, she certainly couldn't manage to relax just yet. She was ready for a new day, and the stories would come back when they were ready to be told.

Raabia Qadir is a Pakistani storytelling enthusiast via the written word or visual media. She has headed a design department that produced interactive software for children and adults, curated exhibits for museum dioramas, international expos and festivals. With a background in animation and design, she focuses on stories for the underrepresented. In 2023, she created games and digital videos about making choices and fostering conversations.

Chapter 16

Esmerelda's Heartfelt Christmas
by Lisa Heidke

Christmas Present

I remember being alone. Heart pounding, crying and frightened.

Just as I'd lost all hope, enormous hands pulled me from the darkness into light, wrapped me in a warm blanket and stroked my fur.

'Little darling,' a soft voice I would later recognise as Hazel's cooed. 'Sweetheart, you have the loveliest emerald eyes ever. We'll call you Esmerelda.'

If giants Hazel and James hadn't rescued me weeks before Christmas, fourteen cat years previously, I'd have been left to die in a dumpster.

You'd think, given the circumstances, I'd love the festive season–twinkling fairy lights, sparkling stars, hearts brimming with love and stomachs filled with abundant fish morsels and all-you-can-eat prawn heads.

But no, I feared it.

Here we were again, and I was feeling even less Christmassy this time. Yes, several jolly, highly decorated trees of various sizes dotted the compound. There was bark to scratch and more than enough shiny baubles for me to whack and paw with pure delight as they crashed to the ground. I'd ingested enough tinsel that I pooped gold nuggets and had kneaded soft Santa cushions until several hundred threads had been pulled, and said cushions destroyed. But it wasn't remotely satisfying.

Outside, I panted from heat exhaustion, yet I froze indoors where Hazel had set the air conditioning to arctic. My fur was dishevelled. I had muck in my eyes. And despite Hazel dressing me in a ridiculous red faux fur collar with jingly bells, I wasn't feeling merry.

I clawed at the silver tinsel hanging from a branch and it tumbled. Satisfaction.

Hazel scooped me into her arms and nuzzled my neck. 'I put a lot of effort into trimming that tree, you rascal.'

I returned her love by biting her wrists and clawing at her shirt. Petting Aggression 101.

Hazel set me down gently on the grass and sighed.

Served her right. Nuzzling me! Next time I'd spray her.

A kitten I hadn't seen before caught my attention as she danced with brightly coloured streamers. Up and down. No cares. Innocent fun. Had she been abandoned too? Had Hazel rescued her like she'd rescued me?

Hazel sat down beside me. 'That's Shirley, our newest addition. I hope you'll make her feel welcome, sweetie. She reminds me of you. Had a tough start and a closed heart.'

Why? Why did giants mistreat us?

Felines are intelligent, calming and charming. Okay, so we also have loud voices, can bite, be aloof and cough up fur balls. But is that any reason to dump us in dustbins?

I meowed loudly. Despite my horrid behaviour, Hazel patted me, stood and continued with her celebratory decorations. I watched Shirley and thought back to the day I was rescued.

Christmas Past

Freed from the bin and ensconced in my new home, the first blow hit hard. I wasn't Hazel and James' only feline.

The second? It quickly became apparent that I had a nasty affliction. *Fleas.*

That week, even if I hadn't been in isolation, I would have kept to myself. I was miserable, covered in welts and an angry red rash, in no mood to meet the *others*.

Quarantine completed, my coat clear and shiny due to a steady diet of oily fish, I felt fabulous and confident. Me, a black and white short-haired mutt. Certainly not beautiful, but not without charm.

Though I was ready to mingle, most cats were fearful. Not only had I carried fleas, but I sometimes lost balance when I tried to jump or sprint. I'd never known any different.

And yet I was. *Different.*

The others were agile, darting up ramps and catwalks, racing through tunnels and across swinging bridges. But my hind legs lacked strength, which in turn made me terrified and then angry. Confidence faded. I couldn't have kept up had I tried.

I ate alone. Slept alone. The only affection I received was from Hazel who regularly checked on me, scratched my ears and cuddled me. When the dangling feather and ribbon wands appeared, Hazel gently encouraged me to jump. She urged me to bat and chase scrunched paper balls like the rest of her brood. But due to my thumping chest and tender limbs, I rarely did.

On days when my limp was particularly painful, she'd squirt foul liquid into my mouth and I'd sleep, the ache easing.

'Hey, hey,' a voice said behind me one afternoon as I snoozed on grass in the sunshine. Most other cats spent their time high above on overhead walkways and hidden ceiling booths connected by intricate hidden paths.

My ears instinctively pressed against my head. It was the first time another had voluntarily approached me. He was portly with short auburn fur and the hugest face I'd ever seen.

'Quite a snore you've got there, kitty.'

I blinked, yawned and stretched, somewhat taken aback.

'I'm Gerry. Gerry the Geriatric Ginger. Triple G for short. And you are? I know you're the newbie with fleas, but...'

'Esmerelda. And I don't have fleas anymore.'

Triple G turned to a nearby feline, sleek, fawn coloured, perky ears and a confused expression. 'Carousel! Over here. Meet Esme.'

'Esmerelda.' I corrected and set about grooming myself.

Triple G stroked his whiskers and wheezed. 'Esmerelda is a very big name for a little one.'

Carousel padded unsteadily toward us. 'Pleased to meet you, Esmerelda.' She had an awkward lopsided gait like mine, but an easy welcoming tone.

Triple G flicked his tail to swat an invisible insect. 'Settling in with the hoarders?'

I shook my head.

'The giant cat hoarders?' Triple G said.

Carousel shushed. 'What he means is that we're all boarders. Hazel and James take us in and then, in time, we're adopted by other giants and transferred to our forever homes.'

Forever homes? I didn't like the sound of that. I felt safe with Hazel and James.

'I want to stay here.'

Triple G coughed. 'Don't worry lass. As I said, they're hoarders. Ailurophiles. Cat lovers. Cats here rarely get shipped out. Sampled the catnip?'

I nodded.

'Feel good afterwards?'

'Mostly. Sometimes I vomit.' I turned to Carousel. 'What does your name mean?'

Triple G flicked his tail. 'She's senile. Keeps walking in circles, stopping to stare into space, before starting up again.'

Carousel hissed. 'Hilarious G.' She turned to me. 'He's not, but the gang's mostly kind because he's old. I'm not impressed when he continually gets preferential care. First in line for all meals, treats and affection, even when he's clearly tenth in the queue.'

'You can talk,' Triple G griped. 'You've only got a couple of teeth and are mostly incontinent.'

Carousel lunged at his face, Triple G pounced on her back and then they rolled on the floor spitting and growling.

Another even older cat jumped on them. 'Time out!'

Triple G and Carousel disengaged.

'Sorry, Pa,' they replied in unison.

He turned to me. 'You must be Esmerelda. Name's Otis, but everyone calls me Pa.'

Carousel vigorously scratched her neck. 'Because you're ancient.'

Pa nodded, his salt and pepper whiskers unmoving in the breeze. 'That's why I take no offence.' He stared at me. 'Why aren't you upstairs on the superhighways doing acrobatics and swinging from ropes? It's only we geriatrics who spend time on the ground.' He nodded towards Carousel and Triple G.

'Yeah,' Carousel agreed. 'A whole new world of discovery awaits, Esmerelda.'

I clawed at the grass. 'That's okay. I like having four paws on the ground. Plus, my heart and legs don't work too well.'

With brooding, sympathetic eyes, Pa looked at me and considered his response. 'You're welcome to hang out with us anytime, kiddo.'

At Christmas Eve dinner, I was wolfing down salmon when Triple G scolded me for eating too quickly. 'Stop gobbling, girl.'

My mouth was bulging. 'I hate waste.' A hangover from when I was left starving in a dumpster.

'Hence why you don't have a waist,' he quipped.

True, I was filling out quickly, but I swiped, just missing his nose. I'd never seriously hurt him. Triple G was still one of my only friends.

Behind me, I heard a snuffle, then, 'Let that be a warning, G.'

I turned.

'Blue Eyes at your service, Miss.'

Oh my! He was the most handsome fellow I'd ever seen. So beautiful.

'Cat got your tongue?' Triple G bellowed, much to my embarrassment. He was always the loudest in a room. 'Blue Eyes is our resident lothario. A charming Birman. Captivating sapphire eyes, hence the name. And check out his perfect white socks.' Triple G stretched. 'I guess you could as easily have been called Socks, hey Blue?'

I didn't know where to look and was indeed lost for words. I purred and tried to stand, but my legs gave way and I fell.

'Steady,' Blue Eyes said. 'Esmerelda, isn't it? The kitty with the piercing emerald eyes. I've been meaning to make your acquaintance.'

My heart raced and I desperately held in a salmon fur ball roiling in my throat.

'Have you visited the koi pond?'

Triple G sniggered. 'What a line. Now all you have to do is reel her in!'

Ignoring him, I held Blue Eyes' gaze. 'I don't think so.'

'It's my favourite escapade. Allow me to show you.'

Leaving Triple G tittering into his dinner, I followed Blue Eyes to the gurgling water. I'm not sure how I'd missed it before. My new friend confidently pranced along the rocks, stopping every few steps to examine the fish.

'Join me.' He beckoned as I stared from the side.

Not wanting to disappoint, I tentatively climbed over the nearest rocks. Slipped.

Sensing my panic, Blue Eyes leapt beside me and dragged me back to solid ground.

'Thank you.' I licked my soaking paws. 'Do many fall?'

'Of course.' Blue Eyes purred. 'I've been known to take a dip myself.'

'And the fish?' My eyes widened as I considered several for my next meal.

Blue Eyes became serious. 'No! We respect the pond fish. Pond fish are for observing, not for eating. Have you met Sebastian?'

I shook my head.

You will. Lovely fellow, somewhat careless. Cream and grey longhair. Any hoo, he dipped his paw into the pond a few months back. Succeeded in scooping up a goldfish. He's now banned from the area.'

Blue Eyes began sneaking along a grassy path. He stopped and turned. 'Come on, Esmerelda. We're off on our next adventure.'

I couldn't believe my luck. I wobbled, but somehow kept upright.

He stopped at a nearby bubbling fountain, stuck his paw in, drew it to his mouth and licked. 'Now you try.'

I did as instructed. Delicious.

Feeling full of dinner and giddy from our walk, I yawned.

'Let's get you inside,' Blue Eyes said kindly. 'Tomorrow's Christmas Day, and I can't wait to take you up to the superhighway and beyond. You'll love it.'

'Hmm,' I purred, knowing there was no way I could ever climb up a wall or even a ramp to reach the superhighways.

I was snuggled in my towel-laden laundry basket when Blue Eyes strolled by and pawed my ears. 'Ahem.'

I rolled over.

He licked my neck.

Waking up, I stretched, drowsy. Blue Eyes was sitting in front of the basket, prawn tail in his mouth. He dropped it. 'Merry Christmas.'

I jumped out of the hamper and pounced, swallowing the offering in one gulp.

Blue Eyes groomed his whiskers. 'There's plenty more where that came from.'

We strolled together, following the scent toward our communal feeding bowls where we shared a plate of tasty fish.

Hazel and James were nearby. I nudged Blue Eyes and held up a paw. 'Are the giants pretending to be—'

'Us? I think so. How odd.'

Heads swivelled upward and silent. The giants wore striped costumes with pointy ears, whiskers and long furry tails.

'Is everyone on the catnip?' Neck extended, Triple G's mouth was agape. 'No wonder other giants won't adopt us.'

It was an odd but comforting Christmas. Blue Eyes and I bantered over chicken necks, shellfish and other delicacies. Our relationship so far was all about ponds, fountains and food. Hopefully it would advance to a shared love nest and kittens.

Full tummies and catnip loosened tongues, I met felines including Sebastian, Mrs Simpson and more. We rolled and flipped, hyperactive.

Triple G continually lashed out at James' ankles and often connected, drawing blood, but James seemed amused rather than annoyed. Mrs Simpson bounced up ramps and swung from ropes draped from overhead bridges. Sebastian scratched at trees and pulled down bark, claiming it was payback for not being allowed to visit the pond. And Carousel? Well Carousel walked in circles.

We all needed a long nap. Christmas and life with Hazel, James and a pack of frisky felines was bliss. What more could a girl from the flea-ridden side of town ask for?

I couldn't have been happier until several days later when an interloper arrived.

Cleopatra, a white Chinchilla, sauntered into the compound looking like she'd just stepped out of a grooming salon. Immediately, she saw Blue and strutted over. That's when their perfect azure eyes met. Bam!

Meanwhile, my eyes and heart grew greener with envy.

I'll admit Cleo was gorgeous, her fur, white and fluffy. She had a delicate meow, just loud enough to hear, not so piercing that it was irritating. Her purr was soft, inviting, and the strength with which she clawed at our sleeping rugs seemed harmless, not at all filled with malice.

Too starstruck to approach her, I was shocked when Cleo sought me out.

'Esmerelda.' Her voice was silky and low. 'Blue Eyes has told me so much about you. I'm glad you've kept him company until I met him.' She purred seductively. 'Who knows what the naughty boy could have gotten up to without his sister–that's what he calls you, his sister–keeping an eye on him.' Her voice oozed with oily charm.

That night, Cleo staked her claim. Blue Eyes' attention was solely on her as they shared a salmon dinner.

'I was sick all over my giant's tennis shoes,' Cleo prattled. 'Maybe that's why she dumped me here.' She snuggled in close to Blue Eyes, begging for sympathy.

'There, there,' he consoled.

'What about the freedom?' Cleo whinged. 'There is none. I'm used to being outside climbing trees. I've been abandoned.'

She was definitely a drama queen, but if that pampered princess had spent any length of time outside, I'd be flabbergasted. Cleo was an indoor cat through and through.

'But Cleo, we've got so many overhead runs here.' Blue Eyes glanced above at cats racing up scratching post trees and bounding onto ceiling runs. I watched as they scampered to one of the love nests on the superhighway far from where I could reach.

Yes, the runs were amazing, and had I enjoyed good balance and wasn't afraid of heights and potentially falling and dying, I'd love them too.

Instead, I was lost. Bereft.

Sad and lonely.

Blue Eyes had chosen Cleopatra over me.

Pa tried cheering me up by offering titbits. 'Esmerelda, you have to eat. I don't have much of an appetite these days, so that's my excuse. What's yours?'

'It's hot and I'm tired.'

Triple G sidled up to me. 'You feline sad, Esmerelda?'

I yawned. 'Not in the mood G.'

He swished his tail. 'Clearly.'

With little desire for food, I paced to the bubbling fountain, heartsick. Every turn reminded me of Blue Eyes. If only we could speak. Did he really consider me a sibling? Had I misinterpreted his attention as romantic when he'd simply intended friendship? If so, what was all the licking about?

Feeling a tiny bit brighter after a nap, I found Pa resting nearby.

He looked up; eyes watery. 'Hey kiddo. Saved you something.' He batted a plump prawn my way. 'Please eat.'

Christmas Present

I shuddered. Hazel was scratching my belly, pulling me into the now. 'Bad dream, Esmerelda?'

Eyes closed, I straightened my body and allowed her to stroke me some more. I felt ashamed about my earlier bad temper. After Hazel left, I opened one eye to find Shirley, the kitten, curled close beside me, nuzzling into my fur. I coughed and pushed her with my paw. She didn't budge. I sat up and glared. 'Really? It's Christmas Eve. Shouldn't you be bounding around chasing red laser dots, clawing at inflatable snowmen and jumping out of reindeer box towers?'

She shook her head.

I yawned. 'Guess not.'

'I want to hear more.'

Had I been mumbling in my sleep?

'Please,' Shirley pleaded.

Fine. 'Where was I? Oh yes...'

Christmas Past

Blue Eyes and I never got the chance to talk because the next day, new giants arrived. They fussed over Blue Eyes, signed adoption papers and quickly whisked him away. After he left, Hazel found me at the pond, picked me up and cuddled me. She was crying.

'I'm so sorry Esmerelda. I know how special Blue Eyes was to you.'

That same day, I saw Cleo in the corner sharpening her claws on a side table. Destructive beast. That's what the scratching posts were for. It's not like they were scarce, but no, Cleo was special! The outer layers of her front talons shed, revealing her sharp under claws. Gross. She gouged even deeper, unaware I was observing.

A moment passed and she looked up. 'Esmerelda, I didn't see you.' She licked her whiskers. 'Come. Let's chat.'

It was a command rather than a suggestion, so I didn't move.

'You must be sad your brother has moved on.'

'Blue Eyes isn't my brother,' I shrieked. 'In case you haven't noticed, he's a pedigree, and I'm a mutt.'

She sniffed. 'True. Which is why he's been adopted and you're still languishing—'

'So are you!'

'Not for long.' Cleo purred. 'But about Blue Eyes. You and he could never'—she sniffed me up and down—'have been anything more than casual acquaintances. Me, on the other hand—'

I lunged and bit her neck. I may have been small, but I was fierce. Right then, I realised my life's purpose: to wreak revenge on those who had wronged me. Cleo was my number one target.

She fake howled so much that several cats came rushing toward us.

Triple G squealed with anticipation. 'Cat fight!'

'Have I missed another party?' Carousel squeaked and

continued walking in circles.

'What on earth?' Hazel arrived and picked up a sobbing Cleopatra, consoling her as they left the room.

I only saw Cleo once more, as she was being carried out of the compound by her new forever giants. She couldn't have been smugger.

'Happy now?' Pa asked a short time later.

'No, I should've bitten harder.' I flexed my claws. 'I should've scratched her. The one time I wish I still had fleas so I could have given them to her.'

Pa stared at me and rubbed his chin. 'Esmerelda, revenge isn't the best solution to your outrage and sadness.'

'But—'

'But what? You're living in paradise. Whatcha got to be hissing at? Yes, Blue Eyes has gone, and I'm sorry. Regardless of whatever stories Cleo made up, he was fond of you. You don't get to my age without recognising mutual attraction.'

'But Pa,' I wailed. 'He chose Cleo over me.'

'Nonsense. He was being polite. Sharing his dinner with a newcomer.'

'He'd never have loved me.' I glanced at my hind legs. 'True love isn't my destiny.'

'Rot! You can't leap as high as some. You can't sprint as fast. So what? You've got heart, kiddo, and that's what counts.'

Regardless of what Pa said, I didn't have faith in myself. I'd always be plain and unlovable.

Pa coughed. 'Instead of scratching and biting, try licking and purring first. Or be quiet and pretend to sleep. Retract those claws and chase butterflies.' He leant forward. 'Choose love and honour your heart, Es.'

Christmas Present

I glanced down at Shirley, who'd been silently listening, enthralled. 'Pa's pearls of wisdom,' I told her. 'Now you know why I dislike Christmas. I still miss Blue Eyes.' A howl escaped my mouth.

Shirley moved even closer and licked me.

'I'm being silly. Losing Blue Eyes isn't even the worst. Last Christmas was crueller.'

'I'm sorry.'

Despite not wanting to, I felt a growing fondness for Shirley. Shaking off my sadness, I sat up. 'Have you ever chased a butterfly?'

'I've never even seen a flutterby.'

'Let's find one together.'

Later, exhausted from physical exertion, we strolled to the pond.

'One of my favourite places to retreat,' I told her.

'Have you ever slipped in?'

'Once, almost.' I remembered Blue Eyes saving me. 'Never again. *Respect the pond* has become my mantra.'

Triple G sauntered by and peered at Shirley. 'Who do we have here?'

'Shirley, meet Triple G, our resident funny cat.'

Shirley meowed.

'Pleased to meet you, Shirley.' Triple G flicked his tail. 'Tell me, why was the cat afraid of the tree?'

Timidly, Shirley shook her head.

'Because of its bark!' Triple G theatrically rolled in the dirt, chuffed with his cleverness. Standing, he shook off the excess soil with flourish. 'Christmas Eve. Time to chow down. See you ladies litter!'

Shirley giggled.

'You're hiss-terical, G,' I shouted after him.

'Look at you two getting along so well.' It was Hazel. 'I'm pleased you're looking after Shirley, Esmerelda.'

She picked me up and rubbed her face in my fur before drawing back, rapidly sneezing over me until I was sticky and wet.

What did she expect? It happened whenever she did this. She set me down. 'You need a thorough brushing, sweetie.'

Shirley and I watched as Hazel's huge form moved inside.

'Later, she'll want to groom me,' I whispered to Shirley. 'Wearing her spiky rubber mitt...'

'Does it hurt?'

'Nah. In the past, I scratched and bit when Hazel brushed me. But I don't complain anymore after the day Mrs Simpson arrived – you'll meet her soon enough, a blue/grey Persian – completely shorn except for her tail. What a farcical sight. Her fur eventually grew back but first impressions count. It took her a long time to make friends. Even now, if one of the gang mentions the word *clippers*, she scampers up a ramp, onto the highway and to the safety of a ceiling box.'

Shirley observed me with large black eyes. 'Tell me more.'

'About Mrs Simpson?'

'No. Last Christmas. Why was it so cruel?'

My ears twitched. This was going to be difficult. 'Ready?'

She yawned. 'Yes, I'm not sleepy.'

I licked my paws. 'The previous Christmas...Where to begin? Obviously, I grew considerably. Hungry all the time. Despite missing Blue Eyes, I tried to put aside my anger and revenge fantasies, as Pa had suggested.'

Shirley yawned some more. 'I can't wait to meet Pa.'

My throat caught. 'Christmas morning, Pa brought me a fish tail and even though I'd eaten a sumptuous breakfast, I was determined to put my previous festive season sadness behind me and enjoy the day.

'Pa and I started the silly game we played every time he delivered me a treat. I lunged at him. He turned his back, then I swiped at his hind legs. Missed. He turned and pretended to claw me. Missed. I leapt on top of his back and began playbiting his neck, kneading his fur. He looked momentarily shocked but jumped around, me still clinging to his fur.'

Shirley's eyes widened. 'He sounds like so much fun.'

'Yes. When he dropped the fish and fell to the floor, I assumed Pa was joking, letting me win the prize as he always did. But'—my voice hitched—'but no, Pa's heart had given out.'

'Yow! He died?'

I nodded. 'Though nudging one hundred and fifty, Pa was larger than life. I thought he'd live forever.'

I closed my eyes. 'After that, festivities were suspended. Hazel and James buried Pa under his favourite shrub and most cats retreated to their preferred sleeping boxes, either here in the grounds or above on the superhighways.'

Shirley snuggled closer. 'I can see why you don't like it.'

I wrapped my seemingly huge paw round Shirley's tiny frame and licked the top of her head. 'Maybe this Christmas will be different. It's already looking brighter. After all, I've met you.'

Shirley purred and we drifted into sleep.

I woke alone. Disoriented. Where was Shirley? How long had I been asleep? My head was fuzzy. I had some vague recollection of Hazel bringing me inside and laying me in my favourite laundry basket. I scratched at my neck. I was still wearing that blasted collar.

It was dawn. All was quiet, unusually so. No sounds of cats snuffling, panting, or meowing in their sleep. I was ravenous, having missed the previous evening's meal. I ambled up, found my litter tray, sniffed, did my business and padded in search of food. In the dining room corner, I spied the remnants of smoked ham and devoured it. Delicious.

I coughed.

Perhaps I'd been too greedy.

I shook my head and swallowed, confident my festive feast would remain in my stomach and not repeat itself in front of me on the floor.

Festive feast?

I sat upright, still as a statue.

It was Christmas Day. How could I have forgotten?

'There you are,' Triple G said.

Carousel wandered around. 'We thought we'd lost you.'

They were joined by Mrs Simpson, Sebastian and Shirley.

'Shirley,' I said brightly. 'Merry Christmas.'

'Come on,' Triple G hissed impatiently. 'Let's get on the catnip.'

'Not you, Shirley,' I warned. 'Wait another six months.'

Pouting, she did as she was told.

Cheer up Shirley,' Triple G said after the rest of us had eaten a belly full of potent stems and leaves and were stretched in the sun. 'What colour do kittens love the most?'

'Tell me G, I can't wait.' Shirley had found her voice.

'Purrple.' G's laugh turned into a sneezing fit and soon we were all rolling in the dirt biting each other's tails.

'I've got one,' Shirley said quietly. 'What does a cat say after making a joke?'

'Surprise me,' Mrs Simpson said.

'Just kitten!'

'Good one kid.' Triple G sounded genuinely impressed. He coughed up a fur ball. 'Apologies. Too much of the good stuff.'

'Esmerelda!' It was Hazel.

We scattered.

'James, I swear she was here before.'

'Not to worry, Hazel,' he replied. 'Es'll show herself eventually. She can't resist Christmas ham.'

I poked my head out from behind a scratching post. Ham? No, I'd never been able to resist.

Hazel swooped in, picked me up and pressed me close to her giant chest. 'I've got a Christmas surprise for you, sweetheart.'

I heard another voice, one that took me back two years previously.

It couldn't be. I scrambled out of Hazel's arms, dashed behind a bubbling fountain and silently shrieked. 'No!'

'Esmerelda?' Hazel surveyed the room before finding me.

'What's gotten into you?'

I licked my paws, groomed my whiskers and ears, and emerged from behind the concrete structure.

The cat who'd broken my heart was standing in front of me.

'Blue Eyes is back,' Hazel said, stating the obvious.

I meowed. My heart pulsed wildly. What now? What should I do? How should I behave? Ignore him? Pretend he didn't exist? Or confront him head on?

What would Pa do? I thought back to our conversation after Blue Eyes was adopted. 'Instead of scratching and biting,' he'd said, 'try licking and purring.'

I certainly wasn't going to lick Blue Eyes. Been there. Done that. But I could be civil. 'Merry Christmas,' I purred.

'Mesmerising Esmerelda,' Blue Eyes said finally. 'I've missed you.'

I flicked my tail. 'Really?'

'Yes. I don't know why you refused to see me before I left. I'm sorry I got adopted.'

'That wasn't the issue, Blue. You had no control over that. I was upset about Cleopatra.'

'Cleo, the crazy Chinchilla?'

'Crazy? You two were all over each other.'

He shook his head. 'I was always trying to get away from her, but wherever I went, she was there. At dinner. In the garden. On the superhighways.'

'I remember you saying you'd show her upstairs.'

He laughed. 'I thought I could outrun Cleo but she was a speedy minx. That's why I'm glad we have this time alone so I can explain to you before I confront her.'

'What? Cleo was adopted days after you.'

He laughed. 'That's a relief. I was worried about seeing her again. And terrified you'd no longer be here. I missed you every day.'

'There was nothing between you and Cleo?'

'Never.' His purr was deep. Intense. 'Esmerelda, I've only had whiskers for you. All twenty-four of them.' He padded over and licked me.

I pulled away. 'One more question. Why are you back?'

'My giants are going overseas.'

'I'm sorry.'

'Don't be. I want to be here.' He tugged at my silly faux fur collar just as Shirley arrived.

'Shirley!' I was glowing. 'Meet Blue Eyes.'

Blue Eyes bowed. 'You are the tiniest kitten ever. Has Esmerelda been taking good care of you?'

Shirley nodded. 'I've only been here a day.'

'Ah, a Christmas kitten.'

Hazel appeared. 'I'm glad I've found all three of you together.'

'See,' James said, standing beside her. 'What did I tell you Hazel? These three belong together.'

She smiled. 'Yes.' Hazel bent down and patted me. 'Esmerelda, you're my special forever cat and your home will always be here with us. But it's also time you shared your heart with your feline family. Blue Eyes is here to stay. He won't be leaving us again. As for little Shirley, she's not going anywhere either. Merry Christmas.'

Lisa Heidke's passion is for writing fiction about women navigating friendships, careers, romance, and ultimately triumphing over adversity. Her seventh novel, *Lily's Little Flower Shop* was published by UK's Bloodhound Books in 2021 under pseudonym, Lisa Darcy. It has since been published in France and Italy. Since then, Lisa's books, *My Big Greek Holiday* and *Should You Keep A Secret?* have also been published by Bloodhound Books. *The Pact* will be published by WingsEPress in April 2024.

Chapter 17

Millefiori

by Amanda Beckett

I thought of you recently when, in the clamour of an antique market, one ornament caught my attention. It was there, glinting at me, between a Chinese bird cage and a set of bone-handled butter knives. I stood close to the table, a stream of jostling shoppers at my back, and lifted the glass dome from its place on a creased white tablecloth.

It was yours. I remembered it, the glass paperweight that had once entranced me as a child. It sat on the sideboard of your apartment when, on tippy-toes, I was just tall enough to see it, hands by my side, fingers itching to hold it. Here it was, bending time, layering the past on the present. I turned it in my palm and watched as its treasures were magnified and distorted by the curve of the glass under the pavilion's fluorescent lights.

'Made in Scotland, that was. 1960s.'

A bespectacled man with a grey ponytail rose from a plastic chair behind the trestle.

I smiled, nodded. It was not the only story of this particular anachronism. Inside that crystal orb was a universe, cross-sections of tiny multi-coloured rods pulled together in concentric patterns to resemble flowers. Millefiori–a thousand flowers.

I thought of you and I felt your loss again.

Millefiori

There is a scene in *The Return to Oz*, that eighties gothic reimagining of L. Frank Baum's novel, where Dorothy walks through a cavernous room filled with curios, each one alluring and potentially dangerous. She must choose the correct objects to break a witch's enchantment and restore her friends to life. Three wrong guesses and she will be transformed into an ornament herself.

Sometimes I feel that if I find the right object, a glass paperweight perhaps, you might reappear, that with a murmur of your name and a clap of thunder I might revive you from an otherworldly darkness.

I have wondered if it is this wish that compels me to walk the aisles of such markets, to keep a lookout for Figgjo Lotte dinnerware, Waddington card games and celluloid vanity sets, artefacts of a relationship long gone.

I have only three things that once belonged to you.

Two really. The first was not yours at all, but your mother's. You had no say in my receiving it and, for all I know, you may have objected. When she died I inherited her Art Deco engagement ring, a small sapphire surrounded by tiny diamonds on a dainty gold band. I resized it to fit when I was eighteen but then kept it in a drawer. It was too special to wear.

I've started to wear it again, but my knuckles have grown. It slips on but is painful to take off. Perhaps, like Cinderella's stepsisters squeezing their feet into her glass slipper, I'm not the rightful recipient.

I marvel that more than one hundred years have passed since your mother was presented with that ring. It was 1919, the year in which short-wave radio was invented and Spanish Flu swept the globe. I learnt all about her after you were gone; her role in the Women's Land Army, her penchant for motorcycles. I learned that you remained in England, aged four, when your parents, brother and baby sister returned to the tea plantation in India. You were too delicate, they thought, to survive exposure to tropical diseases.

I picture you, sweet as a button in a drop-waist dress with Peter Pan collar. You are playing hopscotch alone on a quiet street, the chalky lines made wonky by your little hand on the cobbles. In the third square, number three is drawn in reverse and it is on this squiggle that the chalk lands when you toss it. You whisper rules and instructions to your brother, invisible, figmental, beside you. Forwards and backwards you hop until the milkman turns into your street and the clinking bottles on his push-along float cause your stomach to rumble. He stops beside you in his tall rubber boots and you take a pint of cold milk from his outstretched hand. Condensation makes the glass slippery so you hold it to your chest as you walk to the door.

The float has moved along now and, out of sight, you slide the cardboard lid from the bottle and sip cream from the top. You shiver, delighted. Your tongue licks the evidence of this pleasure from your lips before you slip inside the house to look for your foster-mother preparing breakfast.

But, as in a Dickensian tale belonging to another era, instead of boiled eggs and buttered toast soldiers, you find the elderly woman slumped, dead, at the kitchen table. So ends your stay in the first of five homes over eight years. You are shipped from one place to another belonging to people paid to care for you.

I'm sorry they left you behind. I wish we'd talked about it. You told me once that your mother's visits were rare, with the heightened formality of a royal encounter.

'She may as well have been the Queen,' you said.

I'm sure I thought this a romantic notion replete with curtsies and tiaras. I see now the anxiety of restrained emotion, survival through detachment. I understand why, when I was a child, you could never tolerate crying, not even for skinned knees on gravel paths.

The second object of yours in my possession is a book: a 1935 edition of Shakespeare's complete works.

Millefiori

Its opaque pages are bible-thin, its spine slightly loose, the gold lettering on its blue cover vanishing with age. It was presented to you when you were seventeen and a sister-in-training at St Thomas' in London. You told me about that once. I was doing a history project on World War Two and I interviewed you about the Blitz.

Do you remember the way we used to time travel? Over a cup of tea and a plate of biscuits you would make time stretch. We would slide from the comfort of your living room into the vivid dimensions of your memory. One moment I was there, in your apartment, staring at the Perth cityscape beyond the river, the next I was hurtling through space.

I like to think of you in September 1940, making ward rounds on the night shift.

You find one of your young charges awake, eyes glassy, lip quivering, and you pull a book, my book, from the deep pockets of your apron. You choose *A Midsummer Night's Dream*, with its fantastical creatures and human follies. But no sooner is Bottom transformed into a donkey than your quiet words are swallowed by the urgent wail of air raid sirens. I imagine you sweeping children along in a current of dust and panic, your movements slow, dream-like, red light casting monstrous shadows on crumbling walls, your silhouette like a fairytale goblin at midnight. The grinding engines of German bombers reverberate overhead, punctuated intermittently by gunfire, the whistling tune of earth-bound bombs and the thick groans of collapsing buildings.

'Come now,' you say to the children, 'to the basement, like we've practised. Keep moving. We'll be fine.'

Shattered glass crunches underfoot as you pass the void where an arched window had been. Sulphur is carried in on the breeze. You catch sight of the horizon and your skin prickles. It is a scene that will etch itself forever in your memory. Flames dance uninterrupted while pink smoke billows above brick ruins. In the red shroud of the sky you see brilliant specks of flashing light where anti-aircraft shells burst like falling stars. You are winded by the dazzling spectacle of savagery. Below, the white light of bombs sparkles on the Thames. Fire is so close you can hear it crackle; hear the shouting of firemen from the shadows. Across the river, the Houses of Parliament take shape, glowing in this artificial dawn.

But here I am, turning your stories over, changing the focus and restoring colour to the film. It is a tendency I have, to create, reshape. You survived those days, those months, of unrelenting Luftwaffe assault on the city. While volunteers pulled bodies from beneath rubble, shopkeepers swept ash from sidewalks and flipped signs to 'open'. You assisted in theatre by day, attended dances with allied soldiers by night and listened for doodlebugs in your sleep. That was the unreality of your reality. The ordinariness of chaos.

'Australian soldiers,' you once lamented, 'had such awful manners. And their accents! So uncouth. Never would I have imagined my grandchildren would have that accent. No, I was more partial to the South Africans.'

You carried your stories across three continents and you laid them down for me: a curious collector of words, the repository of family history.

The third object is a photograph of you and Grandpa circa 1950, two tiny portraits in a foldable, worn-leather holder small enough to fit in a pocket.

It sits, opened, on my bookcase, petite but conspicuous in its age and fragility. You are each framed by a gilt border but the images themselves are cut from the same photograph. Grandpa is squinting, laughing at an off-stage hilarity. Your toothy grin is wide and your short hair is set in soft waves. You are both bathed in a sunlight I imagine is only possible in Kenya, where you met and married. Is that the wing of a small aircraft behind you? Perhaps you are going on your honeymoon.

I must have found this trinket on one of those many nights I slept at your house as a child, when there was always a collection of poetry, and a book of puzzles, by the lamp of my bedside table, when the fused smell of mothballs and perfumed drawer liners felt so reassuring.

On those nights you would set up the projector in the lounge room and regale me with slideshows of your life in Kenya. Grainy monochrome images of safari adventures in a Volkswagen beetle, a succession of Jack Russell terriers, and two boys sporting sandals and sun-bleached hair. Perhaps Grandpa found me looking at this photograph in his study and bid me take it. I must have squirrelled it away for safekeeping.

I've since learned what took place in Kenya in those years you were there. The camps, the violence, the bloodshed. You didn't show me those slides.

I picture you in a bungalow with a wide verandah, your boys thousands of miles away at boarding school, nought but the maid for company. You pace the rooms, smoothing bed covers, puffing cushions, sorting photographs at the kitchen table. The day is airless, the heat stifling, the dry palm fronds of the maid's broom a scraping metronome. You are writing a letter to a nurse friend in London, reporting rumours of the rebellion, when a stirring at the edge of your vision breaks your concentration. The gardener's boy is grinding a stick in the dirt beneath an umbrella tree across the lawn. You stare. A span of sweeping seconds pass before you drop your pencil and stroll over.

'You shouldn't be here. You should be in school,' you say, frowning at his bare feet and grubby tunic. It is not a stick he wields, you discover, but a walking cane. He lays it beside his withered leg.

Then you notice the drawings in the dirt – an elephant, an ostrich, a dog that must be a jackal – and your face softens. You teach him the words for these animals in English. He gives you their names in Swahili.

Long after you leave Nairobi and find yourself on another

continent, you will fold notes inside letters, sending this boy – and then his children – small reminders of friendship.

At the market, I replaced the millefiori paperweight and felt the antique dealer's hopes deflate. I realised that what I want is not for you to be resurrected by the magical touch of a glass paperweight – I have no stomach for ghost stories – but for such objects to serve as portals to an imaginative space, the only place the dead can live.

Perhaps, after all, that is the appeal of antiques: the narratives they evoke, the pleasure of feeling two temporal planes coexist.

I want to find myself enveloped in the plush floral armchair of your dark lounge room, the painting of a Maasai warrior above my head, Scrabble tiles littering the coffee table, sunlight dancing on the brown river beyond the window, the cinnamon smell of stewed apples and rice pudding drifting from the kitchen, and your voice, posh, British, insisting that I really must try a cup of tea.

And if I can't find you there, then I'll give you this.

I'll hold you here in these words, fluid as molten glass, these shape-shifting memories, in these translucent images tinted by time.

Amanda Beckett is a secondary English teacher and a writer living in Perth, Western Australia. She holds a Master of Arts in writing and literature, and won the 2021 Armadale Writers' Award. She writes short stories for both adults and children, creative non-fiction and academic essays. She is currently working on a novel of historical fiction.

Chapter 18

Losing Harry

By Anne-marie Taplin

It can't be true: The first thirty days

Where are they? The sounds of our intermingled lives, the subtle rhythm of mother and son, enriched over nineteen years like ivy in the brickwork of our century-old home. Your steel-capped boots on our polished floorboards as you leave for work at dawn. Your endless requests for food; the harsh bark of your gaming voice from your bedroom, or the whir of power tools from the shed you built in our garden.

Sometimes, wilful self-deception doesn't cut it; I can't pretend you're just away on holiday – I want you here, to see and hold, to hear your voice, so gruff and deep now. Like a man, like a young man in the prime of his life.

I want to hear the radio humming as you tinker with your latest car project. I want you leaning, arm raised above your head, against the wall by the fridge as you survey the contents. I want to relish the sight of you relaxing on your bed, a safe nest away from the world; your eyes on the laptop searching for the next bargain, the next car or motorbike. Planning, always planning for *the next thing*.

When you were four, I'd say, 'live for the moment, Harry!

Enjoy what you have, without always looking for what happens next.' You'd look at me as if I was speaking another language. You had things to do, quickly. Twin desires for problem-solving and perfection battled it out in your head. Your nature was indelible, both endearing and exasperating, my rambunctious, demanding, exhausting child.

I worked hard to accept you as you are, the firstborn son destined to challenge me beyond any secret fantasies of calm, joyous motherhood. Like every other inexperienced parent, I learnt on my feet, and from my mistakes. Now, they haunt me – that time I shunned you and sat on the floor, heavily pregnant with your brother, in a corner of my bedroom, desperate for solitude. I needed a moment's peace from you at almost three, needy as a vampire. Or that time I hurled your spade at your back, every fierce instinct to protect your baby brother alive in my veins; a moment's rage that a four-year-old did not deserve. I have other regrets, more complex and murky. Knowing, even at the time, that I was caught up in my own desire for perfection in that heart-wrenching vocation of mothering. I'd enlisted willingly, even if late in my fertile years, which made the stakes all the higher.

You taught me to love with my whole, pulsing heart wide open – all the bliss, fear, entangled attachment raw and visible and fully lived. Your vivacious energy sustained and propelled us through those pre-teen years. Then I became wary of the tangible aura of your frustration when things did not go your way. You'd emit an ominous cloud of hormones; occasionally, there was a broken object or a hole in the wall. You fought and bickered with your brother, resentful at his intrusion, even years after his birth. My role evolved – I became your steadying ally, your calm harbour where you could always drop anchor and ride out a storm.

I've never stopped learning from you, Harry. These recent halcyon days, the late-teen, working-young-man days, were mostly filled with awe, bursting maternal pride. I was learning about who you are, who you might become. I was learning to let go, although I wasn't ready. I saw your commitment and dedication to your career, your work ethic, your entrepreneurial spirit. I saw your success with projects, your passion for your hobbies, your fiercely independent nature. (That did not stretch to cooking your own food or doing your own washing. 'I could if I wanted to,' you'd say. 'It's not like I'm dying to do the washing or housework, or make you a cheese toasty, Harry,' I'd reply with a smile.)

I saw your faultless, shiny beauty; youth's dewy complexion and lithe limbs grown so tall; the rosy blush on your cheeks; the way your dusky-blond hair grew so thick, just like your father's.

You needed a haircut when you were killed, instantly, on that peaceful afternoon in the rolling, redgum-studded hills near our home.

Headline: *Teen Killed in Motorbike Crash.*

Fact: A television reporter on the scene seconds after local police, asking the mortuary driver, 'Can I ride with you and ask some questions?' The TV news showed footage of your twisted, wrecked motorcycle. A niggling, erroneous preposition – you did not lose control 'at' the corner; it was two hundred metres down a straight stretch of road. Weeks later, when I saw the clip and read the newspaper, I focused on the difference a little word can make, because it wasn't true. *None of it was real.*

And yet, I am told you died on impact. You met that gnarled, ancient eucalypt with no knowledge, no clue of your destiny. 'It takes two and a half seconds for the mind to comprehend danger and act,' the Major Crash investigator told me later that evening. 'Harry only had two seconds at the most.'

Each time I visit your roadside memorial, I am compelled to retrace the path outlined in blue spray paint during the forensic investigation. It begins safely on the far left of the narrow gravel road. It ends in a shallow, loose gulch to destruction. I witness the damaged bark on that mighty tree. I see, in my mind's eye, your body's thunderous impact, before it is hurled twenty metres across the road onto the lime-green October grass. The crack of your helmet, which rips apart. My imagination stops here at this point – *because it isn't real*. You flew, you soared away, out of your body, into the universe, at one with the stars and angel dust. You *became* an angel then, or something; something other than *dead*.

Headline: *Hoon Drivers in the Hills*.

My blood boils at the injustice, the insensitivity, the newspaper's sensationalist desire to neatly wrap up the long weekend's road trauma, including the two fatalities near us. Two people not going home to their families that night. Apparently, your age marks you at fault. 'It is not known how fast the teenager was travelling.' Never mind that you were a home-loving, shy young man at the cusp of adulthood. Never mind that you were a finalist in two categories for our region's Apprentice of the Year Awards. Never mind that you were a beloved son, brother, friend, grandson, cousin, and workmate.

These days are a strange kind of living nightmare. My heart dies a thousand deaths, over and over. My tear ducts sting.

On autopilot, I plan your memorial service. Unbelievably, that dreary, drizzly day arrives (although it still isn't true; *you're at work, or at your dad's*). My compassionate helpers arrange the flock of red helium balloons in the old church hall I hired. We carefully place and light the candles; the vases and vases of fresh flowers; the photos and special mementos of the phases of your life. The socially distanced chairs fill the hall to capacity. Your precious, late-nineties Honda Civic marks the entrance, decked out in more balloons to match its glossy red.

I hide in the hall's kitchen. I'm numb. I struggle to breathe. The hall is filled with mourners, and a heavy silence shimmers like a bated breath. Your old classmate sings in your honour and her music pierces every single heart. I've taken my seat at the front, below the stage where my old friend, now your funeral director, opens the ceremony. I start to sob; my eyes frantically search the cathedral ceiling but see nothing. *It can't be true.*

'You've got this,' she says, holding my gaze. As I climb the steps to the stage, I withdraw into my core, my sombre face a mask as I speak those four thousand words of your eulogy.

Tears leak out as I listen to the other nine speakers, but I am not fully present, though I accept embraces, gifts and condolences. The first bars of the songs we chose to accompany the visual slideshow of your life are my undoing. I imagine you – incredulous, awestruck – that so many people *care*. My humble, introverted young man, how proud I am of you. How much I love you, deeper than the deepest ocean, wider than galaxies – and back.

It is peaceful here, at your tree. We have dressed it in a bold, red cloth banner with your name emblazoned in yellow. There are bright flowers at its base and rustling grasses in the paddocks; grazing horses, boisterous flocks of galahs overhead. I lean back in my fold–up chair and gaze upwards through twisting branches at the endless sky. I imagine this as your view, after you landed.

Fact: my child, a ragdoll projectile travelling with bike, landing face down. Broken.

I've heard about the poor man who found you, still traumatised. Your left leg and arm were not right, he told Triple Zero. He gently turned you over. 'There's no point doing CPR. He's definitely dead.' I want to find him and thank him, though I'm not sure what for. I think I just want to extract every tiny detail of the accident and live vicariously through him, wishing I'd been there. *Why didn't I know?*

It was your first trip out on the bike in six months. I suspect you planned to sell it. You'd had fewer than thirty hours' experience; still on your Learners. Your inadequate training – a mere ten hours over a weekend on a government bike at low speeds on a purpose-built bitumen track – now feels like an insult. What kind of irresponsible law allows this to happen?

But things could always be worse. You could have been brain-injured or left comatose, likely so damaged you'd never feed or care for yourself, never stand or walk. My mind plays games with other outcomes, but it doesn't matter. This is the outcome I have.

Fact: The words that stopped my world: 'I'm sorry to inform you that your son has been killed in a motorcycle accident.'

The visceral *sound* inside me! I never knew that shock and grief felt like that, the booming otherworldly terror, the searing pain, vacant disbelief, so intense that there are and never will be any words to describe it.

'It must be a mistake! It isn't true! It isn't true.'

The first time I met you, after an emergency caesarean section and a traumatic birth. The perfect picture of a healthy, angelic newborn. Lashes like palm fronds, a crown of messy dark hair, baby blues ocean-deep. A knowledge in you, a soul connection that spoke to my very cells: blood of my blood, I will always love you.

How has it come to this less than two decades later? This early grief is enduring, limitless and soul-altering. People say that I will learn to manage it, and perhaps there will be whole days when I will not think of you. Unimaginable, now. My mind is exhausted by re-running your last five seconds, or the churning over and over of your echoing absence.

But I cannot live in this state of overwhelm. I have your brother to care for, to raise to be the man you will never fully make. The impact of your loss will be measured in months and years, as with mine, but unique to your own peculiar sibling relationship. Always a younger brother, he is now a singleton.

But where is he? The second thirty days

My boy is taken from me, that much is clear. Harry was adored, cherished; he taught me the full spectrum of immeasurable, unnameable maternal feelings. They haven't changed despite his absence in our home. His bedroom, across the hall from mine, is silent. Though I take calls from the coroner's office and the police, *it still is not real.* The memorial service and the farewelling of his exquisite, damaged body are behind me. I have noted the passing of 'the firsts' – first aching, sobbing evening without him; the first month.

What has happened to him, to his essence, his soul? His body is now reduced to ashes in the pearly blue urn on my bedroom mantelpiece. His images line my walls, face me in the kitchen, on doors. His work jacket hangs in the hallway. I hold his clothes close to my face and just breathe. His scent transports me.

The gap he has left, his absence in our home, is juxtaposed with memories of his powerful, living presence, the energy of him everywhere. I am enraptured by the sound of his voice on my phone's videos. I watch, over and over, a miraculous capture on his last day, less than an hour before the accident, from his father's just-installed video security system. I will know my son's posture, his stance, his gait and his mannerisms forever.

On his final morning, I made Harry bacon and eggs, then watched him readying for the ride. 'Take extra care on the roads,' I said. 'Remember what happened last time.' He smiled – embarrassed, dismissive, invincible. It was a fortunate near-miss, a year ago, when he'd flown over the handlebars as he'd hit a rock hidden in long grass. A foolish, rookie mistake he'd learned from.

He zipped up his motorcycle jacket, then swung his leg over the saddle and buckled his helmet. I saw him, I mean I really *saw* Harry that day. Effervescent on reflection; the poise of his slim body, tight black riding pants and padded safety jacket. The moment is, of course, imbued with otherworldly significance now, but then…he was eager to be on his way and we did not even hug goodbye. He never liked a fuss.

Could I have taken that freedom away from him? He was legally an adult, and it was not my choice, or my life to live. I could not have stopped him, but maybe it could have started sooner, this clipping of wings? I could have forbidden his passion for motorbikes, learned from his father since preschool. I talked about the road toll; so many of our region's young people killed on bikes or in cars. Maybe the sweet lure of danger was in his blood? As a child, like a whirlwind, Harry was a force of nature.

Our last goodbye, post-mortem, is never far from my thoughts these days.

As I entered the chapel, my eyes were both drawn to and repulsed by the dais, sensitively made up as a bed. I remember the howling, a guttural roar of agony erupting from my throat. The touch of my friend, the undertaker's hand on my arm, her gentle pressure. *I am here. I am witness to this horror.* Our children are the same age. She leaves me to my final farewell. This, too, is impossibly hard for her.

I fall silent as I examine him, close, my face inches from Harry's; more intimate than he would have allowed, had he drawn breath. My own breathing is noisy, I hear it with this otherworldly sense of time slowing down. I gaze, I stroke, hold and study my child. I see his neat brows, his smooth right arm; I touch his right hand, frozen-cold. I'd been warned about this iciness but did not expect the unyielding hardness – the insulting opposite of our pliable bodies in life. I realise the awkward, unnatural rise of his chest, his angular clavicle jutting out. All over again, I marvel at his perfection, the shadow side of my delight in his infant self. I allow a ragged cry and tears to ebb and flow according to my own rhythm.

I cannot bear the sight of his delicate skull crushed inwards. What is worse, our imagination or brutal reality? I rip fresh tissues from the box beside me and cover the parts of his face that I do not wish to see. It creates a window that feeds my illusion of peaceful sleep. I avert my eyes from his left side and do not speculate why he is almost a foot shorter than normal. A wave of grief and sobbing overtakes me again, and when it has passed, I lift my forehead from his arm. I tell him that I am bereft; I talk in a flow without thinking, just speaking words direct from my heart without filter, analysis. It is a glacier of sadness at his loss. 'My beautiful boy,' I say, over and over.

Walking out of that chapel, with its soft music and bubbling fountain, was perhaps the most difficult thing I have ever done.

News of Harry's death travels like shockwaves through our small community. People approach me at the supermarket, at the service station, in the street. *So sorry*, they say, lost for words, sometimes with tears in their eyes. Sometimes they simply hug me.

Is it any worse to lose a young person, any more tragic when a teenager is killed? Perhaps so, because we live our fortunate, comfortable lives believing that children outlive their parents; it is an offense against the natural order to have that challenged. I see ragged fear in the eyes of other parents: there's nothing like a pointless tragedy to remind us of our shared humanity.

Fact: two nights after Harry's accident, I woke with a jolt in the early hours to the deep clanging, otherworldly sound of a gong reverberating through my body. I have never heard, or felt, anything like this. *What was it?*

Where is my child, as grief overtakes me when I read the letter from the coroner? He informs me of the timeframe for the official death certificate for 'the late Harry Felix' who died of 'multiple injuries'. How dare they use those offensive words! (*late, died, injuries*) I phrase a complaint letter (that I never send) in my head that night as I sleep. If ever a situation calls for sensitivity to cut through bureaucracy, this is it.

Where is my child, as reminders, *triggers* overwhelm me? Writing his dates on the pile of forms – date of birth, followed by date of death. I am enraged that the span between them is so obscenely tight. I try, again, to process the events of that day where Harry left our home late in the morning, and then did not return.

Grief rises also at comments from strangers on social media, their kindness and the respect or care they have for my boy. I feel the hot prick of tears and yet I cannot look away; I read it all, re-

read my own brief posts to see, again, *that it is real*. It must be true because, look – there, the dozens of expressions of *omigod* shock and disbelief. I have seen the best of people, of friends, family and strangers, through these long days and weeks.

I address the cancer of the sensationalist headline and incorrect reporting from the day after Harry's accident. My strident letter to the newspaper relieves my ire of injustice, and then, barely ten minutes later, I receive a heartfelt call from the journalist. In an Orwellian twist, she offers to edit out digital coverage of Harry's crash under the offending headline. While I am raw and vulnerable, I agree to be part of a feature on the 'lived reality' of road trauma.

I wholeheartedly reject my 'new normal', but just like Covid, I cannot wish it away. No matter how strongly I believe that Harry's energy, his soul, the magic that animated his body *cannot have disappeared*, he still did not come home that night. He is absent from this earthly plane. I devour books, films and near-death experience accounts explaining the miracle of life beyond death, across the veil. Naturally, I seek out a psychic medium, because I want third-party proof. Although Harry continues to come to me in dreams and lucid visitations, it is not enough. It will never be enough.

She gives me solace and undeniable evidence. I am elated for days in an unreal high – the kind of joy that only another bereaved parent could ever understand. I can't let it go, one session is not enough, I need to see others and so I plan the next, and then the next. After every visit at night from Harry, I fiercely clutch at the dream, writing it down in a journal and cementing it so that, like the series of recent memories I regularly rerun, I will never forget him. The living, breathing, moving humanity of him.

It must be true: three years on

There have been many mediums since those early weeks. It has been a journey all of its own, bolstering a new certainty, an unshakable knowledge that Harry and I will be together again one day. There is a new purpose in my life now, new passions I am driven to explore; words I am propelled to write, feelings and experiences I hunt down in my quest for information. I make new connections in all segments of my life and marvel at the serendipity, the calling of hearts and minds across miles, or right in my own city. The desire to see, feel or hear Harry is like a dopamine hit and I am hopelessly addicted.

There is also a sinister black hole that skulks at the back of my thoughts: that I will forget him; that he will become just a photograph; that even his smell will disappear. Rallying against this, every day I inhale the clothes he wore in his final week of life. Miraculously, his unique scent still survives.

In his bedroom, we talk as I lovingly gaze at the dozens of photographs, large and small, that adorn the walls. It's the same one-sided conversation I'd become accustomed to since he turned fourteen.

It's odd that these long months have passed in a nanosecond. I've survived the police visit, hats in hand, that first ghastly night without Harry under our roof. I've survived that last, poignant kiss on his chilled cheek. I've survived the intensity of the memorial service and entered a permanent state of disbelief. I've performed the motions of daily life, frequently re-traumatised with every TV show road accident or crime drama – the bodies, mortuaries, motorbikes or mangled cars. Daily, I hear local sirens and wonder who is dying this time. I see motorbikes of the same make and model and my heart stops; many times, I've considered warning the rider. But what would I say? 'Be careful, motorbikes are dangerous. Death happens.'

There, I've said it. After the first year, something shifted, and my mind finally accepted that Harry is not coming home. It was the end of the beginning of this grief, the loss of that intuition about his imminent arrival. Another blow to the normality of his key in the front door, his footstep in the hall.

Too soon, I tried to watch the video of Harry's memorial

service. I could not bear to see myself speaking his eulogy, nor hear the opening bars of those forever-tainted songs. Sometimes, I still cannot bear for any of it to be real. I cry until my head aches. Only recently, I removed the pillows I'd placed under his bed covers in the shape of a body, to fool my brain or comfort my aching heart.

I give myself permission to do whatever helps – even still telling myself that Harry is away overseas, having a ball! Surely, there's been some sort of colossal mistake? I run over again in my mind – noting the sickening pit in my stomach – the visit from the police, the kissing of his cold cheek, and the holding of his set-solid hand. 'Forever young, forever cherished, forever beautiful' read the words on his memorial service card and on the brass plaque at his roadside memorial. Heartfelt words that gloss over the fragility of the human body.

Fact: We are no match for a tree, for all our feelings of immortality and youthful invincibility.

Although I don't want to remember the damage to his precious head, those memories intrude at times when I least expect it. Instead, I try to focus on remembering my son *as he was*, alive, dynamic, always moving. Bending, squatting, striding, bouncing, somersaulting, vaulting, running, scootering, jumping, riding...all the movements of a life well lived, though tragically cut short. I so desperately want to see his hundred-watt smile that could light up a room.

I want to fertilise my memories of Harry with a rich, composted motherly love. I regret those hours of living in the moment, not breaking the spell with a jarring lens. How is it that I have no video footage from the last four years?! He refused to be photographed, even in a cheeky selfie with his workmates. I ponder the mystery of his adolescent shyness, after his unselfconscious childhood exuberance waned, to be replaced by the visage of a serious, hard-working young apprentice.

There is no roadmap for a mother's grief. I know now that everything, from the date of the accident, will be measured from that point of loss. Every moment of every day and night, images of Harry flicker in my mind's eye. There is a weight to him inside me, an ever-present *absence*, though I know he is here with me, and sometimes I even feel him. It's not the same and it's never enough, but it sustains me. I see him in every rainbow.

He lived.

Anne-marie Taplin is an Australian author, editor, copywriter and artist. Her gift book *Being Mummy* was published in 2007 by Wakefield Press and launched simultaneously with online platform, *Parenting Express*. Curated for more than a decade, Anne-marie published international creative writing about raising children. Her publishing history includes dozens of memoirs, short stories and feature articles across literary and trade outlets, from *MamaMia* to *Overland*. She is the devoted mama of two sons.

Chapter 19

Songs of Yesterday's Tomorrows
by Samara Lo

The *gŭzhēng* propped against the wall sits inside its green, coffin-shaped hard case. Quite suitable imagery for something Anna had buried years ago. Normally, it's easy to ignore the niggling that comes whenever she notices the box collecting dust in the corner, but today is different. It's hard to pinpoint why. Maybe it's nostalgia. Maybe the sight of it doesn't hurt as much.

Layers of dust smudge her fingers as she sets it down, unclasps the latches, and lifts the lid. The familiar earthy scent of lacquered wood seeps out. Inside, twenty-one strings run the length of sixty-four inches of board, set across individual wooden bridges. Smooth carvings of peonies and clouds decorate the compartment hiding the tuning pegs.

A string in her chest tightens and twists as she runs her fingers down the strings. It's been five years since she last played. Five years since she last spoke to her parents.

The sight of the instrument draws up feelings she'd shoved into a deep abyss. Why she'd kept the giant thing instead of throwing it out, like the broken relationship with her father and mother, was beyond her. Maybe a part of her wanted to hold on. Maybe a part of her still believed in the ties of generations where honouring one's parents was important.

She should pack the instrument up, but like a sadist, she chooses to pick at old wounds instead. With faux-tortoise-shell nails bound to the pads of her fingers, she stumbles across a piece written as a serenade to the full moon. She's slow at first, rusty. The notes that had once been memorised scripts in her head have long faded.

Yet even with such a clumsy attempt, she's thrown back into her *gǔzhēng* teacher's home. Scrolled paintings of mountains peeking through swirling clouds hang on the wall. Steam wisps from the spout of a fist-sized teapot on the wooden table, stewing dried leaves of *tiěguānyīn*. It's in this place she felt closest to her parents' home country.

Each lesson, she would pluck out a song that she had forgotten the meaning of, with a name made up of characters she had never learnt to read. But none of that mattered, because music was a language in itself. One she understood. The numbers, symbols and lines running across the sheet music all had meaning and they opened a doorway into another world. One where tea brewing felt like a ritual and each arpeggio and tremolo told stories of emperors, empresses and their people. Thousands of years of history were tied into each note. Her teacher's history. Her parents' history; her history.

And all throughout the lessons, her parents smiled proudly. They were happy whenever she played. Perhaps they too saw the door that opened to a land they'd left but never quite left behind.

She pauses, fingertips throbbing against the hard strings. With a shaky breath, she shifts into the next song with quick, strong plucking. It's the angry pound of war drums, mirroring the battle waging inside. It reminds her of the song that had drawn her to the instrument in the first place. The theme song of a fictional martial arts hero.

During her first lesson, her teacher played it as a demonstration. He'd stopped part way, his weathered hands hovering above the strings.

'I'm too old to play this now,' he'd said gently.

But she was not old. So she practised daily to master each technique. Yet even when she was skilled enough, he did not teach her. So she taught herself. At least, she tried. But her fingers couldn't keep up with the tempo. She didn't know how to read all the symbols. Like her teacher, she stopped part way. But she wasn't old like him. Perhaps it was because she was...

'Lazy.' Her father said it so often it had to be fact.

'A stupid pig.' Her mother smiled each time the words left her mouth.

They were meant to be words of affection. A backwards show of love. It's why she was taught not to tell a baby they were cute because they would grow up ugly or why she should never praise another for their cleverness in case they forgot humility. So she was always ugly, lazy, stupid. They were phrases meant to be embraced as a warm hug, but were a slow death by a thousand cuts.

Her left hand sweeps down. Her right hand follows. Glissandos race rhythmically down the strings. They're the ringing of waterfalls, the rush of a river pushing a small boat downstream, the sweet haze of intoxication and a soft mist blanketing a jade mountain.

They're falling teardrops, a bleeding heart broken by misunderstandings and criticisms, the weight of honouring one's parents but failing, and the exhausted cry of endless overachieving, yet somehow still never being good enough.

Harmonising with the melody are remnants of the eternal questions that she had asked when she was younger: *Who am I? Where do I belong?*

She had always been too different. Too influenced by the culture she'd grown in rather than the one she'd inherited. Too foreign compared to her parents, relatives and neighbours.

Her foreignness was a joke during family gatherings. An accent to laugh at. A behaviour to mock yet forgive, because she would forever be a spectator caught looking in. It only emphasised the fact she was like them, but not quite. That she didn't belong.

Yet neither did she fit in on the other side.

Her dried seaweed snacks were disgusting. Her chive dumplings were pockets of yuck. And then there was stinky tofu and tripe. She loved it all still, even though it had made her an outcast in her youth. These were parts of her that she couldn't hate, just as it turned out playing the *gŭzhēng* was a skill she couldn't erase.

'Mummy? What are you playing?' A small voice pipes up behind her, more beautiful than the song she'd been playing. Tiny footsteps pad into the room and small hands reach across to pluck the strings.

Anna slides her chair back so her daughter can climb onto her lap. She smells of strawberry shampoo and baby lotion. She smells like home.

'This is a *gŭzhēng*. I learnt to play this when I was little.'

She had only been a few years older than her daughter.

Hugging her little one close, she struggles to remember receiving such an embrace from her parents. It wasn't in their culture; wasn't how they showed love.

There were other ways it was done.

Bowls of sliced fruit. Homemade bone-broth soup. A good education. They'd given her opportunities they'd never had by holding down multiple jobs no one wanted to do. Their ways were practical ways. Dutiful ways.

Anna didn't blame them for that. They'd done their best with what they had. It wasn't why a great wall had risen between them. That came later.

When she'd been torn between the idea of boundaries and the notion of filial piety; crushed by the weight of their shame that demanded the erasure of the fatherless child in her belly.

It would be quiet. No one would know. Women like her would've been drowned in a pig cage in the era her parents romanticised.

But Anna had chosen a different kind of love back then. One she now cradled in her lap. It was not lost on her how, by cutting ties to her parents, she'd epitomised the very culture they'd always said she carried too much of. As always, that brought a twinge of regret. One that said her child should've had a chance to meet Grandma and Grandpa even though they hadn't wanted her to exist. The one that belonged to a world across the ocean, re-awakened by each note her fingers had sung across the strings.

'Do you want me to teach you to play?' Anna presses her cheek to her daughter's head and feels the gentle nod. Guiding her daughter's small hands across the strings, they pluck out the opening bar of a nursery rhyme.

After a few attempts her daughter holds up her hands.

'Mummy, it hurts.'

With a nod, Anna lightly kisses her daughter's fingertips.

'It does hurt at first, but then the skin hardens with callouses and it stops hurting.' She pauses, surprised, reflecting on the wisdom her daughter has inspired.

Setting up another chair beside her, she takes out the music sheets for a different song. It's the theme from a Chinese drama, so different from the classical music her teacher taught.

As she plays, she smiles at her daughter who listens intently. It is then she realises that some ties can never truly be broken. Her upbringing may have been different from back in her parents' home country, but the *gǔzhēng*, the music, tied her back to it. To them. Somewhere in the melody were notes of her parents' love, of pain, hurt, rejection, but deeper still, perhaps there was a song of forgiveness—but not yet.

She understood then, that this is who she is and where she belongs. With her daughter, cherishing the piece of her parents' culture preserved by this instrument, while giving herself permission to cultivate a culture of her own. One fitting for her family. A hybrid.

The best of both worlds.

Samara Lo is a past recipient of the Copyright Agency-West-Words Fellowship and Varuna House's Westwords Emerging Writer's Residency. She was a judge for the Aurealis Awards and Living Stories Writing Competition, and has appeared in various panels/workshops. Her short fiction has been published in *Gothic Fantasy Anthologies: Shadows On The Water* and *Immigrant Sci-Fi Short Stories, Daily Science Fiction, The Saltbush Review* and others.

Chapter 20

A Mother's Love Letter
by Anita East

Today is going to be special. We are going out for our first family social outing. Agatha is so excited. Daisy, my baby, is two weeks old and Agatha, my toddler, is almost two years old. Being the older sibling of a newborn can be difficult–all the attention on the baby–so we're making it up to her today.

'Have you got the nappy bag?' I ask.

'In the bottom of the pram,' Toby replies.

'Agatha's banana?'

'In the pram.'

'The muslin?'

'In your top.'

We giggle. He's right; the muslin cloth I use to give Daisy privacy when we feed is still in my blouse from our last feed this morning.

'Bub, we're just going around the corner. This will be fun; we've planned for every eventuality,' Toby says, kissing me on the head, then bending to swap Agatha's sandals onto the correct feet. 'You're so clever,' he says, and she beams proudly up at him.

Outside, I breathe the humid October air. Agatha squeals with delight as she runs through beautiful purple blossoms felled by recent heavy rain. The jacarandas are out, and I haven't even realised. The scent of jasmine is strong, comforting.

Toby pushes Daisy in the pram, Agatha just meters in front of him, and I amble a little behind them all.

'Gee, it's nice to get outside,' I say to no one in particular.

The café is busy, but a table becomes available in our favourite spot beside the open window. We are lucky.

Aching breasts wake me from deep sleep. A morning of fun is too much for me now, it seems. An hour in the café is an exciting outing, but we all needed to come home and sleep.

I look at Daisy, who is sleeping beside me. Pulling myself up, milk soaks my top, and I'm excited as I enter the lounge where Toby and Agatha are playing with blocks.

'Did she take the bottle?'

'No.' Toby is confused. 'I thought you fed her before you both fell asleep.'

'I didn't. I must've fallen asleep. She didn't cry...' I say, still coming to. 'Why is she still asleep?'

'You've both had a big couple of days,' Toby says.

I turn and walk quickly back to the bedroom. 'What's wrong?' Toby calls after me.

'She hasn't fed since 9am!' I respond.

I pick Daisy up. Eyes wide, she looks at me, quiet. Daisy is never quiet; she is a hungry baby, a loud baby.

I rip my shirt up, undo my bra, and put her face to my breast. But she doesn't move, and her eyes stare straight ahead. My nipple is seeping, the deep ache now a painful yearning as her mouth sits so close.

I feel into her nappy. It's dry. Toby stands in the doorway. 'Have you changed her?' I ask.

'No,' he says.

'God.' To Daisy I say, 'Come on, darling. You must be so

hungry. Daisy, darling. Big drinkies now. Come now.' I push my nipple into her mouth.

'What's wrong?' Toby asks.

'I don't know. She's not right.'

I pick up her arm and place her hand on my neck. She likes to roll the skin on my neck as she feeds. But her arm falls. I lift her in front of me, but she struggles to hold her head up.

'She's floppy,' I say.

'What does that mean?' he says.

'It means she's sick. We need to get her to hospital.'

Toby doesn't move.

'Now!' I say. 'Bring the car around. Take Agga. I'll keep trying to feed her.'

He runs out the back door. I grab this morning's nappy bag, still unpacked.

'Come on, baby. Come on, now.'

On the way, Toby drives fast, but he stops at every orange light. 'Drive through them!' I yell.

He's quiet; he always goes silent with an emergency. From my Advanced Life Support training, I'm used to detailing out loud the events of an emergency as they unfold, so that everyone knows what's happening if they haven't got eyes on. Toby clams up and says nothing.

I cradle Daisy, trying to get her to feed. 'Drive me right up to ED front entrance,' I say.

I open the door before he's stopped the car. Running into the waiting area, the triage nurse stands up from behind the reception desk. There's nothing quite like a frantic mother running into ED holding a silent baby. In the world of emergency medicine, it can only mean one of two things.

Locking eyes with the nurse I say, 'She's floppy!'

She thrusts open the door connecting the outside and inside worlds of the Emergency Department. Behind this door is a place of fear and loathing for any parent and child. I understand, I used to work in one.

I look down at Daisy's face. Her colour has changed; she's grey and her eyes are closed. I pull her face to mine, and I can feel shallow little breaths.

'Her last wet nappy was seven hours ago.' I say.

The nurse's bright, colourful badge says *Sylvie*. I'd never noticed how inappropriate bright colourful badges were in a paediatric ED. She extends her arms to me and I nod. Wrapping her hands around Daisy, she pulls her from me.

A voice booms over the tannoy: 'Code blue. Neonate resus team to ED now.' I know they're talking about Daisy.

The umbilical cord, cut only two weeks earlier, pulls tight as Sylvie runs from me with my baby. 'Follow me,' she calls.

People, running from all directions, overtake me. Like some rehearsed dance, we all arrive in the cubicle with the empty crib simultaneously.

Sylvie lays Daisy's still body down. Newborns deteriorate so quickly; I should've called an ambulance instead of us driving her in; I'm such an idiot.

'Who's this?' a doctor asks.

Someone rips open the press studs on Daisy's onesie. She doesn't writhe or wriggle with joy like she does when I undo it. She doesn't move.

'This is Daisy.' I say.

'How old is Daisy?'

'Two weeks.'

'What's your name?'

'Anita.'

'I'm Mark. Head of paeds emergency.'

Someone places ECG dots on Daisy's tiny torso. Another wraps a tiny blood pressure cuff around her arm. I place my hands on the bed to steady myself. The relief as I hear it pick up the beating of her heart is great, but the machine alarms loudly and flashes red meaning her vitals are bad, really bad.

I inspect Daisy's vital signs on the monitor. It tells me that her heart is still working, though extra hard, that her brain is still alive, and that her lungs are still bringing oxygen in, though the amount in her blood is very low.

Someone reads out the values on the screen so everyone in the room can hear: 'BP -120/100, O2 sats - 98, heart rate - 80, resp rate - 50.'

'What's happened to Daisy today?' Mark asks.

Someone squeezes blood out of a tiny prick in her finger.

'Last feed at 9am,' I say. 'Last wet nappy at 7am. No bowel motion since last night. Became floppy at 1pm, I think–and febrile. Not interested in feeding. Pallor.' I continue: 'We went out to a café. She's been quiet all day. I fell asleep.' I trail off, ashamed. I'm such a bad mother.

'What do you do, Anita?' Mark asks.

'I'm a nurse practitioner.' I say.

'Daisy is going to be OK, but she's severely dehydrated and has something underlying at play.'

Someone tries to find a vein in the top of Daisy's hand but can't; her vessels have all but retreated deep into her body. Someone takes blood from an artery in her elbow. Another person taps the top of Daisy's little foot and inserts a needle into her skin. 'I've got it,' she says, and she starts filling tubes and handing them to Sylvie.

'Was Daisy full term?' Mark asks.

'Thirty eight weeks,' I respond.

'A routine birth?'

'Yes.'

Toby appears in the cubicle holding Agatha. When she sees me, she tries to wriggle from his arms to get to me. On seeing so many people in the room, Toby's face crumples–we've been here before, Toby and I, and he still can't talk about it.

When I was in labour with Agatha, the umbilical cord was wrapped twice around her neck. That meant that every time I pushed, which I did for a ridiculous three hours and twenty-five minutes, the cord pulled tighter around her neck. Eventually, her heart rate slowed dangerously, and on the second-to-last contraction, they cut the cord around her neck while she was still inside me.

Before I'd even done my final push, knowing that she was dangerously ill, they called a code, and just like now, people had run in from everywhere in preparation of reviving her. As they worked on her brand-new, just-born body, we waited to hear her cry. It seemed to take forever, but it finally came.

I know what Toby is thinking.

'Blood sugar 1.8,' Sylvie says.

Daisy's blood sugar is too low. She could slip into a hypoglycaemic coma at any moment. I start swaying my body, like I'm rocking her to sleep.

A bag of fluid is connected to an IV line, which goes into Daisy's now-bandaged foot.

Mark places a couple of drops of sucrose syrup on Daisy's tongue. Everyone stops what they're doing and watches.

Suddenly, Daisy starts to scream. Equal to the scream of her older sister as a newborn, it's the most beautiful sound I've ever heard.

'There we go, little lady,' Mark says.

'Oh, baby. Mummy's here.' I press my face down into hers. I feel wet tears–mine–on my cheek, and Daisy's. Her sweet, panting, hot breath.

The room calms immediately, and half of the nurses and doctors leave. Back to their normal wards and units, back to the patients they were helping before we so desperately needed them.

When I worked in the cardiac unit, I used to love being part of the crash team, which sounds sick now that I say it. With each code, a loud, distinct buzzer goes off throughout the hospital and someone states the code and gives its location. Those of us in the crash team drop whatever we're doing and run to the location of the code. It means there is a medical emergency somewhere in the hospital and the medical staff who are close by must step in until the full crash team has arrived.

It was an honour to be on the crash team, and I'm grateful to the team who have come to Daisy's aid today.

Adults are my thing, not kids, not babies. Sick babies really freak me out; I used to look after sick babies when I worked in the Cardiac Catheter Lab and working away on their teeny tiny bodies scared me.

Mark is handed a piece of paper. Barely looking over the values of Daisy's blood, he simply nods. He doesn't really need to look; experience tells him what comes next. Unfortunately, I also know what comes next. I look at Toby and Agatha, who don't know. I want to protect them, in a way, but Mark gestures for them to come further into the room.

'Daisy is very sick. Ee need to test her for meningitis,' Mark says, more to Toby than to me.

Closing my eyes, I nod. My consent is given. Mark, Sylvie and two others wheel Daisy's crib out of the cubicle and I follow them.

I grip Toby's hand as I pass him. 'They need to do this, darling,' I say.

'How do they do that?'

'A spinal tap.'

'Oh God no!'

The double doors to the procedure room close on me, and the team continues in with Daisy. Toby keeps walking to the other end of the corridor with Agatha, trying desperately to find games to distract her, and maybe himself, along the way. Pointing to the bright wall poster of the little girl with a Band-Aid on her knee: '*Ouchie.*' Or the sticker of a large cartoon character holding a measuring tape: '*Let's see how big you are now.*'

He wants to get as far away as possible from whatever is happening to Daisy in that room.

They both watch me like hawks; I am their gauge. Poor

Agatha knows something isn't right, but she can't tell what. This morning when she awoke, we promised her an adventure, and she probably thinks this is all part of the plan.

There is a skinny glass pane insert in one of the double doors, meaning I can just see inside the room to three people in full surgical garb. With only a nappy on, they turn Daisy on her right side and bend her body into a ball. Sylvie and another nurse hold her steady while Mark cleans her back with great swathes of Betadine-soaked gauze, her spine exposed. Sylvie notices me and says something to Mark, who looks at me and smiles, kindly.

Another nurse is suddenly beside me. 'Would you like to sit in the family room and have a cup of tea?' I shake my head without averting my eyes from Daisy.

They need to get a positive result, meaning that they must collect some drops of the spinal fluid from the end of the needle that is now lodged in Daisy's spine. Then they can test for the deadly meningitis disease or, more importantly, they can rule it out. It is the difference between her getting admitted to intensive care or not; it is the difference between possible death or not.

There are risks any time a needle is inserted into someone's spine, especially a two-week-old baby's. A spine so tiny has increased risks; the space between each of the vital parts of Daisy's spinal anatomy are mere fractions of a millimetre. There is the risk of severing her spinal cord with the needle, which would result not only in paralysis but in the loss of organ function, including in her brain, heart, and lungs.

In addition to the risk of respiratory arrest, there is also the risk of introducing infection into the spine–and therefore, the brain–in an already depleted immune system, which would be catastrophic.

I run through each scenario, weighing up the risk-versus-benefit ratio, and I decide the benefit is still in our favour: we need to rule meningitis in or out.

I will that needle hub to drip with Daisy's precious spinal fluid, but no drop comes. Removing the needle, Mark places a dressing over the hole in Daisy's skin. Palpating a little lower this time, he inserts a second needle into her spine. The length of the spinal needle is confronting for adults, but for babies, it gut punches out what little breath I have left.

Sylvie stands beside Mark with an open specimen jar, hoping to catch the drip. But the needle hub remains dry.

What is wrong with them?

Toby stares at me now, hard. He's scrutinising my every movement.

Have they done this procedure before? Does anyone know what the hell they are doing in there?

My breasts are so painful, my top completely soaked through. Toby rushes toward me, leaving Agatha blissfully unaware, eating biscuits and playing with the nurse who tried to escort me to the family room for a cuppa.

'What's wrong?' he asks.

'They can't get any spinal fluid.'

'What does that mean?'

'I don't know,' I say, imagining the worst and a stay in Intensive Care, 'But I want them to stop now.'

Toby bends down to peer through the thin glass pane and sees what I've been watching. He pulls his head back. 'No!' he cries. 'Tell them to stop! Now!'

He's angry with me for letting them do this to her; I need to turn this around. Today has been a series of complete screw-ups on my part; I need to step up.

But it's too late: they've already inserted a third needle into Daisy's spine.

The Swiss Cheese model of accident prevention informs both the medical and aviation professions. It describes a small failure as a hole in one cheese layer, and when all cheese layers have a single hole that lines up, catastrophic outcomes occur. This morning has already seen a few too many Swiss Cheese holes lined up, and I'm scared this could be the final catastrophic hole.

I wave frantically, trying to get the attention of someone in the room, but they're all preoccupied staring at the dry needle hub.

'Stop, please stop,' I say.

Agatha's playmate nurse is by my side again. 'She's too dry,' I tell her, 'They won't get a sample. This is too risky. They've had enough attempts now.'

My arms and legs are heavy. What feels like poison courses through my veins as I notice the periphery of my sight blacken, leaving a cruel spotlight on the needle sticking out of Daisy's tiny spine. To steady myself, I grab the arm of the nurse.

'Please ask them to stop,' I plead again.

I sit in a chair back in the cubicle. I hold Daisy, trying to negotiate all the wires and tubes coming out of her. Toby stands next to me, Agatha asleep in his arms, her head nestled into his neck. Poor Agga, so much for a fun family day. Toby looks old and thin; his eyes are red and swollen. The stress of the last few hours is already etched on his face.

Unable to get a sample of cerebrospinal fluid, they cannot rule out the most dangerous illness for newborns: bacterial meningitis. They must treat her as though she has it, which means aggressive intravenous antibiotic therapy. Rule in until we can rule out: ruling out from the most to least dangerous of diseases is how we roll in medicine. Sadly, I understand it, but I wish I didn't have to test the theory on my own child.

Mark and Sylvie place a large plastic-wrapped box on the table in front of us.

'Anita, we're going to put a nasogastric tube in. Daisy is very weak, and we need to get nutrients and medicines into her,' he says.

After watching them try and fail to take a sample of her spinal fluid, I refuse to watch them insert anything else into my baby.

I'm her mother, and despite my failings earlier in the day, I know what is best for her; I need to take control of this situation.

'No. I will feed her,' I say.

'You can't,' Mark says, looking at Daisy who is barely moving. 'She's too weak to feed.'

'Give me thirty minutes alone with her,' I beg.

He stares at me, but I reassure him, 'I'll get her feeding, and there will be no need for a nasogastric tube.'

I clutch Daisy tightly to my chest, and Mark looks between Daisy, me, Toby, and the monitor recording Daisy's vitals. He recognises a desperate mother, and his body softens.

'Thirty minutes, that is all you have,' he says. 'But if she deteriorates, you press this immediately.' He hands me the buzzer and he and Sylvie leave.

'Are you sure?' Toby asks. Despite me having got everything wrong so far today, he still trusts me.

'Yes! I'm OK; just leave us be for a moment, babe,' I say. 'Maybe go and grab the pram from the car so Agga can sleep soundly.'

Toby leans over and kisses Daisy on the head, then he kisses me on the lips, long and soft.

Daisy and I can do this, for our little family.

Over the next twenty minutes, I try to get Daisy to take my nipple, but she's too weak to suck. If only I can get some of my milk into her mouth! She responded to such a small amount of the sugar syrup, and I know she'll do the same with my milk. If she can get enough energy from my milk to feed, she and I can turn this around.

She just needs to feed.

Over the next twenty minutes, we work hard, Daisy and I. Both exhausted, we know the secret is to keep calm. Two weeks ago, we went through hours of labour together, just the two of us. I have one last chance to redeem myself for not recognising just how ill my baby was, the mistakes I have already made as a mummy to Agatha, and the mistakes I will no doubt make for the rest of my Mummy life.

Mark pops his head into the cubicle. Seeing Daisy still not feeding, he looks defeated. 'Anita, you have five minutes left before we insert the nasogastric tube,' he says.

I nod and he leaves. A moment later, I press the buzzer. Sylvie comes in quickly.

'Can I please have a sterile sample pot and a five-milliliter Luer Slip syringe?' I ask.

'Yes, of course.' She hurries out.

Returning with the equipment, she smiles, and I thank her. It sure is nice to have someone in my court.

I remove the blue lid and start manually expressing milk into the sample pot. Once filled, I insert the syringe and draw up some of the milk. I adjust Daisy so she is now more upright, and I insert the syringe into the side of her mouth and squirt in a small amount. Milk doesn't run out of her mouth, and she doesn't choke, meaning it must've gone down her oesophagus. I push the plunger and empty the whole five milliliters.

Refilling the syringe, I squirt a little more into Daisy's mouth, and like a miracle, her little tongue starts moving as she tastes it.

So focused on what her mouth is doing, I haven't seen that her eyes are wide open, and she is watching me.

'Hello, babycakes,' I say. Her little eyes sparkle. 'Baby Daisy. Are you hungry, my darling one?'

I squirt more milk from the syringe into her mouth. She tries to latch onto the syringe with her lips, and then it happens; she starts shaking her head back and forth, searching for my nipple.

I drop the syringe and sample pot onto the table. I can't miss this moment; I need to get my nipple into her mouth, and fast. As soon as I do, she latches on beautifully and drinks. And drinks. And drinks. A day's worth of milk, spilling out from the corners of her mouth, she plays with the skin on my neck, rolling it between her fingers. The hard lump in my throat finally starts to soften.

I look up to see Mark and Sylvie smiling at me. Their eyes fill with tears as they both watch Daisy hungrily feed.

'Well done! You're doing good, Mummy,' Mark says. 'Daisy and Agatha have a wonderful Mummy.'

For three days, Daisy is injected with four types of intravenous antibiotics, at four separate intervals each day. I lie on the hospital bed beside her crib and watch the nurses and doctors come in and out. On the fourth day, her results come back negative for meningitis and positive to adenovirus, a virus that was spreading through Agatha's childcare centre.

All but one of the antibiotics is stopped, and we are sent home to return daily for three more days until the course is complete.

In that emergency department cubicle, after Daisy started feeding again, I lost the use of my legs. I'm not sure why; I guess the massive surge of cortisol and adrenaline pumping through my body might have had something to do with it.

Once I knew that Daisy wasn't going to die, I no longer needed to fight or to fly, but my body, still suffering the effects of birthing only two weeks earlier and enduring the most frightening experience of my life, decided to shut down. I used a wheelchair while we were inpatients in hospital and, once home, crawled from room to room until I was strong enough to use my legs again.

My hope is that any time I doubt my mothering skills, I remember what happened and let it be a love letter to my children and to me: we're doing good. I'm doing good.

Anita East is a nurse practitioner in aesthetic, skin, and integrative medicine. An award-winning author with her book, *Beau-*

tiful Unique Faces, she frequently presents at meetings worldwide. Anita hosts the podcast *Difficult Conversations About Beauty* and has created an affirmation card deck and two skincare lines. She is a professional actor, and has worked on TV shows like *Neighbours* and *Offspring*, and as a presenter for Sky Sports and BBC.

Chapter 21

Delivery

by Andrea McMahon

'Took their time,' mumbles Todd, eyes fixed to the TV screen and the Friday night footy match between Collingwood and Geelong. Amy rises from the sofa to answer the doorbell. It's the pizza delivery boy, the same one as last week. Amy smiles. The boy smiles back.

'Hello. How much do we owe you?'

'Thirty-six dollars,' replies the boy. Amy feels a surge of anger at the cost. Todd phoned up for the pizzas; asked for them to be delivered even though the store is only a ten-minutes walk from their flat.

'Took your time, mate.' Todd has shuffled to the door. Amy can hear the jingle of a television commercial in the background. It must be quarter-time at Kardinia Park. Todd takes the pizzas and shuffles back to the sofa as Amy hands over forty dollars in cash.

'I am sorry. It is busy tonight.'

Amy is embarrassed by Todd's words, seeks to reassure the boy. 'It's okay. It's Friday night, everyone wants to watch football and eat pizza.'

As the boy searches for change, she looks at him; decides he is about her age. She wonders if he is an international student.

'Are you a student at the university?' she asks, already having concluded that delivering pizzas must be his part-time job and that the rest of his time is taken up with lectures and books and the hard work needed to make a better life for himself.

'No. Refugee.'

'Oh.' Amy is flummoxed for a moment. 'Where are you from?'

'Pakistan. Quetta.' The boy is looking at her now, her four dollars resting in the palm of his hand.

'Quetta.' She repeats the word. 'That was your hometown?'

The boy nods and smiles. 'Yes. I come with my family. Six months.'

'Hobart is your hometown now. You like it here?' Amy smiles as the boy hands the change to her, their skin touching for the briefest of moments before she signals that the coins are for him.

'Yes,' he replies softly. 'It is safe.'

Amy closes the door and returns to the sofa. Todd has eaten half of one pizza already. He is already onto his fifth beer. For her, perhaps, it will not be so safe tonight. Not that Todd has ever hit her. Not once. Not yet. But he has barred her exit from the house, kept her trapped in the bedroom, pinned her to the bed with hands that could so easily have tightened around her throat. More than once. Mostly when he wanted money.

She earns it at the Chicken Barn; Todd spends it. That is Todd's expectation of their relationship. She has come to accept this.

It wasn't always this way. Not long ago Todd would come over to her parents' house after work, his curly blond hair still damp from showering, and gossip with her mother in the kitchen while she finished off a school assignment in her bedroom. Todd would stay for tea, and after they would lie in each other's arms on her bed, making plans for the weekend. Todd would leave early so she could get back to her homework. She took her homework seriously. Todd knew that.

But then twin craters opened up simultaneously in both their lives.

Todd's father, a builder, took a fall that led him down the path to early retirement. A slump in the building industry meant Todd was unable to find another carpentry apprenticeship. Her own father took a fly-in fly-out job as an electrician with a mining company in Western Australia. The increasing amount of paperwork involved with owning his own business had been weighing him down for some time, he'd informed his family one night at the dinner table. He'd get more money and less stress working for the mines. All the family thought it was a good idea.

But it wasn't. Her mother was not a woman who liked to be alone as it turned out, and so it wasn't long before she took up with her mixed doubles partner from the tennis club. Her father took it stoically. After he'd had time to get used to the idea that he was a single man again, said he wouldn't mind spending his three weeks off in Perth rather than cold, old Hobart. When the mixed doubles partner took a job in Launceston nine months later, her mother put the house on the market and went with him, taking any vestige of their family along with her.

Amy moved into a share house with two classmates from the country. Todd would stay over sometimes, and then suddenly he was there all the time, watching television, drinking beer, and eating everyone else's food from the refrigerator. After a couple of months, tensions spiralled in the household. Amy knew it was time to find a flat for her and Todd. This was three months before her final exams. It became too much; she dropped out.

It makes her sad to think about how easily, how quickly, it all fell apart. How what had appeared to be a robust family built on rock solid foundations had been no more stable than a house of cards. One decision, not really a momentous decision, changed everything. She was meant to be at university this year. She'd thought that she and Todd would get married one day and Todd would build them a big house by the beach. They'd even talked about it, or joked about it, because no-one their age could talk seriously about something like that. Todd had seemed so perfect. Hardworking, generous, funny, happy. He'd been happy.

'So what do you think of the shelves?' Todd demands, ripping open another tinnie.

Amy knows there is only one answer to this question. 'They're great. We needed more storage space.'

'Floor to ceiling. Huon pine. Do you like the finish?' Todd gets up now, runs his hand down the side of the shelf as if it were the body of a woman, responsive to his touch.

The shelves are beautiful. Todd cut the logs himself in his father's workshop. Todd is not lazy. He still works hard every day: measuring, planing, sanding, hammering, drilling. Drilling holes into the walls of their rental home which, Amy is sure, will cost her the bond when the time comes for them to leave.

Amy knows that if someone were to come by and offer Todd another carpentry job he would change back into the boy she so adored, just as a run-down house can be transformed to its original glory by a loving renovation. Gone would be the flaky bits, the rotting bits, the dangerous bits.

When the going got tough, Todd had reverted to a lesser being. That was the truth of it. But then hadn't she also? She'd abandoned her own dreams, given up her independence, given up on herself, when all she'd had to do was boot Todd out of the share house.

She can't blame Todd without blaming herself.

'I'm gonna build you a nest of coffee tables for your birthday,' Todd says, taking another swig of beer. More tables, she thinks. Her life lacks many things, but coffee tables and bookshelves are not amongst them. 'Not telling you what the timber will be.'

'I like surprises,' she replies, as Todd reaches for her on the sofa, pulls her down on top of him. She wants to push him away. She wants to scream, but she does neither. What she does as he pulls down her jeans _grinds his body against hers, inserts himself none too gently into her–is think about the pizza delivery boy. How she felt when he smiled at her.

She sees the boy at the library the following week. She has finished her shift at the Chicken Barn and come over to the library to use a computer away from Todd's prying eyes. The boy hasn't seen her. He is with his mother and two younger sisters. He is carrying one sibling; his mother pushes the other in a pram. His mother is dressed in a flowing black outfit from head to toe. The family are Muslims, Amy realises. She wonders if the mother is a widow, or if all Muslim women from Quetta dress in this manner. She has no idea.

It's so strange for her to see the boy, for that is why she has come to the library today, to research Quetta, Pakistan. She thinks now she will search for Muslim refugees from there. As she passes the family, the boy looks up. He smiles in instant recognition. It is a smile that flows through her body like a cool summer breeze, cleansing and pure.

At the computer she clicks the images tab. In the search box she types 'muslim refugees quetta pakistan'. She is shocked by what materialises on the screen. Images and more images of devastation and death. Images of pain and suffering; blood and fire. She forces herself to keep scrolling down the screen, succumbing to paralysis every so often when confronted by a mutilated face, or by row after row of corpses. She breathes in deeply when she finally closes the window but knows she can't stop. In the search box she types once again 'muslim refugees quetta pakistan'. She follows link after link, reading news reports describing Quetta as 'Hell on Earth', until the library lights start to flash on and off, signalling it's closing time. But she has learned enough now.

The boy is Hazara, an ethnic minority originally from Afghanistan who practice the Shia form of Islam; religious beliefs for which they are persecuted by militant Sunni extremists. For which they are slaughtered.

You are safe now, she whispers to the boy. *You are safe.*

She gets up early the next morning. She feels so far away from home; like a displaced person. Or how she imagines a displaced person must feel. A displaced person who has never suffered from hunger or been in fear of her loved ones being murdered, she reminds herself. But still, she doesn't belong anywhere. She doesn't belong with Todd or her mother or father or her world-weary older brother. She doesn't belong at the Chicken Barn; she doesn't belong in their dingy one-bedroom flat. She belongs in a family. She belongs where she can breathe in the enticing aroma of an evening meal being prepared amidst the sound of laughter. Amidst love.

She thinks about the boy, the boy's mother, the images she has seen. She wonders if any of the politicians who want to 'turn back the boats' have seen those images. She wonders if the boy and his family made the journey to Australia on one of those unsafe, people-smuggler boats. She wonders if the father, the husband, is dead, a victim of a bomb blast in Quetta. The mother's black clothing must surely be the attire of a grieving widow?

Many of the women in the images she looked at were not wearing black. They were wearing bright, colourful clothing and patterned headscarves. There is a special word for the Muslim headscarf but she can't remember it. She locates her old computer under a pile of empty take-away containers and searches. *Hijab*, that's it; the veil Muslim women wear to dress modestly.

She scrolls down the screen, randomly clicking on links until she discovers a story on Muslim women's fashion in Australia. The women in the images are beautiful, stylish. In their faces there are no signs of the anguish and suffering of the women of Quetta. She clicks on a video and listens to a woman speaking with a confident Australian accent. Some, judging from the colour of their skin and facial features, must have had ancestors who migrated from the same cold-climate countries as her own ancestors.

She learns that the hijab can not only be multi-coloured and embroidered, it can also be worn in many different styles. She closes the laptop suddenly and walks with purpose to the bedroom. There is no need for stealth; she knows nothing will wake Todd from his alcohol-induced stupor. She opens up a drawer and pulls out a handful of scarves, carries them with her to the bathroom. She compares each scarf to determine which will be most suited to its new purpose. She chooses a pale green scarf that is larger than the others, a casualty of her mother's migration to the north of the state. She places it over her head, tying it this way and then that way. She decides she is neither beautiful nor stylish, but she likes what she sees in the mirror. She likes how it makes her feel. Like she belongs.

When she dresses for work the next morning she chooses an embroidered blouse instead of the plain t-shirt that would've been her usual choice. At the Chicken Barn, a tomato-red apron covers her from top to bottom but she is not dressing for work today; she is dressing for when she knocks off. She will walk over to the library hoping–praying–that the boy will be there also.

He is not there. She books a computer and spends the first half hour aimlessly trawling the internet, every few minutes rotating her head three-hundred-and-sixty degrees in the hope of spotting him. As the time passes she becomes increasingly despondent.

What am I waiting for? she thinks, banging the keyboard in exasperation, her eyes filling with tears that she refuses to let spill down her cheeks. She is well into the second hour of her computer booking. The malaise of disappointment has enveloped her like a thick coating of artery-clogging cream. *I must try to make use of the time*, she thinks, but the malaise has taken hold, lifting her hand to type is like lifting lead. *I must search for information on teacher training courses*, she tells herself. *I must search for information on the life I was meant to lead.* She is so immersed in misery and self-pity that she fails to notice when the boy sits down beside her. She is startled, suddenly jump-started back into life at his greeting.

'Sorry...I scared you.'

His simple words are as powerful as the claws of a bird of prey. A great weight is lifted from her shoulders, taken up, away. 'Oh...hello...I was deep in thought.'

'You are busy?'

'No, not busy.' *Just relieved*, she thinks. 'I'm looking up teacher training courses. I'm going back to school next year.'

It is the truth. She can feel the resolve gripping her like vice as she speaks. She is going back to school next year.

'Me also...next year.' The boy is smiling now. 'School is good.'

'My name is Amy,' she says, smiling back at the boy.

'Amy,' he repeats softly, the dark of his eyes holding onto hers. Onto her. 'My name is Hamid.'

Andrea McMahon's stories have been published widely, including in *Island* and *Forty South*. Prize winners include 'The Cuckoo's Nest' (2023 Lane Cove Short Story Prize), 'Damselfly' (2020 Tasmanian Writers' Prize) and 'Delivery' (2014 Beaconsfield Festival of Golden Voices). Andrea's short story collection, *Skin Hunger,* was published in 2008 (Ginninderra Press). She lives in Hobart and has worked as a librarian and library adult literacy practitioner. See more of Andrea's writing at andreaswriting.wordpress.com.

Chapter 22

The Women in White

by Sky Harrison

I was born to a mother-who-was-never-my-mother and a non-father who saw his infant daughter only once. It was a common occurrence back then, but unlike many other children in my predicament, my mother-who-was-never-my-mother actually held me. It must have been a great comfort to my tiny self in those first few moments of life. Perhaps I even took it for granted before I was whisked away by the women in white who saw me only as another chore–something I suspect I picked up on with a newborn's instinctive perception, because it was at that moment I started my protest by refusing all attempts to feed me. For two days, not a drop of milk passed my lips. The women in white suggested I was lazy and got around the problem by widening the hole in the bottle teat, so that I was forced to suckle, my message overcome by the pangs of hunger brought about by the milky formula cascading into my mouth. Clearly, I needed to shift my protest. Left alone in the sterile crib, I focused all my consternation at my lack of mother on the inner workings of my digestive system. The tubes between my bladder and kidneys twisted in despair. Perhaps if I'd had a longer-term vision, I'd have chosen another form of protest. If I'd been able to talk, I could have told them I would not be happy until returned to the comforting arms of my mother-who-was-never-my-mother. If I'd been more cunning, perhaps I would have smiled at them cutely and elicited the love I was craving. At the time, I did the best I could. If they wanted me to stick around, they would have to prove it. It seems unwise now, but at two days old, the memory of birth must have been so fresh, and I was still longing for the fleshy, warm confines of the only home I'd known for the past nine months. Would I have entered the world if I'd known what I was in for? I've never been one to knock back an opportunity or to cower behind walls, no matter how warm they may be.

The following eight days must have been a misery, with my energy focused on the damage spreading through my body, as I worked hard to hold everything in. I wasn't ready to let go; wasn't ready for this cold and unfeeling world of women in white with too much to do and sore feet and no sympathy for my affliction, or of mothers-who-were-never-mothers who took their love away when it was needed most. But then, on the tenth day, something miraculous happened, or so it must have seemed to me. The women in white picked me up not to force me to feed, but to swaddle me in cotton and a soft baby blanket, and hand me over to a smiling couple who gave me a new name and fell in love with me at first sight.

All I knew about love at ten days old was that I didn't have it. For my soon-to-be-parents, that invade-your-heart-with-full-force kind of love was a rare but not unknown occurrence. They had experienced it with equal voracity four years and eight months earlier, when they had stared into the face of my soon-to-be-brother, who seemed much less surprised by their love than I was. My soon-to-be-mother had experienced it once before, when she met her little sister for the first time, but I'm not sure my soon-to-be-father knew it until he held that little chubby boy, although maybe he had loved my now-mother right away.

If so, it wasn't reciprocated. They had met at a dance hall where my mother and her cousins escaped their sepia-toned lives on Saturday nights, dressed in the good outfits they kept for such occasions, made of starched taffeta and crêpe, their hair curled and teased, shoes too high and too pointy for the long walk home on tired, danced-out feet. My mother secretly loved to dance but was born with no rhythm, so she stuck to the wall with the other wallflowers. My father, in contrast, was dressed in an oversized electric-blue jacket that went almost to his knees and was working the room as if he wasn't anywhere near as short, stocky or balding as he was. He wasn't looking for a dance partner but gullible people he could scam out of the entry fee. While some people look a gift horse in the mouth, my father reached in and tickled its tonsils. His sense of mischief must have been a breath of fresh air for my sensible mother, because she eventually let her cousins coax her into dancing with him. No one could have predicted that dance would lead to love.

Love wasn't something my mother was used to. Her first taste of it–in the reassuring arms of her doting father–had been cruelly taken away when he was killed in a motorbike accident. She was only 10 months old. I don't know if she found a way to protest. Her mother was inconsolable, left with a child to remind her of the husband she adored. Homeless, they moved in with her grandmother, uncle and aunt, and their three children.

The already-overloaded house was the centre of all family activity, drawing all into its orbit. Aunts, uncles and cousins all lived within walking distance and visited daily, and in the evenings, half the neighbourhood came by to continue drinking after the pub around the corner closed. It was noisy, messy and crowded, furnished with opinions, arguments and post-war trauma. The women were the loudest, and they broke up the nightly punch-ups by getting into the middle of it with a hands-on-hips stare. No doubt there was also laughter–especially when the men were out or when the local children gathered to play in the street–but none of it made up for the loss of her father.

When she was thirteen, she gained a step-dad when her mother remarried, but it was more for convenience than love. Their relationship was built on sarcasm and long periods of hurt silence. My mother didn't care, because into that silence came her little sister. Some people might wonder how a child can be born of silence, but my mother knew right away it was because of the cherry stones. She'd been burying them in the backyard ever since her uncle, who took her outside every night to show her the star in the sky that was her father, told her they were the secret ingredient for babies. Her little sister didn't realise it right away, but she had two mothers–the one who gave birth to her, and the one who made her possible with the cherry stones.

My father never planted any cherry stones but somehow he got four younger sisters, which was a lot for any young boy to deal with. He'd had a brief reprieve when his brother was born, but the sickly child didn't make it past a few months, and left him to fend against the feminine tide alone. His father was no help, lumping all the children together with a 'don't be seen or heard' approach to parenting that saw him spend most of his nights alone with his war medals and several bottles of beer. So my father sought attention elsewhere, quickly gaining a reputation in the small country town as something of a rascal. His mischievous streak filled his childhood with pain–from beatings for racing his mother home after she dropped him at school; from being hit with brooms by nuns after he asked for holy water to make hot cross buns; from saltpetre wounds gained while stealing the neighbour's apricots; and sore legs from running from drunks who'd realised the wine he'd just sold them was actually piss.

At sixteen, he ran further than he ever had–all the way to Adelaide, where he landed work repairing cranes that unloaded cargo from ships. He attended dances where he tricked people out of their ticket fees. But his greatest trick of all was turning a reluctant dance into a romance, and the uneasy stare of a strait-laced girl into the coy smile of a fiancée.

But perhaps it wasn't a trick at all. My mother craved a quiet, neat life, away from shared bedrooms and closing-time violence. Maybe the trick was her seeing through the charming prankster to the warm, reliable man beneath–a man who, having escaped his own family, dreamt of creating a happier one. Or perhaps it was he who was caught in my mother's spell, seeing her practicality as the grounding force he needed. All I know is, my father's love is of the unconditional kind and by that time, my mother had learnt how to spot it, seeing it in the face of her little sister every day. Whatever the case, they fell in love, and my father convinced my mother's family that he was acceptable by often, but not too often, beating them at cards.

My mother hated her wedding. She hated her dress, the church, the reception hall and most of all, the attention. Everything was decided by the women in the family, from the location to the flowers. She got through it by dreaming about how quiet and organised her new home–a small, rented flat only a few blocks from the family home–would be, and of the house they would save up for, and the children that would fill it. But even when the hassle of the wedding was a distant memory, and long after the 'sold' sign had been removed from their front lawn, there were no children. Even the cherry stones hadn't helped. The cousins married, gave up their jobs and produced plentiful offspring while my mother trudged to the haberdashery store and sold fabric for others to decorate their nurseries. She took days off for intrusive tests and degrading medical examinations that made her feel less of a woman. She couldn't bring herself to speak about the results. The cousins labelled her selfish for continuing to work, never knowing how she mourned the loss of the children she dreamt of giving birth to. When it became clear there was no hope, she and my father turned to adoption. They lost years to paperwork.

My brother was put into their arms by a nun who knew he was the one for them. He was three weeks old. What did he think of his new family after those weeks with the doting nuns, who had grown so fond of him they cried when he left? Moved from one set of adoring arms to another, maybe he didn't notice any difference. Or maybe his seemingly inherent belief that he was so loveable was a clever defence enacted the moment he left the womb? Whatever the case, it was a smarter decision than mine, and carried him through the subsequent years with few scars to show for it. It did, however, cause a problem. Upon discovering his new parents, he decided to discard his past and simply block out anything he didn't like. And just like the baby logic that kept me ill long after the women in white were gone, he kept blocking everything out even when external circumstances dictated otherwise.

When you're the child of a mother-who-was-never-your-mother, there's a part of you that will always fear that no matter how much she wants to keep you, no matter how loving your new family is, you aren't enough. And so we try to fight that knowledge with the only weapon we have–our bodies. Our cries say *feed me, change me, hold me, sing to me,* but our hearts say *don't give us away.* Perhaps if we were wiser, we'd be the sweetest, most obedient and patient children, but you work with what you've got. For me, it was my kidneys and bladder. For my brother, it was a hearing problem, letting his ears do all the hard work so he didn't have to. Maybe it's a backhanded way of seeking reassurance, testing our new parents to see how far we can push before they confirm what we most fear? *Prove you really love us,* we say. *Don't think for a moment we don't see through those loving smiles and sweet lullabies.*

My brother's blocked ears weren't the only way he tested them, though. For the first five years, he hardly slept, and when he did, it would last only as long as my mother would let him stroke her face. It would be nice to say it was because he wanted to keep an eye on them, but in fact, the opposite was true. His first steps were an attempt to run–he never bothered crawling. As soon as he found his feet, he was off. My exhausted mother would find him on top of wardrobes, running along the corrugated iron fences that lined the property, or playing on the roof. Occasionally, he'd make it to the local playground. He wasn't even two years old. By the time my father got home from work, my mother was at breaking point, her formerly neat home neglected as all her energy went into keeping the little escape artist safe. To this day, his childhood remains the stuff of legend, for he never suffered a broken bone. Yet no one stopped to ask him *why* he ran. Perhaps he couldn't have told them. Perhaps the only thing he was running from was himself–the part of him that knew, no matter how much he blocked it out, that his mother-who-was-never-his-mother didn't want him enough to keep him. Even today, he walks ten paces ahead of everyone, as if he wants us all to prove that we love him just by following him and not running away while his back is turned.

I guess I should be grateful he kept my parents so busy. It meant they paused their search for a little sister for fear they'd have a daughter with the same sleep schedule and penchant for running away. It took three years before they dared consider adding another child to their family. Two more were lost to paperwork and government checks. When they finally looked upon my tiny sleeping face, they instantly fell in love, even though they had no idea yet how much their prayers had been answered. And yet without knowing it, they were taking home a dud.

Love is an amazing thing–it can transform ugly into beautiful, meaninglessness into purpose–but can it transform sick into healthy? Basking in the glow of my parents' affection, did I set about overcoming my illness and rebuilding a healthy body? I can only say that baby logic is somewhat obscure when looked at through the wisdom of later years. The fact is, I've never been one to throw things away, and I kept my illness close. It was a souvenir to remind me that I was unworthy of a mother-who-was-never-my-mother's love, that I was just another chore for those in charge of my care. I wasn't yet two weeks' old, but I had it figured out. These new people seemed okay, but just to be sure, I'd keep their attention firmly on me. If they were busy dealing with my illness, they wouldn't have time to consider giving me back to the women in white.

So they took me home to my freshly painted pink room, where they dressed me in nightgowns knitted by my grandmother, and wrapped me in my pink-sheet-lined cot. I was warm, I was loved, and I was so very tired. Those first ten days had been really hard. I just needed to sleep.

And sleep I did. Grandparents, aunties, cousins, neighbours visited, excited to meet the newest addition. I slept through every visit. My mother indulged their complaints that I was never awake, but secretly she rejoiced. My brother was at school, the house was tidy and organised again, and she could hold me as long as she wanted, without any fear that I would try to get away. And as I slept, the illness I had planted in myself grew, liking its new home as much as I did. So when I finally opened my eyes, it was accompanied by high-pitched cries of pain. The family doctor suggested homemade ointments and patience. His offsider said it was colic; another told her I was just looking for attention and to ignore it. She sought more opinions, only to be told that she was making a mountain out of a molehill. But she persisted, knowing it was a mountain. And then, just as her prayers of having a healthy son and then a quiet daughter had been answered, so was her prayer for a doctor who took her seriously.

I was three years old, and I was back with the women in white. Ice-cold x-ray machines, blue dye fed through needles with butterflies on them, intrusive catheters, stainless-steel instruments, plastic sheets on vinyl beds and that overly clean smell of industrial disinfectant–these became my regular companions. I was six months away from losing a kidney, from a life of daily dialysis, from spending the rest of my days with women in white. Surgery was scheduled to correct the tiny tubes between my kidneys and bladder whose twists mirrored my fate and sent fluids in the wrong direction.

I've always been blessed–or perhaps cursed–with a strong memory, but some things stand out more than others. Those ten days I spent in hospital with the white women are vivid to the minutest detail. Their starched uniforms and white-stockinged legs, the mock-concern on their faces as they woke me for another round of needles, the reassuring voices they used to keep me compliant—it's all as fresh as yesterday. Just like the first ten days I'd spent with them, I refused to eat any food they offered me—they put milk on my Weetbix instead of butter, filled my dinner plate with vegetables I'd never touched—so my parents had to bring food in from home. Dad snuck in lemonade. I tried to be brave when they left, but without my mother's skirt or my father's jokes to hide behind, I had nothing to protect me. I spent the long, lonely non-visiting hours watching the seconds tick by on the old wall clock until my parents would return and I'd be safe once again. The major surgery my three-year-old body had just undergone seemed a mere trifle in comparison to their absence.

On the tenth day, I eagerly waited for my parents to arrive with my going-home clothes, doing my best not to engage with the women in white as they made their way through the ward. I was sure if I didn't look at them, they wouldn't be able to trap me any further. When my parents arrived with my favourite dress, I changed as fast as I could. We made it to the corridor before one of the women in white stopped us. She asked if I was going home and I nodded.

'I'll miss you so much I'll cry,' she added with obvious sadness. For a moment I was confused. Perhaps I had got them wrong? Perhaps they did care about me after all? But no, it was a trap. I gave her what I hoped was a reassuring smile and continued on my way, knowing that as soon as I was gone, she would forget me. It didn't matter, because once again I had escaped them. I made my way towards the exit, my dad holding one hand, my mum holding the other.

Sky Harrison has been writing and editing for the Australian media and corporate sector for three decades, including many years as a magazine editor. Currently, she works on custom publications for the food and wine industry and in corporate communications in IT and cyber security. Her free time is spent crafting stories from the heart, pursuing publication of her speculative fiction novel and as roadie for her son's funk fusion band.

Chapter 23

Not for This World
by Pat Saunders

'Tis a curious thing to realise one is not meant for this world.' You are not where you should be. A creeping suspicion had seeped into her head, then solidified in her brain that she was somehow different. From the people she worked with. The people she passed every day. In the shopping centre. On the street. It gnawed at her persistently, insistently. Frustratingly, she couldn't quite put her finger on it, but she strongly suspected she and the rest of the world were, in fact, mutually exclusive.

When did the world start hating her?

She tried to pinpoint it, and failed. People annoyed her. Made her angry, when they didn't think. When they didn't use common sense. When they did stupid, ridiculous things. Stupid people doing stupid things had worn her out. She wanted nothing to do with these people.

'Cheer up! It might never happen!' older, tubby men told her. She'd lost the urge to smile. Lost the willpower to pretend she was happy when she wasn't. When there wasn't anything to be happy about. How did other people do this?

Her mother would've dismissively told her to stop 'moping around.' Just as well she wasn't around anymore.

Small things niggled her. Irked her. Cars at night without

headlights. Cars at night with headlights on high-beam blinding her. Dogs being walked without leads. Being bitten on the backside, by a dog when not on a lead. The neighbour's cat catching birds in her tree and depositing the remnants on her back doorstep. The odd course grey hair speckling her otherwise auburn head; she hated those. Her neighbour talking loudly in the middle of the night, outside on the phone, on speaker, next to the fence, metres from her bedroom window when she was trying to sleep. Healthy options at fast food restaurants. When did that happen? Ads on the tele. (Except that chewing gum one with the two chicks in the car kissing–where did that come from?) So much so she'd pretty much given the tele away and rediscovered reading.

The library was her new favourite place. Luckily, she didn't have any friends to speak of, as that would undoubtedly be something they'd give her a hard time about. The old guy on the bus flying to the floor when the driver brakes suddenly. Other passengers rush to his aid, flapping around. 'Just fell off the seat,' he splutters helpfully, awkwardly attempting to gather himself.

'He'll bruise tomorrow,' the woman behind the driver comments, as he wheels his walker down the ramp at the stop. 'He'll be black!' The young Asian woman sitting opposite peers out the window, noticing red on the man's knee. 'He's bleeding!'

The girl checks her phone. She was definitely going to be late. She tries remembering the last time she was truly happy.

There used to be a framed photo in her Dad's study–one of five hanging above his bookshelf dedicated to his only child–of her, aged six and a half, straight blonde short, home-haircut hair and blue eyes sitting on her father's knee. He holds her snugly, his right arm wrapped around her, his left hand brandishing a huge bunch of plump, shiny red grapes–the very first from their own vine!

Despite her face telling the story of a painfully camera-shy kid, she recalls fondly the comfort, warmth, security she felt nestled in Dad's large muscular arm, his Santa beard (bushy and black rather than white) nuzzling her cheek, his eyes beaming proudly from behind his black-rimmed spectacles. The grapes were lovely. If they were the only two people in the world, how perfect would that be?

She couldn't remember the last time she laughed. Perhaps comedians at festival shows on the tele? Even then, it seemed an effort. Laughter used to be rather more natural and easy to come by. She'd find humour in the silliest things. The word 'kumquat,' she once thought hilarious. She couldn't recall why.

She felt…muted, flatter-than-normal. Her battered, bruised heart had lost hope. Trodden on, trampled like it was nothing, the blood it pumped metronomic, once bright red with vitality, full of life, felt discoloured and stale. It dripped into ventricles like a tap with a worn washer. Days melded into weeks which floated by like leaves on a breeze. Each day she felt the final drop getting closer and closer.

She was over feeling this way. She'd played the game, tried her best…and wasn't good enough? At night she cried large silent tears which left her pillow moist, her eyes dry and swollen.

Her last relationship had ended badly.

Kat cleared her things from the closet, carefully packing them into her worn black suitcase. She watched from the bed, numb to what was happening. Was it not merely hours earlier, she'd held this person in her arms, felt her sweet breath on her neck, heard ecstasy pour from deep within, soaked in every sweet molecule of her being?

Zipping the case with two swift movements Kat avoided her gaze until they were at the front door, forced to stop to open it.

'Why?' she pleaded, 'I don't understand…'

Kat sighed like it was all too much trouble to deal with; like she was too much trouble to deal with. Eventually, turning to her.

'You just…' (she paused, meeting her eyes) '…make it so hard to love you.'

At work she'd been going through the motions for some time. People there didn't respect her. It was the little things; derisive looks, snide comments. She was sick of work. Sick of having to work.

Her boss Rebecca spoke in loud, barking, nasal monotones; had a permanent scowl plastered on her resting bitch-face, always appearing to indicate she was wanting to be anywhere else than where she currently was.

'Once you're done with [insert current menial task here] would you mind getting on with [insert another menial task here].'

Hey Rebecca, would you mind not constantly being such a complete and utter bitch?

She wondered how someone like her got through life. Behaving the way she did. Speaking to people the way she did. Surely she couldn't have any friends?

She'd always had a really good way of compartmentalising stuff into little metaphorical boxes and dealing with each one on its merits, not letting any one problem or issue affect any other aspect of her life. Now though, it felt like everything was a jumbling mess. The world was closing in on her. Whatever she did to try and recalibrate, seemed only to make things worse.

She sometimes found herself driving, late at night, for no particular reason. Alone on empty highways, freeways, following white lines, rather than cars, not knowing how she got there.

And to top it all off, they were in the middle of the first heatwave of summer and it was only November. Bushfire-inducing easterlies rattled loose street signs. Cravens with their beaks open, sheltered in the shade of eucalypts. Sweat pooled in places it shouldn't. Bloody climate change. She wasn't interested in baking through another Perth summer.

She'd learnt the hard way that having thoughts and opinions and daring to express them was not what people wanted. Her boss. Her colleagues. Every statement needed drafting, re-drafting, subbing, re-subbing, censoring and sugar-coating. It irritated her, the way people didn't say what they meant. Her brain hurt just thinking about it.

She's fibbing when she tells her computer she's not a robot. Turn up on time. Don't take sick days. Keep your mouth shut. Don't have a thought. Don't even think. Blend into the background. Hide in the shadows. Behind shoulders. Flatten yourself against walls. Hug rooms' circumferences. Don't have an opinion. Only speak when spoken to. On the back foot, not the front. Be a wallflower rather than the sunny variety and definitely not a rose.

Don't care at all. Go under the radar; unobtrusive; entirely forgettable and most importantly, keep your thoughts and opinions to yourself.

Let the spotlight shine on those who seek it–go-getters intent on making a name for themselves, bulldozing anyone stupid enough to get in their way. She'll stand to one side, silently observing from the sidelines. Head down. Bum up. Get the job done. Go home. Simple. Come back the next day and do it all again. She was a tap washer. Worn down each day. At night, dripping, leaking a little more.

She felt more lost every day. This wasn't the way it was meant to be. This wasn't the way she should constantly, consistently feel. She barely spoke to anyone. Took her breaks outside alone, away from the smokers, sitting on the cold, hard brickwork, unable to stomach the endless meaningless minutiae her colleagues exchanged. The people she worked with didn't get her. Didn't think the way she did. Why did they not see the world the way she saw it?

She was sick of people. She was sick of having to deal with people. She wished she didn't have to deal with people.

She should sell up, she thought, move to the country and buy a quaint little cottage in the middle of nowhere. She remembered at school how many people she would speak to in the course of a day. Now, she could count them on the fingers of one hand, if she was lucky. Man may well not be an island, but she figured in a court of law her case would be thrown out on a technicality.

When did she begin avoiding people? Avoiding interaction, conversation? She listened more, she thought. She listened and observed a hell of a lot. It was true what they said about the loss of one sense, heightening the others. Since her 'quiet phase' had begun, she seemed to see so much more. Interactions between people; the subtle tells. She wondered if all quiet people were the same. Dreading someone asking, 'Are you ok?'

She'd rediscovered writing. She liked working, playing with words. 'Wanking with words' her year eleven lit teacher called it. She'd warned the class not to do it when writing their essays – using fancy words that meant nothing – but she wasn't writing essays anymore, her scribbling now free verse. Words, unlike people, were extremely malleable, easily manipulated. She could control words and make them do what she wanted them to do. It intrigued her how easily she could spout pages and pages of thoughts and feelings–her thoughts and feelings–but when it came to talking to someone, seemed barely capable of stringing two words together.

She retreated into herself, sleeping a lot.

She pressed her index finger inside. Her other hand caressed her breast, cupping and massaging the nipple until it hardened. She rolled onto her front, squashing her breasts in a way which made them feel larger than they actually were. Her finger continued to work, gradually building the tension, until finally, feverishly, she released, her finger sticky with pleasure. Her sheets stank of the sex she wasn't having.

On cool, clear nights she'd wander down to the local park, lie on her back in the middle of the cricket pitch and stare at the moon and stars. Police sirens wailed in the distance. Occasional drunken yobs blathered indecipherable nonsense stumbling the outskirts. A hotted-up V8 roaring past leaving dirty black tyre trails. Her nostrils flooded with pungent rubber. She didn't move. Didn't flinch. Continued staring at the moon until she swore she could discern distinct craters. The landscape she thought she saw, a trick of her mind, recalling countless Hollywood interpretations. Cicadas perpetually chirped until finally the couch of the wicket tickled her bare legs sufficiently and she heaved herself up, dawdling home.

Dirty dishes accumulated in her sink. Bench tops wore a film of dust.

She began shopping like an old person—boxed microwave meals filled the freezer. Anything that took more than ten minutes to prepare wasn't worth the trouble. Her stained coffee mug had a crusty build-up on the lip of one side, forcing her to drink from the other. She used the same bowl for her cereal each morning, rinsing it daily. Her legs, underarms and bikini-line competed for the prize of most attractive body hair on a forty-something. Her floors screamed for a scrub. Cobwebs dangled, capturing tiny flying bugs that seemed to appear from nowhere.

She couldn't be bothered getting dressed properly, wandering around in her underwear. She hated it when her Dad did that when she was a kid. Ugly dark shadows underlined her eyes. Outside in her garden, the overgrown jacaranda, wilting lilac bells, stood sentry over a scraggly weed-ridden lawn littered with leaves which the local bird life waded methodically, meticulously through. Beaks picking, probing, punching through paper-thin blades into the soft fertile earth below. Magpies, the most eager, unafraid. Dancing right up to her front door, expectantly awaiting tasty treats to be tossed from within. The slow-moving deliberate bin chickens rifling through foliage, flinging it aside with their long hooks. Pink and greys screeching, perched on fences surveying the landscape. Kookaburras cackle high atop light poles.

She'd begun having these weird visions. When she was driving, on a freeway overpass or across a bridge, a thought would enter her head – What if I just drove off? Over the edge? What would happen? Her car barreling through the safety barriers into the air where it would momentarily float like a gull on the breeze, before plummeting into the blue below. She saw her face through the window, eyes closed, her heavenly hair wafting peacefully around her as the car filled. She'd never looked so beautiful, so calm.

For five songs on the radio, she peered at herself in the mirror, turning her head this way, then that. Moved closer to the mirror until she was millimetres from her reflection. Stared deep into her eyes until the colours bled and they weren't eyes anymore. Splashed cold water on her face, dampening the vague burning behind her cheeks. Flicked a fleck of white fluff from the shoulder of her faded black t-shirt. Her fingers tingled. Plucked a rogue eyebrow hair. Limbs were heavy. Tweezered a zit. Felt rooted to the spot. Inexplicably, ironically, she felt...alive.

Deep breath...Fiddled with the razor until it felt comfortable in her hand. Deep breath...

Her childlike toothy grin beamed at her glistening pale skull reflected in the dimly lit bathroom. She'd shaved it all off, after wanting to her entire life but never being game enough. (What would the boss think!) Things were different now though– employers couldn't sack you because they didn't like your haircut. (Well, they could, they just needed to think of an adequate justification that had nothing to do with your hair!)

She chopped her ponytail off. Trimmed what was left back to a buzz. Then the whole way. The bald look suited her, she thought. Made her look tougher somehow. Fearless. No one is gonna step on me no more.

Her new look attracted comments. 'Nice...' 'That's... different...' 'What the hell ...?!' and a variety of looks and glances from her colleagues. The dark, mousy chick who kept herself to herself did an obvious double-take. The blonde loudmouth sneered openly, sniggering with her lookalike mate as they passed her in the hall. Most of the guys thought she was coming out, as if that was even a thing anymore.

She felt, on that first day, like she was on show; on display. Everyone was looking. And staring. And checking her out some more. Studying. Evaluating. Judging. Good, bad, indifferent? Made her ears look big. Had a funny shaped head. Eyes were more piercing. 'Makes your lips look thinner.'

Yeah, cos that's what I was going for. Thinner lips. That's what everyone wants and needs isn't it? Thinner lips.

She pursed her thinner lips, studying them in the work bathroom mirror. She turned her head slightly to one side, evaluating her shaven profile, then the other.

She didn't care what anyone thought, what anyone said, she liked it. The rawness of it. Freedom born of the rejection of conformity infused her. She felt luxuriously relaxed, like a cat spread-eagled on the driveway soaking in the sun. The more she looked at herself–the new version of herself–the more she liked what she saw.

Her previous thick, flowing locks had the unwieldy wave she'd allegedly inherited from her father's side of the family. That's what her mad aunt had told her, dispelling any hopes that she was, in fact, adopted. She'd always had long hair. Her mane required constant care and attention. Shampoo. Conditioner. Blow drying. Hairspray. Gel. Hair lackeys. Headbands. Clips. The list of products was endless. And for what? To have a shower. Go to bed. And do it all again the next day. It was more trouble than it was worth.

She wondered why she didn't realise it sooner. She found herself absentmindedly reaching for her ponytail. Her hand left grasping air; her phantom ponytail serving only to remind her of the deadweight that had been lifted, banished along with her wavy locks.

'I like your hair,' a quiet voice came from nowhere.

She glanced in the mirror's reflection, to the side, where a slight movement caught her eye. It was the dark, mousy chick who kept herself to herself.

'I mean...' she fidgeted with her hands, 'I like your haircut.' She peered at her in the mirror, awkwardly standing, avoiding her gaze.

'Thank you.'

Mousy Chick moved shyly forward, becoming larger in the mirror's frame. 'Can I...' she hesitated. 'May I...touch it?'

She'd heard more come out of Mousy Chick's mouth in the last minute, than she had in the entire time she'd worked here.

Curious, she turned from the mirror to face her, who despite their nearness seemed unable to tear her eyes away from her freshly-shaven head. 'Go for it.'

Mousy Chick tentatively reached out and timidly–exquisitely so–ran her coppery index finger along her scalp, front to back.

She felt a kind of shiver go through her as Mousy Chick carefully spread her fingers, like cautious, gentle tentacles, across her head and moved her palm silently forwards, and back. Stopping; almost cupping her scalp, side, to side.

Another shiver. She relaxed into Mousy Chick's warm hand, as a cat might position itself for maximum owner-scratching satisfaction. Mousy Chick peered at her, gazing in wonder at her pale shaven scalp. She had the most gorgeous green eyes she'd ever seen. How'd she manage to miss that?

Mousy Chick seemed to feel her stare, and abruptly, self-consciously removed her hand. She caught it on the way down, their palms colliding, twisting, fingers pointing upwards intertwined. Slowly, she guided it back to once again rest on her head. She held it there. Her thumb found the pale webbing of Mousy Chick's hand and gently, almost imperceptibly, rubbed it.

The air between them stilled. Their eyes found each other, and held. Fine dust particles shimmered around them. A dripping tap reverberated, breaking the silence. Mousy Chick's fingers twitched to life, delicately stroking her scalp once again. The mirror's reflection revealed two growing grins. Her cold heart lifted, together with the corners of her thin lips.

Pat Saunders is from Western Australia and studied film and television and creative writing at Curtin University. She has twenty six years' experience in the Perth film and television industry including fifteen years at the Australian Broadcasting Commission. She spends her time editing news stories and sorting mail for Australia Post. She hopes to continue creative pursuits until she dies.

Chapter 24

Sky Chase

by Nina Cullen

Danny could hear Daisy singing from her cot in the room next door. It was a soft trill but soon it would wake her sister and then things would ramp up as Lucy ran around the room finding things to bang or blow. The walls were thin and Danny needed to get them out of the house. Fast.

Skye rolled over and faced him. He thought she was awake but her breath was still slow. She wore ear plugs and an eye mask to create night for at least a little bit longer. Her shift finished at eleven last night. She was on another late today and needed the sleep. He really needed to get the block out blinds they'd been talking about.

There was a loud bump as Lucy jumped out of bed. Danny sat up and rubbed his eyes. Okay. Look smart. Another day had started. Only six more hours until nap time. When he walked in, Lucy was running a wand along the cot bars, so Danny picked her up and zoomed her around. The wand dropped and she was too busy giggling to notice. Still contained in her cot, Daisy held her hands out for a pick up.

'Hold on pumpkin,' he said, swapping Lucy so he had her like a barrel under one arm. Then he scooped up Daisy. He deposited them both on the couch, as far away from Skye as their small house allowed.

If Danny made breakfast there would be noise. If he tried to get them changed there would be noise. If they stayed in the house there would be noise. He grabbed their dressing gowns, quickly sourced some yoghurt pouches and hustled them out the door.

'Where we going Daddy?' Lucy asked from under the giraffe hood of her dressing gown.

'An adventure.'

'Ooooo!' Both girls were in. It was a better sell than the reality which was maybe get some petrol, pick up a few groceries and find an early opened café for babyccinos while he quietly clock-watched and Skye got some more sleep.

He didn't know the where and what yet but was keen to get them into the car while cooperation was high. He tucked and tied dressing gowns, made sure they had slippers on their feet and a favourite soft toy to cuddle.

'Molly.' Daisy stamped her foot and pointed to the yellow pony squashed under a couch cushion.

'You chose Melon, bubba. Just one each.' He needed to get this out of the lounge and into the car before it got any louder. Daisy stood and eyed the pony. 'Come on.'

Danny saw it could go either way. He could jolly her along and they'd move on with life unsnagged or he'd miss the window and there would be tears, tantrums and hyped up craziness. And that kind of craziness was contagious. It would transmit from Daisy to Lucy and somehow what had once been a scene of proud domestic peace would now be chaos and high emotions. Then he would have to calm and cajole two kids and for the rest of the day Daisy would bring it up again, the left-behind soft toy, unfinished snack or shortened playtime, whatever the fixation was. Again and again. That kid could hold the same grudge across multiple days, which came as a surprise after Lucy's general cheeriness.

'I'm coming in to pick up my cargo.' Danny swooped in to

pick up Daisy, blew a raspberry on her tummy and that way, got to the door. He was only just learning that there was no point reasoning with a toddler. As much as he wanted logic to win, it just didn't.

Everyone was strapped in and beaming.

'OK Luce, which way should we go?'

She pointed out of the driveway.

'And after that?'

'Past the park.'

'Yes, ma'am!'

That had them in stitches. Daisy held Melon up to the window and talked her through the route. It's lucky Melon understood, because a lot of the time Danny and Skye still had no idea what Daisy was saying. Lucy tucked Softy, her rabbit into the seatbelt with her and gently stroked her ears.

'Your turn now, Daze. Where to next?' Danny put his hand behind him and tickled Daisy's foot.

'There! There! There!' She pointed past the park and kicked her legs around. Danny and Lucy followed her finger and saw hot air balloons in the sky. There were four of them hovering like a trick in the distance, red, yellow and two with coloured patterns.

He drove in their direction. In the rear mirror he could see Daisy with her nose mashed up against the window and Lucy bobbing her head around to try and find the best view.

It was quiet this early, just the dog and pram walkers and a few tradies. It felt like this quiet world was just for them and Danny needed to remind himself that Stop signs and traffic lights still counted, even if he was the only car around.

'That way! That way!' Lucy was pointing to the left and had the better view now out her side. 'Catch them Daddy! Sky chase!'

The balloons were heading to the city's north, away from Danny's rat runs and known routes. When he had a chance to look longer, it seemed like they stood still in the sky but then he'd follow a street to get closer and the balloons were always just beyond them. Danny put the windows down and the girls reached their hands up to touch and grab at the air. They screeched with the wind in their hair and the thrill of the chase.

A rubbish truck took its sweet time in a narrow street of terraces and instead of backing up and executing a cranky three-point-turn Danny sat for a moment, hands resting on the wheel, head craned forward looking up now with the same wonder as his little girls. Those balloons stopped time for them. They were all suspended in this airy wonder together, imagining what it might feel like to float and fly away in any direction.

Someone sat on their horn behind him and the rubbish truck was turning the corner. Danny held his hand up in the universal driver's sign of apology. He turned in the opposite direction of the rubbish truck and was fed into a railway tunnel.

'Dark Daddy, dark!'

'Bwahahahahahaha! Spoooooooky!' They were all finding it hilarious rather than scary and it was a shock when they came back out into the sunshine.

'Where are they Daddy?' Lucy twisted her head and scanned the sky. There were telegraph poles, five-storey buildings and patches of blue but the familiar round shapes of those shifting colours weren't there.

No one said anything.

Daisy started to cry. 'Gone, Daddy.'

It was a loss. They'd felt like a guiding force, something to follow, something they all wanted together. He couldn't bring them back home broken and bereft.

'We'll find them again, Bubba. Promise.' Don't make promises you can't keep. He saw Skye waggle a finger and announce that he could clean up the fallout. It was an unnecessary word that he'd tacked on to the end. It just came out sometimes.

He needed to get out of the mid-rise residential. You couldn't see enough sky. A few wrong turns, some streets which were getting leafier and wider, a strip of shops where they could stop on the way back and finally there was sky again on all sides.

'Eyes peeled, girls. Where are they?'

Concentration was audible with these two. Lucy whispered to herself while Daisy clicked her tongue. Danny took a couple of turns but without the chase it was just a lonely way to learn new streets in your city. They may as well stop somewhere so he could orient himself. It was nearly seven. Skye wouldn't sleep much longer anyway.

Daisy was banging on the glass, probably getting ready to kick off. Danny decided the ring road would be the best way to get them home. There were more cars driving now and he didn't want to get caught in the pre-peak peak hour with two hungry girls both a little sad at the sudden end of their sky chase.

'There Daddy! Over there!' Lucy had paid more attention to Daisy's banging, which was actually pointing, and the balloons were back in sight again. Danny's hand loosened on the wheel and he settled back into his seat.

'OK!' He got them in the right direction and this time it was like he was following a preordained path. They got green lights and long straights and for the first time they caught up to the balloons.

'We're under them!' Lucy screamed and both she and Daisy tried to twist their heads against the window to look straight up. They waved madly as much as little arms could and Danny tried to slow down to see his next move.

The red balloon was going lower, followed by the patterned two and then the yellow one sunk down too. Danny followed them to a huge park and stopped the car. He got the girls out and they all stood together, Lucy tucked into his leg and Daisy light in his arms as they watched the balloons slowly return to earth.

Nina Cullen is an Australian writer based in Newcastle. Her writing has won prizes and grants and appeared in publications such as *Australian Book Review, The Big Issue Fiction Edition, Meniscus, Island, Sleepers Almanac, Taste – Fresh New Writing, the Sydney Morning Herald* and *The Guardian.* She has completed a collection of linked short stories and is working on a novel. She publishes book reviews monthly at *Bedside Bookstack* ninacullen.com (@ninacullen).

Chapter 25

Building Something New

by Ruth Morgan

I thought being married would make me happy. I would be loved, worthwhile, complete. So firmly blinkered by my pursuit of an illusion, I dived in at nineteen, saying yes to the first man who asked. I knew no other proposals would be coming my way, so I grabbed my only opportunity.

Four decades on, I realise that so much that influenced everything I did, thought, or felt was locked away in my memory. Experiences and events were stuffed in iron trunks, studded with bolts, and securely wrapped in chains and padlocks. Boxes, pushed into the deepest dungeons of my mind, leaked beliefs about who I was and what I was, their influence insidious.

When I think of that naïve, wounded child, I want to tell her that she was then, and is now, *enough*.

She didn't need to sell her body and her soul to someone without the ability to treasure either. But it's a waste of energy best directed elsewhere; I can't change the past, or renovate the disaster area left behind. The only solution is to dig within to find the courage to leave, to walk away, and to not turn back to see the ashes.

Bravery can be learned if you're prepared to dig deeply

enough, and to discover that the cost of staying outweighs the cost of leaving.

A trusted friend–a psychic–said I had two choices in how I left my toxic marriage. In a pine box or on my own two feet: the decision was up to me. I chose the latter. I waited until I had a clear run. And then I ran.

Cowardice, or sense, made me wait until he was visiting friends. Days and days of endless hours doing, planning, packing, until my brain felt like it was moving through a thick fog. I had no help; I could trust no one. There was only an endless list of things to do.

I planned, packed up my life, put the tear-soaked lessons into a black plastic bag and moved towards something that had the glimmer of a future. I kept my decisions to myself and, to protect those who were vulnerable, I boarded my cats elsewhere.

There has always been a chasm in my head between what I think I can do and what I actually can; something else filtering into my life from the past, a thought designed to make me doubt and hesitate. Regardless of my own lack of faith, I knew that, now, I would do whatever was necessary, even if I lost my sanity–or my life–trying. This time there would be no turning back.

The night before the Removalists arrived seemed endless. My dream of a happy life was dead; my marriage was a failure, so was I. The new world was nothing more than a mirage, and I felt numb, methodically plodding towards the next step, a combination of exhaustion, and fear.

The truck was packed, and I watched my world be pulled apart. Though 'he' was five hours away, there were spies in the street, and, as the movers packed, I panicked, wondering if he would come flying back in a cloud of tyre smoke and anger.

Then the truck left and I was alone, a taste of what the future held.

I packed my car, one thing after the other, with space left on top for the birds, and the cats.

At the end of a long hot day. I'd planned to reclaim my freedom and sleep in the wonderful enclosed sunroom on the back of the house, to prove to myself that I wasn't scared, but I couldn't relax, thinking every car driving up the street was him coming back.

Gathering up the cushions to put on the floor in the empty bedroom, I locked the door, curled up in my sleeping bag, and cried myself to sleep. Outside was peace: I could hear a mopoke in the distance, and I felt the breeze blowing on my face, carrying the faint scents of salt from the ocean.

Morning. Another frantic day.

Time to finish packing and to collect the cats from their secret hideaway. Lock the house and take the keys to the agent. Someone would live in the shell I'd left behind; they might succeed in making it a happy home. My ex would come home to find it empty. A reflection of what he'd tried, and nearly succeeded, in doing to me: making me a hollow thing, filled only by what he approved of. At his beck and call, panting like a starved dog for scraps of affection.

No more. Leaving was hard. Staying was no choice.

I drove down the street, pausing before turning right–away from the past and towards whatever was to come. I handed over the keys to the agent, and then took my feline family for tranquilliser shots to reduce the stress of travel. I wished I could have one, too.

Three cats lay in baskets piled onto the mountain of stuff on the back seat, and the fourth sprawled alongside me, on the floor of her cage, eyes unfocussed and drooling, occasionally stirring sufficiently to cast me a puzzled look.

Ahead, a town, a location I didn't know. No friends, no contacts. A street directory when I went shopping.

As every kilometre passed, something within me changed. I tentatively dipped a toe into the waters of independence. There was nothing solid, secure, or certain, except a determination to make a new life and do it well.

The only known was the house that would, I hoped, become my home.

I'd found a home of my own; the first house I'd ever bought alone. The agent remarked that it must be challenging house hunting solo, but he was wrong. Everything that led to that point was so much harder.

As I drew closer, the scenery changed. There was a turning off ahead; I could keep heading north, sticking to the highway, and adding another hour to the trip. Or I could turn left, cross the hump-backed bridge, and use the road the locals chose.

I'd already passed through one set of cross roads, what was another?

I took the back road. It's rough in sections, bumpy, and winds blowing gently through cane fields, the faint smell of sugar in the air. I wound down the windows, allowing four still groggy cats to smell the fresh air.

As I drove towards my new life, those ever-present tears ran down my face. The countryside was so beautiful, and I felt I'd come home. My home. *Our* home.

Into town, and up the hill, through the cutting, and towards my new address. I went left to the bottom of the road, panicking because nothing was familiar; where was my house?

Then it struck me; I needed to turn right at the roundabout. And there it was: the little house with the big view. I found the keys and stumbled up the stairs. The key fitted into the lock, but the door wouldn't open.

I'd come through everything, fought for my freedom and my future, and now the key wouldn't let me in! I wanted to sit on the top step and sob my heart out, but instead I wiped my face dry, and took a long, slow breath. It wasn't just me who wanted to get inside, after all. After a jiggle, a wriggle, a spit, and a swear, the door swung open.

Alone for a moment, I wanted to see, to look, and to feel my new sanctuary.

I removed each basket containing a tired, hungry, and now cranky cat, and I carried them upstairs, one by one by one by one. I put down their litter trays in the bathroom and unpacked the cat food.

Each cat had, according to their personality, done what they normally did when stressed. The babies – Champurrs and Muscat – bolted under the bed. Whiskey – known as Madam Cranky Pants – disappeared into the spare room, somewhere behind the boxes. Coco, the youngest, was in heaven; a whole new world to climb over, play with, and hide behind.

Leaving them to explore, I went into town in search of roast chicken. And wine.

Back at home after my shopping trip, I found a plate and a knife and sat on the floor, surrounded by my family. They ate from newspaper, and I drank wine from a cracked coffee mug.

This was our new life.

As the sun set, we all went to bed. I was about to drop off to sleep when the realisation struck me: I wasn't afraid. I didn't have to get up and close the bedroom door to feel safe; no longer would I have to sleep behind a locked door with a pair of scissors under the pillow.

When the sun rose, so did the cats. Four, hungry, somewhat confused felines who didn't give a stuff about my epiphany, wanted food. And they wanted it now. But I couldn't move; my tank was empty.

Cats are individuals. You need to live with and love them to see that. When they realised starvation would intervene before I got up, they set to work. Each cat approached and did their thing: first,

Muscat tried to push me out of bed, and, failing, retreated. Next came Champurrs, feet always radar-guided for a full bladder; no success. Coco, the smallest, decided he would climb the curtains; failure. Whiskey, the boss and bossy, raced all over me. Another failure.

Instead of being overwhelmed, I lay in my new bedroom, chuckling quietly and wondering what came next.

Suddenly, I realised that there was silence from the feline family; that was never good.

Then, just outside my bedroom door, I heard the second biggest cat fight in history. Without thought, I flew into the corridor ready to intervene, but there was silence–and four cats heading for the kitchen, and breakfast.

I swear to this day that they sat together, worked out a plan, and then acted.

While they ate, I found the kettle, the powdered milk, and the coffee. I rinsed the red wine from the only mug I could locate, and I made myself a cup of coffee.

The last seven years have taught me how to live.

Every part of my life is different; now there is richness and laughter, and joy and diversity. I follow with a passion the things that set my imagination and my heart on fire.

I still have three cats, my feline family who keep me sane. They gave me a reason to get up when I had nothing left. I look outside now to see the green paradise that continues to develop around me, and I smile. I wake in the night and hear the mopokes down in the valley and see the moon shine into the sunroom.

I hear the gentle purring of cats. I sleep with my bedroom door unlocked and a handkerchief, rather than scissors, beneath my pillow.

I am content.

Ruth Morgan loves telling stories of the characters and outback country she knows and loves. Her preference is crime fiction with a twist, her stories set in rural and regional Australia. The harsh landscape with its vast open spaces, floods, trees and isolation are essential elements. Ruth's first collection of short stories, *The Whitworth Mysteries*, was released in 2021.

Chapter 26

Sisters at Heart

by Juliet Madison

'But Mummy, I want to stay with youuuu...' Zac whines, pouting as he grips my wrist with two hands and surprising strength for a five-year-old, almost displacing the cake I'm struggling to hold.

'I have to look after the cake stall along with another mummy, sweetie. Grandma and Grandpa will take care of you.' I widen my eyes and nod in reassurance.

He cautiously turns his head towards my dad, who bends forward and holds out a lollipop of swirling, jarring colours.

Dental decay and hyperactivity to look forward to–thanks Dad!

Zac's uncertain eyes glance back at me, then back at his Grandpa. He releases one hand and holds it out to the lollipop, while Dad inches back slightly so it's just out of reach. Zac sighs and removes his other hand from my wrist, his pout soon replaced with a smiling red stain on ripping open the wrapping and licking the treat with gusto.

Bribery. Works every time.

I smile and wave, walking away quickly before he changes his mind and comes running back to reattach himself to my wrist. Like he did the first day at kindergarten last month.

But at thirty years old I should know by now to look where I'm going. A fallen branch snaps underfoot and my ankle rolls outwards, lurching my body and the cake onto the ground. A sudden whiff of grass shoots up my nose and I sneeze, bumping my head and blowing away some amber leaves.

Hysterical giggles burst from children nearby, and my cheeks flush warm as I pick myself up, flicking clumps of dirt from my white (of all the colours to wear today) tee-shirt and denim capris. I try unsuccessfully to reinsert a loose strand of hair into my pony-tail, and then bend back down to retrieve the cake, which despite its trauma has remained intact beneath its tightly cling-wrapped prison.

I wish it hadn't.

I approach the cake stall and my mouth almost gapes at the competition. My modest apple and cinnamon cake (courtesy of Betty Crocker, but who would ever know?) looks like roadkill compared to the delectable towers of sponge with blankets of smooth icing displayed proudly on the table. All made from scratch too, I'm guessing.

I thought I'd do better with a packet mix, but I still stuffed it up. A lopsided brown mound with a lightning-shaped crack, slapped onto a paper plate. I doubt I could even give it away, let alone sell it. But maybe some kind soul will take pity and part with their money, if only to support the fundraising efforts of Tarrin's Bay Primary School.

I'm used to things going wrong. They say three of the most stressful events in a person's life are a family death, divorce, and moving house. I've experienced all within the last three years.

Add embarrassment from lousy baking skills to the mix and my stress levels must be at the terminal stage by now.

'Hi, you must be Carrie,' the woman behind the cake stall says with a smile, her dark hair floating around her face. 'I'm Deanna, but call me Dee.'

She holds out her hand and I check mine for remnants of dirt before giving hers a brief shake.

'Hi, Dee, sorry I'm late. My son,' I glance briefly in the direction from which I came, 'he doesn't like me leaving him.' I press my lips together in a hopeless smile.

'Ah, no problem. Come, take a seat.' She motions towards a stool, and my backside accepts it gratefully.

I go to shove my cake behind the others, but Dee places her hand on mine. 'Yours should go at the front, because it's smaller. No one will see it back here.'

That's kinda the point.

'And it needs a name,' she adds, reaching below the table and pulling out a sticky label and permanent marker. 'Like all the others.'

I stand to examine the titles given to the cakes: Coconut Bliss, Raspberry Rendezvous, Vanilla Heaven, Chocolate Delight, and I'm thinking mine should be called Cinnamon Catastrophe or Apple Blunder.

'It's just a basic apple and cinnamon cake,' I say with a shrug.

'What about...' Dee taps a finger on her lip, then points it to the sky. 'I know-Apple Adventure!' She slides the label and marker along the table towards me and I oblige, emphasising the word 'adventure' with a thick underline.

An hour later no visitors to the fete have taken up the offer of an adventure, but plenty have opted for delights and rendezvous.

'So, why did you move to Tarrin's Bay?' Dee asks, her hand shading her face from a laser of sun sneaking in from the side.

'Just looking for a fresh start, I guess. Be near the ocean, leave city traffic behind,' I reply.

'Plus, my parents live here.'

'Have you or hubby got work here?'

I shake my head. 'I'm looking for work, and my husb – I mean, Derek and I, finalised our divorce before Christmas.'

No need to tell her I've moved in with my parents for now, and that as well as the lack of spouse, money, and housing, I have no friends whatsoever in this small town and am in desperate need of a social life.

Dee tips her head to one side. 'Oh, I'm sorry, Carrie.'

I nod a thank you, and as Dee bends forward to retrieve her water bottle, the neckline of her dress gapes, and a long brown scar marks the middle of her chest. I must be staring, because she pauses, and then realisation dawns on her face.

'You're wondering how I got this, right? It's okay, I'm used to it, although sometimes I forget it's even there.'

I apologise and tell her it's none of my business, but she tells me anyway.

'I had a heart transplant.'

Words try to form but jam in my throat.

'Pregnancy didn't agree with my wonky ticker,' Dee continued. 'So it was all downhill after that, but luckily my number came up. A perfect match.'

'Wow,' is all I manage.

Dee's hands cover her heart and her eyes roll skywards. 'I'm so grateful I live in a time and a place where doctors can perform these miracles. Otherwise, I doubt I'd still be here.'

The widening ray of sunlight reflects off the glossy sheen of her eyes, as a stinging warmth creeps into my own. Not only for hearing Dee's story, but for the harsh injustice that no miracle saved my sister, Lily.

'I've got an interview tomorrow, Carrie!' Lily had squealed into the phone the day before she died. 'At 'DeLuscious', can you believe it? The hippest, most amazing restaurant north of the city!'

And she would have got the job as head chef, I'm sure, had she made it to the interview. But two blocks shy of DeLuscious, her car got sandwiched between a delivery van and a telegraph pole. She was still alive on arriving at the hospital, but not for much longer.

Like the little girl moving backwards and forwards on the swings opposite the cake stall, my mind flits backwards and forwards from the amazing outcome experienced by Dee; this woman, this mother–just like me, to the horrific outcome of my sister's accident. The swinging in my mind stops when a woman approaches the stall and points to the Vanilla Heaven cake.

'I've got to have it!' She rifles through her purse and pulls out some coins. 'I'm guessing you made it, Deanna?' Dee smiles and packages Vanilla Heaven into a cardboard cake box.

'You made that?' I ask, which is silly considering I already know the answer. Creamy white icing embraces the tall sponge cake, with flecks of fluffy coconut, and a circle of mini meringues framing the top.

Dee nods. 'A few others too.'

She points them out and mentions those that had sold. 'My husband and I own From the Heart bakery, have you seen it in town?'

I recall the flourishing pink and white lettering of the bakery's signage in my mind, and mouth-watering cakes on display in the window. 'Oh yes, I have. How wonderful.'

'Drop in next time you're nearby,' Dee suggests, and I nod. Dee's gaze washes over the remaining cakes on the table and she shakes her head. 'You know what's weird? I had never baked a cake in my life until after my transplant. It's like my new heart gave me a whole new life, a new passion. I can't get enough of baking and cooking now.'

A bubble of curiosity rises in my stomach. 'How long have you had the heart, Dee?'

'Almost three years.' She smiles and her eyes become glossy again. 'I'll never forget the day–fourteenth of April. It was pouring rain, I was unwell and miserable. But then I got the call.'

The bubble of curiosity pops and my body stiffens. 'You had your transplant on the fourteenth of April...three years ago?' My voice falters at those last three words.

Dee nods.

'Which hospital?' My question is almost a whisper.

'North Sydney, why?'

The noise of children laughing, seagulls squawking, and parents chatting is drowned out as my gaze locks with Dee's. And somehow, I know, I just know, that the blood giving a red flush to Dee's cheeks is coming from the same heart that once flushed red the cheeks of my sister.

My own heart beats faster and faster; a clenched fist punching repeatedly into the wall of my chest, and I pant, struggling to take a proper breath.

'Are you alright?' Dee's eyebrows draw together, one hand on my forearm and the other gesturing for me to sit on the stool. 'You probably need something to eat. Here, I brought extra.'

She lunges under the table for a plastic container. The lid opens with a pop, and she hands me a cupcake with swirly pink and white icing.

My head is spinning, my surroundings are one big, colourful blur. My shaky hand delivers the cupcake to my mouth and icing sticks to my top lip as I bite into the soft centre. Each bite brings me further back to the present moment, to reality, although my nerves are trembling.

'I get low blood sugar from time to time,' I explain, and even though I was probably due for a bite to eat, low blood sugar had nothing to do with the surge of shock that just ran through my body. Trying to appear normal, I hold up what's left of the cupcake.

'This is delicious,' I say. 'I wish I could bake like this.'

Dee straightens her shoulders. 'I'd be happy to teach you. Come to the bakery on Monday morning and I'll show you how to make our signature 'Love Cake'. It's the same as what you just ate, only full size.'

'I'd love to, that is...if you're sure I won't be an occupational hazard to your staff?'

Dee tips her head back with a laugh. 'Don't be silly. You won't be in the way at all. I'd love to share this with you as a welcome to the town.' She smiles, and my body softens.

I can't stop eyeing Dee's glowing skin, bouncy hair, and chest rising up and down. It's bizarre, surreal, and I'm wondering whether to tell her about Lily. Unknown words try to form in my mouth, then I bite my bottom lip.

Maybe that story's best left for another day, I decide, as a man and small boy approach.

The man points to a cake, and the boy shakes his head. He points to another, and another. More shakes. 'What's that one called, Dad?' the boy asks, as he points to…

What? He's pointing to my cake!

Dee discreetly nudges my side. 'Apple Adventure.'

'Can we get it?'

'Of course,' his dad replies, flipping open his wallet before looking at me. 'It's strange, Lucas only likes food that's brown, beige, or white. This is perfect.'

I chuckle, and as we exchange smiles, a glimmer of hope sparks inside.

It was the right decision, moving here. Maybe fate played a role too. I know things are going to work out… Tarrin's Bay isn't called The Town of New Beginnings for nothing. I may have lost a husband and a sister, but I've gained a friend.

And Lily may be dead, but her heart is still beating.

Juliet Madison is a bestselling author of books with humour, heart, and serendipity. Writing both fiction and self-help, she combines her love of words, art and self-empowerment to create books that entertain and inspire readers to find the magic in everyday life. From the picturesque south coast of New

South Wales, Australia, Juliet dreams up new stories and follows her passions – being with family and doing minimal housework!

Chapter 27

Wallaby

by Vanessa Hardy

BBC 23 October 2013

A wallaby has set up camp in Highgate Cemetery in north London.
The marsupial was first photographed at the cemetery–famed as the final resting place of Karl Marx–on Sunday...
It is a mystery as to where the creature has come from. No animals have been reported missing from nearby Golders Hill Park Zoo...
[A spokesperson] said there were no plans to move the wallaby, which they are going to let settle and see how it gets on. Staff are leaving out fruit and vegetables.

Is it a mystery where I have come from? Not to me. Where I come from is embedded in my bones. My home, on the other side of the world, where I know the meaning of every leaf, each sharp grass, the rocky outcrops and rustling plains. Where my ancestors sing, and I sway along. I was taken from that. Although I could tell you the story of my escape, the mystery to me is not where from, or how, but why. Why am I here? And why is this place? This place of short damp grass, of twisting vines and weeds that grow around the large stone markers.

My bones ache for a day of bright hard sunshine. Something I can stand up to and fight. Instead, I have the dappled light between these unfamiliar trees. And the voices. The voices piercing through my ears and ringing in my head. Even uprooted to this unfamiliar landscape, my connection to the senses and spirits beyond the world that can be seen is still strong. So many voices, over 170,000 of them, these crowded strangers, sharing 53,000 graves. Each stone pillar or plaque is set to 'remember'. Are these people so forgettable? Why must they be remembered by being piled together?

Can you hear that voice? I lay my head near to the earth and feel his words rise. He is speaking of other things that have been taken from where they belong.

'Arrowheads, bronze bands, iron blades, marble reliefs, tomb chests, marble sculptures from tombs, twenty-seven cases...'

I am not the only one. Maybe he knows why so many things from far away need to be brought to this small island or how I might return.

'I am homesick,' I whisper, hoping he might comprehend the pinching pain that settles between my eyes.

'From Troy, from Xanthos, Lycia, Lydia, Mysia, Bithynia, Phrygia....'

'Why not leave these things be?' I ask, louder now. I wait for shame to colour his voice and stain the dirt around us.

'Discovery...' he begins.

'But everything you discovered was not yours to find.'

No shame.

Not him.

He smells like a thief, taking the memorials of others as a prize. He is but one of many, celebrated and well rewarded for it. No tomb sculpture of his own, his stone reads simply:

Sir Charles Fellows
Died 8 Nov 1860

I scratch at the ground as my breath escapes in a snort. I will not learn here how to get home. All he can teach is the arrogance of love that requires possession. My love of my home doesn't require that I possess it. He trades in separation, but I remain connected.

I wish I could explain this to him.

'The River Xanthus, Pisidia, Pamphylia, Caria...'

I bound high to escape his continued litany, mouth dry as I push faster to block the sound. Each word another cut into my flesh, seeking to sever hope. Branches slash at my face, stones grip at my toes as I race away. Far away. Stopping when the pounding in my chest is too strong.

In my true home, I bound beyond any obstacles. I can leave behind boulders, fallen logs, and even the long thin strands of a barbed wire fence. But here, my feet hurt. The paths and stones limit my freedom. Nothing feels right. My fur never feels clean when damp with this wrong rain.

Why do you need such a place to remember the dead? In my world, the dead and living are as one; here, the living are so afraid they will forget the dead that they build monuments and bundle bodies into this cramped place. In my home nothing is ever gone, there is no need to 'remember' what is always with us. When I die, I return to the earth and nourish the tall grass in the wide open spaces, and in turn, the grass nourishes my offspring and their offspring. We are part of the great ongoing, the everywhen.

Not here.

Here people are boxed up and stopped from returning directly to their earth; prevented from being part of a natural cycle of things.

Though I travel with my ancestors' words, I am without the camouflage of the grasses, the rocks, and the sweeping dust of grass plains they meant me to know. Instead, I peer from behind large monuments. I watch them, the ones who walk. They leave me food to eat. I take it and fill my stomach, but inside me the emptiness remains. Is this to be how I must spend my days? If they catch a glimpse of me, they smile, heads shaking. I am not what they expect to see. I can't speak with the living. They can't dance to the music I can hear, and they don't want to bound away.

They do not hear the voices.

I twitch my ear as a gentle breeze of a voice calls to me. Hope sparks again.

There is someone here who knows how the dead and living are joined. She sprinkles her words like soft leaves in front of my feet. I stop to breathe them in.

'Immortality…' she whispers.

'A choir invisible to live eternally, to be a cup of strength for those who follow.'

At last. Some understanding. Was she hailed, elevated, rewarded with a special resting place?

Not her.

'Why not?' I ask.

She tells me she did not care for made up connections, she would not marry. Seeking equality by taking a man's name did not stop them from banishing her from a loftier grave. At first discarded in a part of the land reserved for those who escaped the cage of popular beliefs. One hundred years later, they deigned to include her, disturbing her rest to place her in their poets' memorial corner.

This is how they treat the ones who know. She defied them anyway. No celibate catacomb for her in life or in death; her love is buried beside her.

Her stone reads:

OF THOSE IMMORTAL DEAD WHEN LIVE AGAIN IN MINDS MADE BETTER BY PRESENCE
HERE LIES THE BODY OF 'GEORGE ELIOT'
MARY ANNE CROSS
BORN 22 NOVEMBER 1819
DIED 22 DECEMBER 1880

Slowly the rain seeps into me along with strength as I sit beside her. My teeth press together and tightness travels down my tail. My capacity to not belong grows in her presence. I see now, many strive for a kind of immortality with their art. Some are rejected in their lives, but in death the bows and ribbons of convention and fashion can be removed, the truth of connection revealed. All is as it should be in death, if not in life.

As the days pass, I am more accustomed to this place. Becoming accustomed only takes time. Understanding takes something else. I have found places to hide. I rest, limbs heavy with the weight of all that is missing.

A dripping echoes in my ears. At first, I take it for the rain falling from the leaves. But it is his tears. The one I have been avoiding. The voice that speaks to me most often. I have heard him, even as I avoid his crowds of living visitors. I am too tired to fear what they might do. They have already done their worst. But to understand him I must wait until there is no one standing beside his tomb. The wait is long. He cannot be left alone, even in death. He is the only one watched over day and night by a camera. Are they worried he will escape?

In the dark, as the damp scent rises so do his words.

'Unity,' he cries.

'Yes. Unity,' I agree. 'My kind are as one, not only with each other but with the ground beneath them and the sky above and everything in between. The living, the dead: we are all one.'

He replies that unity is not a concept that comes easily. People who seek to unite too many are despised and their words are twisted and used to divide. Uniting one mob against another can sometimes be achieved, but it does not lead to harmony, or peace. There is no peace and no forgetting here.

The giant sculpture of his head makes me picture him in life. His stone reads:

WORKERS OF ALL LANDS UNITE
KARL MARX

THE PHILOSOPHERS HAVE ONLY INTERPRETED THE WORLD IN VARIOUS WAYS. THE POINT, HOWEVER, IS TO CHANGE IT.

All those who come to him, do they come here to unite, as his marker suggests?

Not yet.

They don't even all come to remember or to ponder his words. Some scrawl angry words in thick red paint, they attack his grave with hammers...and yet they come.

'Do they think it will help to remove your pillar?' I ask.

'Conflict and struggle are defining...' he tells me. But he is lost to know how to change the conflict and struggle his words have left behind. He is not forgotten, nor are the acts committed in his name. Do they hold him responsible? Is that why they hate him? And why do they still come?

He laughs with me that, in death, people must pay to see his grave. He has become a means of production. We laugh so hard I am not sure if we are crying.

When he cries for too long, I remind him that there is unity in the fate in store for every one of us. No ideas or words, utopian or dystopian, can change that; we can only strive to understand the ways in which we are connected, and then wait for the levelling force of inevitable decay.

Before the sun can rise, the alien cold seeps into my ears, my feet, my eyes, into the depths of my marsupium, this pouch – no longer destined to hold the next generation of ongoing. I know I am not to return to the earth of the land where I belong, I will never see it again or hold its air within me; that familiar air, flowing in and out without effort. Each breath in this place is a cold chill deep inside me. I am ready to die here. If I must. Knowing I will not be alone. Ready for the force that clears away divisions: home and unfamiliar, living and dead, peace and war, belonging and possessing–all gone at last.

Finally, I understand why this place exists, why your urge to remember what should never be forgotten is so strong. The knowledge that is buried here cannot be possessed, only heard. This invisible choir that sings to me will sing to anyone who puts an ear to the ground. The voices of the past do not hand out easy lessons–they merely speak–but still, they want to share, and to connect us with their knowledge. Some of them tried imperfectly in life. In death they are united: they need the living to listen.

After years of writing archaeology reports, Vanessa Hardy wrote her first novel manuscript, set in the world of urban archaeology. She also writes short stories and a blog, which explores her fascination with human behaviour. When not writing, you will usually find her on the sidelines of her son's sporting events, or at home on Australia's unceded Gadigal/Wangal land with a glass of wine.

Chapter 28

Palimpsest

by RS Morgan

I've been having this recurring dream – ever since my divorce – where I wake up in the early hours of the morning, back in my childhood bed. I think I'm about twelve but I'm not at all surprised by the fact. I've been here many times before, each time exactly the same and the same and the same.

'Look out, Phoebe, you're going to crash.'

Sarah mumbles from the other single bed, her voice thick with urgency in the semi-darkness of our shared bedroom. I close my eyes and listen, holding my breath, but she quietens quickly and I exhale in a rush. My sister is ten right now, but the sleep-talking is a habit that clings until she's at least twenty-five. I remember it used to annoy me so much that I sat on her once to stop the chatter. My weight scared her awake and from then on she insisted on a nightlight so she could see me coming. I don't think that's happened yet.

I don't get my own room until I'm sixteen, but that's not important anymore because in the future my sister and I don't speak. I haven't heard her voice in six years and suddenly wish I'd listened to her more growing up. I justify it as the self-absorption of youth. It doesn't make me a bad person.

Maybe it makes me a bad person.

I stretch my hands above my head, stroking the embossed wallpaper I'd forgotten until now. My arms are mine and not mine. They're soft and slim, unmarked by the tattoos that'll eventually trace a complex narrative across my skin. Marking achievement. Marking time. Reminding me to be resilient, as if I need reminding. My bare fingers are strangers too. The rings are gone and so is the tell-tale imprint that faded too slowly after I took them off, a silvery reminder of what was. Or what will be.

In my dream I've woken up from another–like a whisper wrapped in an echo–and I know what's coming. I see my future laid out as clearly as train tracks. A life I haven't lived yet. Vivid memories unfold in front of me, unwritten but as indelible as ink on paper. Each and every pivotal moment clearly signposted as though signalling when and where I'm supposed to get off.

Predetermined. Is that the right word? I'm curious to know what might happen if I bypass stations I know have a broken lift or dangerous cracks in the platform. Will intentionally missing my stop mess with the schedule, maybe even derail the train?

I think about Mark and wonder if I can still call him my ex-husband if we haven't met yet. Haven't fallen in love. Haven't figured out how to hurt each other in exactly the right way. Haven't discovered how to ease the hurt either, but we never really did. Or is that do?

Past tense. Future. Certainly never perfect.

At this moment Mark is a gangly sixteen-year-old, on a bus somewhere in Sydney's western suburbs, heading enthusiastically to an apprenticeship he'll one day loathe. He doesn't know I exist. Unlike me, he has no idea what's coming. All he knows is what he's already running from.

There's no point resisting. I let myself fall into the familiar loop, thinking about what I might do when I eventually reach 2009. What I would do if I was a good person, that is. Perhaps then it'll already be too late. I make a mental note, 2008 would be better. I should write it down–2008 is twenty-one years away–but something tells me I won't forget. Not this.

Two-thousand-and-eight is three years before Mark's wife dies. Not me, obviously. The other wife. The first one. Abigail. I remember being told the cancer takes two years to do its dirty work. If my calculations are correct. I sound like Doc from *Back to the Future* but push aside thoughts of fucking up the space-time continuum and instead imagine 2008 me, walking up the steep driveway of their house. Our house.

I picture it in my mind–suburban and solid–even though in 1987 it's nothing but bushland. I see pale pink brick, the tall portico and the shade sail that was torn on one side before I came along and never gets fixed; the invisible cracks in the walls and in the people behind them. Cracks that won't show themselves until it's too late and not just figuratively. It's a house that won't belong to me then and never really will, even long after Abigail is dust.

I'll hesitate before knocking on the familiar front door and Mark will answer and he'll look different. Younger but not by much. He'll have that terrible long hair that I'll laugh at one day when he shows me old photos. He won't have a clue who I am. But he'll look happy, I'm certain of that.

The sound of his kids will ring from inside and they'll be smaller and louder and brighter because they haven't had the rug pulled out from under them yet. They haven't learned to be angry and spiteful, haven't had to navigate being broken. They don't know how much they're going to hate me, or why. Or that I'll hate them right back, even though they're just kids, because their rejection of me cuts more than I want to admit, and maybe I'm a terrible person after all.

I try not to think about those brief months near the beginning when, carried away by new love and ill-fated optimism, we talk about trying to get pregnant. Daydreaming about making a baby together as if it'll somehow cement the life we're trying to build. Fill in the cracks. We try names on for size and wonder whether it would be a boy or girl, and I choose not to say to him that it doesn't matter as long as our hypothetical kid doesn't turn out like either of the ones he already has. I should have known then.

But we try, we really try. Caution carried away by the hurricane. And each month the same result. The universe senses our failure before we do. No baby for you. One less complication we'll have to deal with when the end comes. Hope turns to disappointment and then resignation. Never really regret. But I feel more for our pretend baby in those months than I do in eight years of battling to connect with his actual flesh and blood.

When I hear his kids' laughter through the door, it will make me wonder if things might be different if I knew this version of them. But there's really no point in *what ifs*, is there? Only in what I know is going to be. So I'll somehow convince Mark that–although he doesn't know me–I have things to say. Things he needs to hear.

Curious, he'll walk outside and we'll sit on the broad steps that won't be broken by the postman for another six years. The pavers will be hot under our legs because it's afternoon and the sun always fixes its gaze on that side of the house, baking the bricks until the air ripples above them in almost invisible waves.

He won't believe me at first. Of course he doesn't. He's not one for magic or fortune telling or anything that requires suspension of disbelief. Which is ironic because I know how much he wants to be an actor, even though he won't have realised it for himself. Not yet.

Mark's suspicion is hereditary because his dad was a policeman. But I won't tell him about losing Irving in 2018. I won't tell him when or where it happens–or how it causes an irreparable rift in his family–because there's only so much future grief you can hand a person all at once.

Instead I'll tell him I know about him hiding as a kid–at the house on Finlay Street – to avoid Irving's drunken anger. That he used to take his *Star Wars* figurines into his dog's kennel and that he still has those same plastic figurines and that Darth Vader is his favourite because there's something about the dark that he likes.

I'll tell him I know he doesn't display them the way he wants to. They're packed away in a box because his wife thinks they're childish. She's older than he is and doesn't appreciate toys, not the way I do. But I won't say that last part as it's something he doesn't need to hear. It's not why I'm there.

I picture his confused face as I tell him more things a stranger shouldn't know. The quiet rage that still hides inside him. His love of lizards and the knotted appendix scar he'll one day try to pass off as a knife wound to impress me. I'll offer it up as proof.

See, I know things. Believe me.

Then I'll become an oracle, a portend of doom, and I won't relish it for a second because there's no going back once I say it out loud. The space-time continuum is completely and utterly fucked. I'll be ruthless and tell him Abigail is going to die, that she doesn't get checked when she should and she knows–she actually knows–but she doesn't do anything about it. I don't know why. But I do know when.

I'll tell him it'll be awful and that he'll try to take care of her but he'll fail and he'll break and so will their children and it won't be like the movies, not at all. There'll be no heroics and no revelations. It'll be brutal and messy until there's nothing left. Until she's gone.

I'll want to scare him so that–even if he thinks I'm crazy–it might plant enough of a seed to change it. And then it'll be worth it. The house will stay their house. Their children will never have to hate me. The postman might never break those bricks and Han Solo and Princess Leia will have to stay packed in that box.

And I'll never know what it's like to fall asleep in his arms.

But.

What if it doesn't change anything? What if she still dies? There's something else and I have to warn him. It's why I'm really there.

I'll say to him, 'Run, don't walk. Sell the house and leave. Take the kids and go far away with them and make a new life. And whatever you do, no matter what, don't fall in love again too soon. Even desperately joyous love that promises to fix everything. You'll know her when you find her, but trust me, don't do it. You'll destroy each other. Because sometimes love isn't only love but distraction and control and manipulation and regret and it's trying to fill a hole that can't ever be filled and–more than anything–sometimes love isn't enough to make up for all the things I know are going to go wrong.'

And in that moment, Mark will realise I'm talking about myself. He'll think I'm even more insane, but it won't really matter. I'll leave not knowing if I've made a difference and–just in case–three years later I'll try to avoid the place where we're supposed to meet. I'll derail the train to save us from the wreckage.

Try. I sabotage myself before I've begun by wondering if I'll be brave enough to do any of it. I'm not sure it's enough to know I'd be giving the kids back their mother, saving them all from the grief and the unstoppable avalanche that follows. It should be, but I think I've established I'm probably a terrible person. Selfish. I know this.

I don't think I'll be strong enough because I still remember how he tastes and that he's going to love me–and I him–with an incendiary power that lights us both up as much as it burns us down. I know we'll get drunk in Paris and we'll fight and make up again and again and again without learning a goddamned thing. We'll love a lifetime in a matter of just a few years.

But we'll also end. And it too will be brutal and messy until there's nothing left.

I wake up for real before I can decide. Every single time. And every single time, it's already too late. It can't be overwritten. As sleep fades, the morning sun is clear and hot on my face.

I'm always right back where I started.

At the end.

And at the beginning.

RS Morgan is an award-winning fiction writer, screenwriter, musician and producer. A former entertainment writer and recipient of the Josephine Ulrick Literature Prize, her screen credits include *Wanted* (Matchbox Pictures) and *Mako Mermaids* (Netflix). Regularly juggling fiction and screen projects, she still dreams of being a pop star and is passionate about story and living a big, juicy, creative life. She loves hot yoga, tattoos and cheese.

Chapter 29

Yiayia's Doesn Madder Policy
by Katherine Lykos

My grandma *Yiayia* was like a second mother, the affectionate, kind, caring, loving type. She would often ask us grandkids, *How much does Yiayia love you?* In which we were to reply: *From here to the sky and back.*

She was the type of grandma who was one-sided (or you might say blind-sighted) by any wrongdoing caused by any family member. Even when my cousin Trevor confessed that he'd accidentally killed a poor duck when casting his fishing line out into the lagoon she lived beside and which bobbed around for the next week: *Probably it died by flying into a rock or something.*

But she wasn't all softness and warmth. There was an inner viper that she released in times of need.

One such time was when Mum finally saw her boyfriend Con for what he really was (an actual walking, gangly-armed dick). Mum broke things off with him, but the guy wouldn't go down without a fight, even when there were no mitts or boxing ring anywhere to be seen. We were given strict instruction: *If he calls, hang up; If he comes over, call the cops.* (The local police station number was placed in our Telstra phone speed dial under slot one).

Looking back, I kind of feel a teensy bit sorry for Con. He

would've been oh so unprepared when he rocked up with his heart on his sleeve only to find a viper he thought was a sweet kind Yiayia morphed into a heart-devouring demon. I mean, let's face it, no one wants to be handed their arse by a woman (let alone an old woman).

She just so happened to be sewing curtains at the time that he came bellowing from his car window that he was sorry. Yiayia had never been one for small talk. She walked out, so calm, so collected, her face a hidden mask, her hand not so much with those lethal industrial-size fabric scissors clenched in her fist. She shoved the gleaming tip in his face through the car window and hissed, *If you ever come here again, I will kill you!*

That was the last time we ever saw Con.

It shouldn't surprise me that she turned out the way she did, no coward would've survived what she went through, events that she wouldn't offer up unless asked, like almost starving when the war broke out. She was just under ten when the Nazis took up residency in their farming village on the island of Rhodes, Greece. The cow that her parents had been devotedly fattening up for the past year was taken to feed the army, added to their provisions, their greater need. The locals survived by quick thinking, by burying and hiding nonperishable essentials like grain and oil, along with their knowledge of what mushrooms and wild greens you could eat from the wild mountains that the village butted against.

If asked, Yiayia would tell of the time she was in the old city, on her way to school, wearing the compulsory new uniform, a white shirt with a silver M to commemorate the occupying Italian's new dictatorship, when the air raid sirens went off. Her terrified screams couldn't save her as the panic stricken crowd shoved past. A stranger took her small hand and led her into a half-sized door where a dozen others squatted around ancient ammunitions left behind by the Knights Templar, a reminder that the place had been victim to many types of past raids. It might have given comfort, if they'd known that the ancient city would withstand, that to this day it holds.

The same English led air raid took out the hospital Yiayia's aunt had been sent to in labour. No one expected to find them… except that they did. By some miracle, she was there, surrounded by rubble and clutching her newborn son, afterwards dubbed *Lucky Yianni*.

There was one relative she didn't like to recall, no one liked to talk about him, as if mentioning his name might bring *the evil eye*. Her grandfather Kola (pronounced *collar*), which even though I never met him, I find it hard not to spit the name when reciting it. No one mourned when his failed attempt to steal a goat from the Nazis resulted in death by firing squad. Certainly not his wife, my great grandmother's mother. She wouldn't have so much as blinked from her grave, considering it was by his fist that she was there. Yiayia's father despised Kola so much that he wouldn't receive the body afterwards, and told the army to dispose of it in whichever way they saw fit.

You might coax Yiayia to tell of the time she was held at gunpoint and almost shot point blank by a Nazi soldier for venturing to the water pump after the sundown curfew. But a memory she didn't part with easily was when recalling the beautiful Jewish family that made the most exquisite furniture on the island. She had been honoured by being flower girl at one of their weddings. It was a friendship strong and pure–until the day that their shop was ransacked, leaving behind nothing but broken pieces of furniture, like remnants of the missing souls taken and never returned.

If the war wasn't enough of a test for Yiayia, she had an arranged marriage to a drunk and then a sail to the other side of the world with their three children that he'd left her with when he came to Australia for work. Not only did she endure a two-month voyage to a foreign country where she would be greeted with an enormous language barrier, she left Greece with a different kind of barrier slammed into her back, because they all assumed this was goodbye forever.

She not only farewelled everything she'd ever known, but parents who had already lost five of their eight children to disease and illnesses. Those mass deaths she would recall, of a whooping cough epidemic that spread through the village. Two of her siblings died within two weeks of each other. You would never question Yiayia's decision to camp overnight to make sure her own children were first in line for mass vaccination drives.

Cooking was always a kind of therapy for her. She would pour every part of herself, her love and devotion into every meal. Not for herself to eat, but for others to enjoy...and if we weren't around to receive these culinary delights, she would offer them to a neighbour (I say *offer* very loosely). Whether she knew the neighbour's name or not, they would take the food, full stop!

She was never good with names. There was one neighbour who she called Chester for years, which he probably didn't pick up on or correct her for because her accent covered for it. I remember thinking, *huh odd name for a guy not born in the 1800s*. That is, until I found out (the embarrassing way of course) when I called him Chester and he replied with, *Actually, my name is ah Justin*.

'Oh. I see.' *Oops*.

The biggest *oops* moment came when Yiayia asked me to help write her Christmas cards. I was down to the last one, to be sent to my uncle's mother-in-law, my cousin's German born grandmother (who I'd only ever known as Oma). With pen in hand, I asked, 'Who am I addressing this card to?'

Yiayia stammered, then stuttered, then told me she couldn't remember the woman's name. With a finger tapping her bottom lip she said, 'It sounds something like cannelloni.'

'You're kidding right? Like the food, cannelloni?'

'Né, Né (*yes, yes*), similar.'

'Well similar is not the same.'

She didn't agree. 'Just write it,' she told me.

'You're sure?'

'Yes!' She fluffed a hand like fluffing away a smell, desperate to get the cards over with for posting *yesterday already*. What choice did I have? I shrugged and wrote the bloody card, addressing it to the cheesy pasta tube dish: 'Dear Cannelloni, how you make my taste buds sing.'

You can guess what happened can't you? *AFTER* we posted it to Leonburg, Germany, we found out from my mother what her name actually was. I shouldn't have been surprised that it was *not* similar to Cannelloni.

My reaction was: 'Oh no, what have we done?!' I turned to Yiayia's nonchalant face, wondering why she wasn't as horrified as I was that we'd just sent a Christmas card to *Cannelloni* instead of *Hannelore!*

She fluffed it off too and in her thick accent said, 'Ahh doesn madder...she can't speak English.'

I slapped my forehead, there was no point explaining that German and English shared the same letters, and if by some miracle she *couldn't* read it (because um, I don't know, maybe her glasses were broken), she had plenty of people around her that *could* read English–like her grandchildren who took compulsory English lessons at school!

I guess there were certain things that mattered to Yiayia in life, such as projecting her warmth and love, striving to be an integral part of her community and family. Learning names and pronunciation was way down on that list, as nitty gritty as small talk.

Maybe life would be less boggy if we all took a pinch of Yiayia's *Doesn Madder* policy.

Katherine Lykos is a Greek Australian writer with a professional background in ecology and natural area restoration. She lives in Sydney with her three kids and 'Big Fat Greek' extended family. When she isn't bushwalking, birdwatching, cooking up an exotic feast or reading and watching adventure stories, she devotes herself to writing. This story was inspired by her passion for multiculturalism, family, cooking and, of course, her amazing grandmother, Yiayia Katina.

Chapter 30

A Winter's Warmth
by Darry Fraser

A dream of horse and rider galloping on the wild, windy moor ...

The thunder of those hooves startled Jan out of her sleep.

Horse's hooves? Surely not. Must be possums dancing on the roof. She glanced at the clock. Large unblinking green numbers glowered at her. Three-thirty in the morning. On a clear winter's night. Bright as daylight. Almost.

Sleep, sleep. Anything for sleep.

Without sleep, the muse wouldn't come. Worrying that the muse wouldn't come kept her from sleeping. She couldn't write a damn thing. She was in a funk out here, had been for months. She was blocked, empty of words, a decrepit, poor excuse for a wordsmith.

Groaning, she turned over. And saw a silhouette, of man and magnificent beast, backdropped by a brilliant three-quarter moon spilling its silvery light.

Jan's eyes widened to saucers.

The stallion reared on his hind legs and over the roar of the ocean crashing to shore at the bottom of the hill, she heard him snort and paw at the ground. Could see his eyes rolling as he fought for independence from his rider.

Rider. Darkly shadowed against the soft-lit sky, he steadied his mount, glared at her, wheeled then charged off into the wintry night with fire and flame at his heels.

Some dream, Jan Ayrton. Best one yet. She sat up in bed and reached for her nightgown, slipping it over her head. As cold as it was, she preferred to sleep naked except for knickers, but a warm nightie was handy for midnight-and-beyond trips to the loo.

She padded to the window. Definitely a moonlit night. She hadn't dreamed that.

No horse and rider in sight. *Silly woman.* The thumping of his hooves must have been the thudding of her heart as remnant dreams stirred her senses. She hadn't eaten before she went to sleep last night; hunger kept her restless.

Sighing at the futility now of trying to sleep, she reached across her desk and switched on the computer. No sense wasting good writing time. She'd try to tease the Muse through the whorls of mist in her head.

Next night and again the startled waking. Horse's hooves. Dark rider. The ocean relentless in perpetual motion. The moon, nearing its fullness, illuminated the starry sky.

Out from under the warm and snug bed linen, her gaze was fixed on the vision. She eased out of bed and slipped into her nightie as if sudden movement might startle the visitor, or at the very least, wake her up. She had to be dreaming again, for sure.

But no, no. A mysterious, magnificent horse and rider were out on this clear night.

The horse pawed, snorted. Then Jan heard a quiet voice.

'Settle, Mes. Settle. There's nothing to worry about here.'

It was a soft voice, melodious. Kind. The horse danced in agitation.

'Steady, fella.'

Jan drifted to the glass door just outside her room and opened it. The chill of the June night air slid past her.

'Good, sweet St Mary!' the man bellowed, his voice echoing through the night. 'I wasn't expecting you outside.' He calmed the horse then leaned forward in the saddle, high above her. 'What the hell are you doing?'

Jan gave him a scoff. 'I could ask the same of you. This is another night you've come pounding into the early hours to wake me. And it's private property.'

He squinted. 'So it is.'

'And so are my dreams.'

'They are. What are you doing here?'

She shivered as the breeze whipped past her. Pulling the nightie tight over her chest, she was suddenly aware her nipples had puckered in the chilly night.

'I'm a writer. I rented this place to finish a book.'

'Name?' he barked.

'Jan Ayrton.'

'Well, now. That means I am indeed in the right place.' The horse danced a circle and the rider pulled him back. 'Are you not afraid to be out here on your own?'

How did he know she was here on her own? Jan swallowed the first ping of fear. *There's nothing to be afraid of*, she said, and willed herself to believe it.

'It's just that you woke me.'

He leaned back in the saddle, his hands draped over the reins. 'I would offer that something has to wake you,' he said.

'I beg your pardon?' Jan clutched the night-gown more tightly about her then scowled at this...apparition. 'What do you mean?'

He looked down at her. 'You have talent, Miss Ayrton, but no heart. You need a big heart under that...chemise,' he said waving a finger at her, 'to thaw the winter's cold you keep inside, to allow your muse to find you.'

A blush fled over Jan's face and she took a step back under the verandah. The light was behind him and his hat was pulled low; she couldn't make out his features, but she wished she could.

The horse danced closer as a brutal blast of sou-easterly whipped at the man's long-coat. 'Go back to bed and mull over that,' he commanded, then horse and man charged off into the dark night.

Jan pressed a hand to her heart. Warmth had started low in her belly despite the gusty, chill wind that flicked leaves and twigs around her bare feet.

It was just a dream, just the machinations of her overworked mind. And how perfectly ridiculous it was, too.

It's the same old thing, she knew. Writer's block would eventually drive her mad. That elusive *emotional punch* the publisher's always cited she lacked. *Skilled and well-crafted, but no heart.* So now she was conjuring up ghosts to mentor her. She would not go mad. And there were no ghosts. *How perfectly ridiculous.*

Jan stepped back indoors, heading for another stint on the computer.

The phone rang, jangling her out of the furious pace.

'Hi Jan. It's Toby.'

'Toby?'

'From the greengrocers. I'm ringing for your supply order.'

'Oh yes.' Jan rubbed her eyes and reached for the grocery list she'd made.

Toby was a nice guy, a little bit strange. When she'd first met him, he looked at her as if he'd seen a ghost.

No, no, no. No ghosts.

She had to stop all that, concentrate on her work. Or go completely mad–if she wasn't already. Last night's distraction was proof she probably was.

And writing was all she needed, if she could just push through the great chunk of granite that stopped her imagination stone cold dead. The only thing coming in was a trickle of pesky thoughts of fulfilment and...other things.

And ghosts.

Not that she hadn't noticed Toby's attention, and the way he looked at her, that dark-eyed, dark-haired man with the handsome face. But it wasn't to be. She just couldn't seem to be open and friendly. Despite lively conversations in his family's store, and chit-chatting on the phone when she needed to place an order, she kept him at arm's length.

Well, she didn't need a man. She had her work.

She placed her order with him.

'Right. I've got all of that,' Toby said. 'I have to come out your way on Thursday for other jobs so how about I bring your stuff with me?'

His voice curled around her, low and rumbly.

'Would save you a trip in,' he said, and added tentatively, 'especially as the weather's about to change for the worse.'

'Is it?'

'It'll be pretty bad. Squalls from the southeast for two or three days. Lots of big rain, maybe flooding out your way.'

Jan didn't want to think about tackling the already boggy roads. And if Toby came out, it would certainly save her a two-hour round trip. 'I should offer you lunch when you come, then,' she said, and wondered where that had come from. Wondered how much writing time she'd lose by doing lunch. By chit-chatting here instead of silently willing words onto a screen.

'Great. Looking forward to it.'

Jan showered, got on with her day. Thursday was the day after tomorrow.

Why was her heart thumping so oddly now?

That night, she dropped off to sleep without anticipation. The day had been a good one, plenty of ideas. Her publisher would be pleased. Who needed heart? Her work was inspired, crisp and...boring. She groaned. *She had nothing, had done nothing.* Mundane words sat on the page, bland as weak tea, accusing her as an imposter. What on earth was wrong with her?

Writer's block, no doubt about it. She hadn't been able to

magically conjure *heart* much less anything else and so nothing of depth was put to page.

Sleep, sleep, sleep.

Loud, short, repetitive gusts of wind woke her. Except it wasn't wind, but the horse, snorting against her window.

'Miss Ayrton?' the rider called brusquely, silhouetted against the gleaming moon.

Jan reached for her nightie, not worried he might've caught a glimpse of breast, or slim waist and legs as she stepped out of bed into the chilly night air.

He isn't real, after all.

'Ah, there you are,' he said and sat back in the saddle, satisfied. 'I wanted to tell you that your hair reminds me of someone else's from long ago. Long and wavy.'

Jan blinked. 'Does it?' She touched her hair, a little surprised. 'You've come all this way to tell me that?'

'Hmm. I have. A fine woman, too. She knew who she was, where she wanted to be. A woman who could teach a man…a thing or two.' Then as if a little embarrassed, he sounded as if he could have been clearing his throat. If ghosts actually did that. 'She had a big, strong heart, moral courage, you know.'

'What does she have to do with me apart from our glorious locks?' She could have fun with a ghost. *I mean, who is going to tick me off?*

The horse scuffed the earth dangerously close to her feet. He certainly was a huge animal for a ghost. Seventeen hands, she estimated. But of course all big, black muscly stallions were seventeen hands. Any writer knew that. She didn't step back this time.

He peered at her. 'You're not frightened by me and Mesrour, are you?'

There was no baying hound nearby so Mesrour had to be the horse. 'I'm not. Because for a start, you're not real, are you? How can I be frightened of something that's not real?'

'How indeed?' He laughed delightedly.

'Just what is it you think I'm frightened of?'

'Ah, Miss Ayrton. It's not just a severe lack of words, now, is it?'

He even knew that. Amazing.

Ignoring it, she concentrated on the lilt of his accent. She must capture the inflections of it for her next story. One about a ghost and a black stallion. And a crazy woman all by herself wearing only a thin nightie, standing outside on a crispy winter's night.

The horse danced suddenly beneath him and he straightened. 'Think, Miss Ayrton,' the gentleman insisted. 'It's spirit you're missing, pluck and pith. You're losing yourself. Think hard.'

Jan thought hard.

A fiery flame zinged through her. *If he were real, I'd lose myself to him.*

'I see you won't answer me,' he said. 'Well, to answer you, I am real. I'm as real as that heart which beats in your chest.'

One of his leather-clad fingers stabbed at her. 'Fear is within you. It makes you cold. You fear success if you let yourself go.'

For goodness' sake. All right, yes, she feared she'd have to trust, and have to hope, and have to take leaps of faith all without a safety net. She'd have to believe in herself, or worse, in things of the heart. All of which she did not believe in, though she longed for it. She wasn't going to tell him that.

'I'm only cold because I'm out here, loopy, talking to a ghost,' she said.

He laughed again. Mesrour's hooves pumped the ground and the rider sat forward.

Jan glimpsed his face as he towered over her. He wasn't handsome but he was craggy, rugged. 'If you're real, who are you?' she asked.

'I'm Rochester, from Thornfield.'

The breeze whipped around her ankles, snaked under her nightie and chilled her face. She shivered. She didn't know him, though there was something vaguely familiar about him.

Right, Jan. Something vaguely familiar about a ghost.

'Go back inside, Jan Ayrton,' he said with some exasperation. 'I'll visit tomorrow, my last for a while. The moon wanes thereafter.'

The moon wanes?

She didn't want him to leave. 'But – tell me why're you here?'

He smiled and her heart rocketed. He was so fine to look at on his majestic stallion, all fire and life and sensuous masculinity – both of them. Despite herself, she stepped away from their heat, preferring the reality of winter's frosty bite.

'Perhaps just to waken you, sweet Jan, like I was once awakened.' He pulled off a glove, leaned down and a cool, callused finger stroked her cheek, touched her lips. 'Perhaps to help bring you some winter's warmth.'

Jan reached up to touch the hand on her face, but Mesrour backed up a length, the rider pulling on his reins.

'Till tomorrow,' he rumbled, and they charged off.

She didn't write that morning. Her tummy twisted and her brain fogged. Each time she thought of her visitor her heart wrenched and her hands shook. He was the biggest man with the biggest horse. *The biggest ghost.* Although to be honest, she didn't know too many ghosts. Well, not any, really. And he'd touched her. His calluses had felt real enough, a rasp on her skin.

Heat kindled and a flame come to life, snatching away her air.

Sleep claimed her early that night, and there he was once more, waiting under the supreme brilliance of the full moon.

Mr. Rochester. On his big, black horse, Mesrour.

Of course – *Jane Eyre*. Why hadn't she picked that up?

Was her subconscious drawing on that classical, wonderful story? If so, why? No reason, she chided. It was sleep deprivation coupled with an avid imagination and a lack of food.

'You need something more than you have, Jan Ayrton.' A smile flashed from under the hat drawn low over his head again. 'Something to keep you warm on these desolate nights.'

'I keep myself warm,' she flared. 'I don't need a man.'

'Interesting.' He cocked his head as he considered that. 'I didn't mention you needed a man.'

His silence had her blushing before he spoke again.

'But every healthy woman needs to find her warmth. It's buried deep in her soul. You need to reach it, Miss Ayrton.'

Sensual feathers of heat fanned her bones. Indignant, she said, 'I don't need to do anything.'

Mesrour snorted derision as he danced on his forelegs.

Oh, and even the horse has an opinion.

'But you do. You need to feel. Have heart.'

It was true. And she did but why did it have to be for him, for an apparition, for a figment of her imagination? For a drop-dead, gorgeous ghost (*what?*) wandering around in her head, or somewhere, ordering her to find her heart, her warmth–

Wasn't that exactly what her publisher wanted from her?

'There's change coming.' His flashing gaze swept over her. 'You might not *need* a man, but he too is coming. Be ready.'

'Oh, and I suppose he'll be just like you, riding in and out on a fine steed, floating the air and philosophising?'

Ghost or not, she clutched at the neck of her nightgown.

Patience personified, Rochester looked up at the moon and for an instant, she saw his face. He really was beautiful. More beautiful than not despite his craggy, rugged features.

'Maybe he *will* be just like me.'

Huh. So, male ghosts have big egos too.

He shrugged, tipped his hat then smiled broadly. 'He comes highly recommended.'

In that moment, moonlight and wild things crowded her heart and soul. She clasped her hands over her chest, holding on to the utter joy it brought.

He galloped off, his coat whipping around Mesrour's mighty flanks. A fierce wind gathered speed in their wake.

She went straight inside and plopped on the lounge. Hugged herself. Slapped herself. It was absolutely sleep deprivation, that's what it was. She was only light-headed, her mind was overworked. Her body underfed. She rocked back and forth on the couch.

Good thing Toby was coming with her supplies today. She'd feed her body; she had to. She certainly couldn't afford this frivolous dalliance with ghosts. She'd be a ghost herself in no time if she didn't take stock. And she didn't want that.

She curled up on the large settee which faced the roiling, rollicking ocean. The drapes were open and the lunar glow spilled in. Against the howl of a gale-force southerly, she closed her eyes and dropped into a deep, undisturbed sleep.

'Jan. *Jan.*'

It was him. He was back. Damn persistent man. *Ghost.*

Sleep was keeping her gluggy. Jan's eyes flickered open and she squinted into weak sunlight filtering through the big glass doors. It was daylight.

But it was Toby's large, warm hand on her shoulder, shaking gently.

'Are you okay? I could see you but when you didn't get up to answer the door, I came in.' His dark eyes were under a frown. 'I was yelling for so long, hammering on the door, I got a bit worried.'

'I had a rough night.' She rubbed her eyes, not looking at him, embarrassed to be seen in the subdued nightgown, her feet bare and her hair messed by sleep. 'I don't feel good.'

'It's too cold in here. You'd be hypothermic, Jan,' he said, exasperated. He scrubbed hands through his hair and as bemused, squatted by the settee. 'Look, that change in the weather came through. You must have slept through it without a blanket or anything.' He tugged a throw-rug over her. 'Wrap up. Get warm.'

Rain slashed against the house, the wind gusted and the windows rattled.

She hadn't moved, just stared at him.

'Look, how about I light the fire and wait till this weather passes by?'

'Oh, please do,' she said, coming back to herself. 'I'll just have a quick shower and get dressed.' She clambered up from the couch and headed for the bathroom. She stopped, turned and looked at him. 'You won't–disappear?'

He smiled. Warm, familiar. 'No way.'

Now hot and cold all over, Jan fled to the bathroom and hurried her ablutions. As she stepped out of the shower, vigorously rubbing herself dry with a big towel, Mr. Rochester's brilliant smile and handsome face flashed before her.

Oh my God – can he SEE me?

Oh dear, she needed food badly.

A big, woolly jumper and jeans would do for lunch with Toby. Her unruly hair–wavy and long *he'd* said–hung in damp ringlets about her shoulders.

Toby had lit the combustion heater and it crackled with life. In the kitchen, coffee was brewing. He'd used her groceries, had thrown together a Greek salad, and had pasta boiling on the stove. The combination of glowing fire, tasty food and a man cooking in her kitchen was irresistible. She should've thought of inviting him out here before. Why had the thought eluded her?

She sat at the breakfast bench facing him as he pushed across a cup of aromatic coffee. Her mouth watered.

'I have something to tell you, to show you,' he said without looking up, stirring the spaghetti before he chopped some bacon, and cracked a couple of eggs into a bowl. 'You'll think I'm a basket case.'

'What is it?'

'There's something uncanny about...well, about you and me. And I don't know where to start.' Then he glanced at her. 'And sorry in advance, I'm going to sound weird.'

Jan's memory tugged at her, as if she was losing her grip on the last haze of a beloved dream.

A man will come.

Her heart rate climbed steadily. She studied him. 'What is it you do?' she asked abruptly.

'You know. The family owns the general store as well as Thorn–'

'Do you own a horse?'

'We've always had horses.'

Her gaze roved over his face. Why hadn't she taken more notice of this face? 'Mesrour?' she asked when she could speak. 'And Thornfield.'

'Mesrour is our stable name for the line we breed, and Thornfield is our stud farm.' He frowned, eyed her, at first uncertainly. Then, 'It's been happening to you too, hasn't it, the dreams?'

'Yes. A man on Mesrour the Great Big Horse.' She gave a desperate, little laugh. 'Now I sound weird.'

'For me, it's a woman with long, wavy hair.'

He reached across the bench and touched her hair.

Jan took his hand, held it against her cheek. Warmth vibrated through her, a shock, stirring deep inside. She let go of him. 'Um, what was it you were going to show me?'

He looked down and she followed his gaze to the sepia photograph close by.

She yelped. 'That's Mr. Rochester!'

Her fingers traced the stained features of the tall man standing by a dignified, serene looking woman.

'And his wife, my great grandmother Jane Airlie Rochester. She was a writer, a woman he found, lost and found again. She's been coming to visit me in my dreams. She's pragmatic, you know.'

Toby took a breath, diligently drained the pasta and tossed it back into the pot, stirring in whisked egg. 'Said I had to be on the look-out for you, that this weather would strand you for days, leave you without any help out here.'

'Oh.'

'She was persistent too,' he said with a little hesitation. 'I always thought you didn't need anything at all. Not even a friend, the way you keep yourself stuck out here on your own.'

Jan was about to retort but thought better of it. Her hands were tingling as if blood had rushed back to them. 'I have to be on my own to write.'

'Oh, really?'

That had been definitely Mr Rochester's snarky question, yet he wasn't making an appearance.

'I mean, I always *thought* I had to be on my own,' she said. Her mouth watered as Toby tossed the bacon into the pasta and began to furiously grate a block of parmesan cheese. 'Lately not even inspiration is with me. It means I get more and more stuck and end up not writing anything. Obsessing about *not* writing.'

'I write,' he said without looking up from the grater. 'We could do a few speed sessions if you like, help get you over that block.'

The tingle was now in her belly. *Oh, the stupid thing–*

Wait. Don't beat it down. Don't dismiss it. Why not do a few writing exercises with him, what would it hurt? Get a little word flow started.

Warm up, woman!

Mr Rochester again.

'Maybe.'

She couldn't look up just yet. Instead, she watched from under her brows as he plated up bowls of comfort food. She licked her lips, felt the first hunger pang she'd had in ages. Dropping her gaze, she concentrated on the photographs. 'You look just like him,' she burst, and touched Mr Rochester's face.

'Don't you see?' Toby asked.

Jan gazed from the photograph to Toby.

He comes highly recommended.

'And you look like her.' Toby tapped his grandmother's image. 'It's us, isn't it? That's the weird bit but what a story we could tell here. You see it, don't you?'

'Oh yes.' Moonlight and wild things crowded her heart once more. 'I see it.'

'Here,' Toby said, pushing a bowl of steaming carbonara towards her. 'Sustenance.' He smiled. 'Something to keep us going till we can get to some words.'

'Grateful.'

She looked down at the photo again, and warmth sailed through her. 'But I don't think I can wait.' Snatching at a pen and paper, always handy, her hand hovered over the page as whole sentences jostled phrases in her head, and rhythm began to beat in her chest. Tone hummed all around her and for a moment words jammed the gateway, maddening, heartening, racing. The glorious muse had returned, bursting forth in a frenzied rush.

'Eat first,' he said, his voice stern.

'All right.' She looked up and grinned with glee at Toby.

He wasn't the only one she saw. Standing behind him was a craggy, rugged faced man, his ethereal features clear against the wild light of a thrashing storm outside.

You may thank me, Miss Ayrton.

Jan dipped her head and strands of long curly hair fell over her shoulder.

Oh, I most certainly do thank you, Mr Rochester.

The Australian landscape is home for best-selling author Darry Fraser, who writes empowering feminist adventures about ordinary Autralians in the nineteenth century, against the backdrop of historical events and iconic landscapes. A lifetime ago, childhood years spent on the Murray in Victoria began her love affair with the river, where several of her novels are set. Darry lives on the Fleurieu Peninsula in South Australia.

Chapter 31

Feeling My Way

by Monique Mulligan

We catch the train from Penrith to Bullaburra in the upper Blue Mountains, an hour-long journey I have not made in years. It is a scenic trip, past weekend-busy mountain villages, riding the top of the escarpment with views of an undulating blue sea of trees. My two sons' eyes are glued to their game consoles, oblivious to glimpses of sheer limestone cliffs that fill me with longing. I have missed this place, this ancient landscape that looms over the Western Sydney valley where I grew up. My fingers drum a discordant, agitated beat on my thighs. If not for my sons, I'd lose myself in those trees.

The garden dances with spring colour: Icelandic and Oriental poppies, lavender, nasturtiums, irises. As we push through groups of well-dressed strangers holding wine glasses, past a photographer snapping photos, I seek out Lara. My sons grip my hands, their uncertainty pushing into my skin, pushing back against the air of anticipation and celebration everyone else seems to feel. I am numb to it. It occurs to me that we three are the strangers, the interlopers, out of place, but it is too late to back out, to tell my boys I have made a mistake. Everyone else is smiling, but I want to cry and howl and fill the weeping wound of me.

I am here for someone's beginning, while a chapter in my own life is ending. It is my best friend's wedding day, two days after I told my husband not to come home.

Endings are only the beginning. On the plane back to Perth, I ponder the meaning of home. The word creates a dissonance in me. I am a woman with her heart on two sides of the country–my childhood home in the shadow of the mountains, and my marital home by the Indian Ocean. And yet. When I visit my mother's brown-brick house, the place that says home after a long absence, I long for the comfort of my own space. The place I now call home. But returning to this home no longer feels comfortable. Or emotionally safe.

Few people know how I wrestle with this nearly every day.

A year before my marriage ends, I am sent to a luxury retreat in Burekup, Western Australia on a writing assignment, along with a friend, a photographer. We, and two other women, are trying to start a new lifestyle magazine; the odds are against it, but for now my dreamy optimism keeps me going. My head tells me I am giving more to this venture than I should. My heart tells me I need this distraction, this lifebuoy on the choppy ocean of my life.

We spend the mornings interviewing the owners, making notes, and taking photos. We climb the hills, sip champagne in the outdoor spa overlooking the bucolic landscape, golden and alive. At night we eat a simple dinner, then wrap ourselves in blankets and sit under the stars, talking about life, dreams, children, marriage. She is one of the few people who knows the fragile truth of me. She is also a practising clairvoyant and that freaks me out. She wants to do healing on me–I suspect she wants it more for herself than me; I am too weak to resist her, but in my head, I pray fervently to the God I still believe in for clarity, peace, wisdom.

After a few minutes, confused and wondering, she says something is blocking her. A white light.

I am face-down on a massage bed, and I think I am relaxed, but the therapist says, relax, no, really relax. I am the most tightly wound person she has seen in a long time, she tells me, her voice as honeyed smooth as the scented oils she is rubbing on my shoulders in firm but gentle circles. I feel lavender-orange compassion soaking into my skin, and I know I don't have to tell her the hurt of my heart. She knows.

When she asks if I want Reiki, I say no. Quickly, decisively. I fear the mystery of it as much as the part of me that wants to say yes. But I am still caught up in what the church says is wrong and right and I don't want to upset God. I'm sorry, I say because I also don't want to hurt her feelings and then the tears come. I should feel embarrassed but, in that moment, I feel love. She talks to me of auras and when I ask what colour mine is, she pauses before saying there is purple in my heart chakra. Heartbreak. But there is a blanket of protection around me, she adds. Perhaps she is choosing words to comfort me, but I interpret the blanket as God sending me a message: good girl.

Most people don't know that I have found myself on a rollercoaster that runs on an infinite track, up and down, upside down. It jerks and twists and throws me from side to side and I hang on for dear life, and breathe when it finally seems to be over, but then it starts again. Something deep inside tells me I need to get off this rollercoaster before it spits me out from a great height, with nothing left to cushion the landing.

There is conflicting advice from those who have some insight: church members, counsellors, friends, his doctor. Some tell me to stay—God would want this from a good wife, divorce is wrong—and they press upon me well-meaning, confusing self-help books. Others, not churchgoers, tell me to look after myself, my kids. They give me books too. There is too much information, and not enough. When I read these books and listen to these people, I hold confusion in my hands, an ache in my heart.

I don't know exactly what I am dealing with.

I don't want to do this anymore.

I don't want to give up.

I am numb.

I cry. I make excuses. I forgive. I have signed up for the long haul, till death do us part, even though I am dying inside. I don't want to break the promise I made in a church; I don't want my kids to grow up in a 'broken home', like I did. And yet. This is not the life I want for myself or my sons. My pastor has heard it all before, he has worked with men splintered by war. He tells me firmly, compassionately, that I will not disappoint God, that this is not what he believes or teaches. That, in his most human and humble opinion, I must change my life to save it. That is what God would want, he says.

End, then begin. I mull this over for months. When your head is so full, your body so tense, your sense of self so weak, how do you know which messages are real and which are just what you want to hear?

One wintry day, two months before I end my marriage, the boys and I escape from a house that is stagnant with a dark and heavy energy, its terracotta floor tiles strewn with invisible eggshells. We find ourselves at the beach where the energy is fiercely alive. The wind has icy fingers, reaching into our ears and up our sleeves, whipping the waves into jagged, white-capped peaks. We can barely hear each other speak over nature's wild roar. We star-jump from sand dunes, hurling prayers upwards. I have prayed countless times over the years, and sometimes it feels contrived and pointless, sometimes I don't know what to say. My head always wants to find a way to say it better, to find the right way, the right words because if I crack that code, everything will be okay. This has always been my modus operandi; I am always puzzled when it doesn't work.

Now, I close my eyes and leap, heart before head. I ask for strength for what I know I must do. For forgiveness. For reassurance that listening to my heart is the right thing to do, that the ending is not the end. And then there is the strangest silence, as if the wind and waves and circling seagulls have frozen in space. I am covered in goosebumps but an inexplicable warmth rushes over me. I hear a distant choir, a joyful harmony of infinite voices. My feet hit the sand; the wind whips my beanie away. My sons laugh; their lips are blue with cold.

Another day, same beach. Rosie, our irrepressibly Pollyanna-ish dog, is off her leash in the dog zone, enjoying freedom from the confines of a small backyard. She bounds joyfully away, almost flying in the brisk sea breeze. Her sights are set on a new best friend, a small, snappy ball of fluff (who, unbeknownst to Rosie, does not want a new best friend). We bolt after her, our desperate calls carried out to sea by the wind, but before we reach her, the other dog's owner kicks our clueless, happy pet so hard she catapults backwards, landing with a thump on dry sand. Her brown eyes are wet and confused as, hands trembling, I reattach her leash and pass her to my boys. Behind me a hulking male rants, his shadow pressing into the shell of me, igniting the shoulds that too often guide me.

I should walk away, this man is not backing down, no, he is advancing; he doesn't care that I am a fraction of his size, that his anger is as overblown as the gathering cumulus clouds.

I should be scared, I should keep my mouth shut, but the sustained pressure I am under erupts like a geyser at the bastard who kicked my dog, and I scream at him for hurting an innocent animal, shaking with rage and hurt and fear and grief and pain. Shaking with the freedom of releasing what I lock inside every day.

Hours later, I am still shivering uncontrollably. It is the adrenaline, I think. I am wrong. I have a raging fever and I am sick for days, stuck inside four walls of sadness.

After months, years of not listening to the messages of my heart, my body steps in. After the flu that knocked me flat comes a sudden bout of labyrinthitis–a debilitating cocktail of vertigo, nausea and dizziness that leaves me bedridden. I am unable to read, watch television, walk; I crawl to the toilet, curl up on the shower floor while warm water gushes over me. The doctor puts it down to extreme stress anxiety, secondary post-traumatic stress disorder; he writes a prescription and wishes me luck.

Months later, the labyrinthitis returns. By then, there has been an ending and a beginning.

The beginning starts before the ending. My remote writing contract finishes, and the magazine venture has come to nothing after all. The first (and only) issue is well received, but the founder has lost interest. My hopes of being paid for hundreds of hours' work fade like the flesh on my bones; I am left with told-you-sos, dashed dreams and an awakening resentment. I walked eyes wide open into a beguiling web of broken promises. I vow not to let that happen again, but many years later, I do. Some lessons are hard won. Some you never learn.

Thrust suddenly into the role of breadwinner, I start applying for jobs. I have two caveats: close to home, close to my sons' school. But rejection after rejection–too qualified, they say–brings me to the brink of despair. I have been making plans for the ending, quietly quitting my marriage, but now there is the real danger of this train being derailed. I pray fervently for divine help. There is only more rejection–not even the local supermarket will have me.

And so, I prepare to look for jobs further from home, even though the thought of not being home when the boys finish school shivers fear to my bones. What choice do I have? There is a mortgage, bills, school fees, swim squad. I rail at God for not helping, for not being there and knowing what I need, and then, the exact second that I open my computer, comes the ping of a new message. It is from a news editor at a community newspaper. Someone passed on your name, she writes. I need a relief journalist. Are you interested?

Six weeks later, the editor offers me a full-time job, a senior journalist role, bypassing the cadet and junior roles. You can write, she says. The other ending soon follows, the door never to be opened. I can't fix you, I say. You must help yourself now. This is difficult, it goes against the grain of being the fixer, the mother, the responsible one. The co-dependent. But of the countless lessons I have learnt in this life season, two stand out: firstly, being emotionally responsible means accepting that the only feelings I have control over are my own and secondly, one of us needs to end this co-dependent relationship so both of us have a chance to thrive.

Endings are searingly lonely, even when you don't live four thousand kilometres from family. Getting through the days until the moment you can remove the mask is all-consuming–ending one chapter doesn't make the next any easier, it just moves the story along. There is resistance, there are pleas and promises, there are boundaries that must be set over and over; these daily challenges test my resolve one minute, harden it the next. I have taken charge of my life, I have leapt into the unknown, but I'm not entirely convinced life will catch me. For a long while it feels like that rollercoaster has shot over the edge of a cliff and I am hanging on for dear life.

Seven months into my new beginning, I am unexpectedly invited to Malaysia, all expenses paid as part of no-expense-spared tourism campaign. The faxed invitation waits on my desk; I am late to work, wrung dry after dealing with earthquakes and aftershocks. Three days in Kuala Lumpur, four at a Club Med resort. My colleagues are envious–they think it's luck; I am convinced it is a gift and I want to believe I deserve it. But I fight off guilt as I spend days swimming, reading, walking, taking photos, making notes. Missing my boys who are with kind-hearted friends. It aches, the missing. Right down to the marrow. On the last day, I opt to take a batik class.

I am dripping hot wax onto cotton when a sharp slap of thunder jolts my hand. The teacher is lost in art–tongue sticking out, hand anchored on the long-handled tjanting; she is unfazed by the lashing rain, the slap-slap of palm branches against the roof. Earlier, I watched the clouds mass over the ocean, pungent and impenetrable. I feared they would birth a monster. I turn back to my batik and try to ignore the defiant blob of wax dislodged by the thunderclap, focusing on holding my tjanting steady, on retreating into myself.

During the break, a woman approaches, keen to chat. I've seen her around the resort, posing by the pool in a bejewelled silk kaftan that probably cost more than the art teacher earns in six months. Are you OK? She's persistent, this stranger with penetrating words and piercing eyes; she sees the subterranean ache of my heart. I turn away, gather pots of dye, a brush.

The sky rumbles angrily, voicing my thoughts, the words I don't allow myself to speak. I'm here to create art. Not to dwell on messy endings and uncertain beginnings. Won't you allow me this one guilt-free afternoon away from my head? Away from worry, away from the throb of loneliness, away from the missing. My hand, traitorous limb, quivers as the brush dives into dye, blood red. My mouth tastes of rusted metal. Reality rises like the roaring wind and I'm rough with the cotton, clumsy with the brush. Red dye blooms under cracked wax.

They arrive as suddenly as the storm, the tears.

I meet him on a bus on the way to a work Christmas party. He is my editor's son. She felt a zing the day she met me, thought of her son. Her husband, a photographer at the competing newspaper, felt this same zing, had the same thought. Our connection is instant but I'm not sure about the zing. It's too early. And yet I find myself thinking about him often.

Am I allowed to do this? I ask Lara. Am I?

Months pass before life brings us together again. I am tentative, scared; my rollercoaster is yet to make a grinding, shuddering halt even though – for me, at least – that door is long closed. I have seized control of my life, and I don't want to give that up. When you have guarded your heart for so long, the unlocking takes time, patience, faith. It takes confidence and perseverance to stop second-guessing, overthinking, worrying. But while the price of letting someone in is high, sooner or later you must decide whether it's worth paying. Sooner or later, you must lean in and listen to your soul. You don't need to ask for permission.

Five months later I am on a bus travelling from Canberra to Sydney. My boys are seated across the aisle, their faces intent and dimly lit by small screens in their hands. I am exhausted–emotionally and physically–and I have not told anyone about the growing sense of foreboding I am feeling. Outside is also dark; the highway is long, and towns are a blur of light and changing shapes.

I text this man in Perth who is becoming part of my new beginning; he texts back that he is sending a hug. A three-letter-word that I feel with every cell in my body. And there it is, a zing. An inexplicable, physical warmth that washes through me, top to bottom, a waterfall of hug. Four thousand kilometres away, he feels it too. We are never able to explain how time and distance shrunk so we were in each other's arms. A higher power? An outside force, an energy pulling two souls together? Whatever that was, it was beautiful, mysterious, and real. And we are ready to leap.

Monique Mulligan founded 'Stories on Stage' and 'Prose & Convos' programs in Western Australia. A former journalist, news editor, book reviewer and publisher, her novels *Wherever You Go* and *Wildflower* were published by Bloodhound Books in 2023. Her work has been published in several anthologies, most recently Reflections on Our Relationships with *Anne of Green Gables: Kindred Spirits* (Cambridge Scholars Publishing). A lover of cooking, photography and flowers, Monique is working on her third novel.

Chapter 32

A Lesson in Loss
by Teena Raffa-Mulligan

'Do you think you'll ever smile again?' my husband asked as we sat in our parked car staring out at the ocean.

It didn't feel possible after the Christmas we'd had.

It was January 1971 and the new year had offered such promise. There'd been so much to look forward to, with our first child due to arrive in February and construction starting soon on our first family home.

Now my world felt like it had fallen apart and I couldn't stop crying.

On 27 December, I had given birth to the son we both wanted. We called him Jason. For months we had talked of him, dreamed of him, planned for him. There was a small chest of drawers at his grandmother's house, crammed with clothes that had been crocheted and sewn with love, packed and folded with anticipation.

When we signed the contract for the house, I had visions of our child exploring the garden, examining ants, chasing butterflies. On wintry nights, I'd snuggle up beside him in the smallest bedroom and tell him stories.

Christmas that year should have been full of joy and hope for the future. Instead, it was a time of deep sorrow. Our son was stillborn. He wouldn't be wearing the clothes, exploring the garden or hearing the stories. I was shattered, even though for months I had been saying something was wrong. I'd told my husband, my mother and my doctor that my baby didn't move much.

However, everything seemed as it should be. I was a picture of good health and impending motherhood and family and friends constantly commented on how well I looked.

'Don't worry,' was the reassurance when I voiced my concerns. 'Some babies are quieter than others.'

I wanted to believe all was well. Yet often I woke crying in the early hours of the morning with the sense that something was wrong with my baby. I pushed it aside and blamed my overactive imagination. Of course, my baby was all right.

A few days before Christmas, I had what I thought was a severe stomach upset.

'It must have been the crayfish I ate last night,' I told Mum.

She didn't think the way my abdomen was heaving from one side to the other looked right. I was whisked straight off to see my GP, who promptly referred me to a specialist.

On 23 December, my husband and I heard the news every expectant parent dreads.

'I'm afraid there's no heartbeat,' said the specialist.

'Your baby is dead.'

He made no effort to soften the news.

'You're young and healthy. You'll have other children.'

It was no consolation. I wanted *this* child.

My husband and I went home to my parents' place and I sat on Dad's lap as if I were a little girl again and cried on his shoulder while he stroked my hair.

That night, back in our tiny flat, I couldn't sleep. It was frightening to think that the child I was carrying was no longer alive. I felt like I was trapped in a terrible nightmare and couldn't wake up.

On 24 December, we returned to see my GP who arranged for me to be admitted to hospital late the next day ready for an induction on Boxing Day. The festive spirit was very subdued as our family went through the motions of celebrating Christmas.

The next morning I survived the induction as if in a dream. In the labour ward I could hear other women giving birth and the first cries of their newborn babies. I clung to a thread of hope that the specialist was wrong and my child too would announce his arrival with a wail.

There was no mistake.

When I returned home several days later it was with empty arms and an emptier heart.

I struggled to make sense of our loss. Unwanted babies were born every day. Why couldn't I have a baby we wanted so much? Had I done something wrong, not looked after myself well enough? Should I have given up work? Or was it a bargain?

I wasn't religious, but the thought crept in: did God hear me that day in Mum's kitchen, the day my husband's birth date came up in the National Service conscription lottery?

Devastated at the thought of him being shipped off to Vietnam to kill or be killed, I'd sat at the table sobbing uncontrollably.

'Don't upset yourself like that,' Mum said. 'It's not good for the baby.'

'I don't care about the baby! I'd rather have him!'

My husband was granted indefinite deferment of his national service because we were married.

And our baby boy died not long afterwards.

In the aftermath of our loss, when I had a copious supply of milk and no babe to suckle, I wondered if God gave me what I'd said I wanted.

Recovery was a slow process.

Losing our baby was the worst thing that had ever happened to me. I felt like I'd been punched to the ground and at first I didn't know if I could ever get up again and carry on. It didn't matter that I hadn't actually watched him grow, seen him laugh and cry and jump puddles, held his hand to cross a road. He had been a part of my life for seven months, and then suddenly he was gone.

Times were different then.

I didn't cradle our lost little one in my arms to say goodbye and let him know how sorry we were that he hadn't stayed with us. Too afraid that his image would haunt me for the rest of my days, I never even looked at him.

I wasn't offered grief counselling in the hospital, or when I returned home without my baby. Telling others was difficult. I would cross the road or duck into a shop to avoid meeting friends who didn't know what had happened.

I conceived again only eight weeks after our son was stillborn. If I hadn't plunged right into another pregnancy I don't think I would ever have had the courage to try again. It was an emotional nine months. I veered from being deliriously happy and certain all would be well, to being absolutely miserable and convinced everything would go wrong.

Fear was my frequent companion. Would it happen again? If it did, could I face it or would it be too much to bear? I was overly concerned about my body and how it was behaving. I regularly prodded my stomach to make the baby move and reassure myself it was still alive.

I needn't have worried. He was, very much so.

Just eleven months after our first son was stillborn, our beautiful, healthy, demanding, eight-pounds-thirteen-ounce, second son was born, naturally and without complications.

His father was there to share the joyful occasion. The birth was quick, easy and trouble-free and I was unafraid going into labour. From the moment my contractions began, I was on a natural high. I knew without doubt I was having a son and that he was strong and well.

Afterwards, I held him in my arms, overwhelmed with relief and happiness. We had a healthy baby son. All my worries had been groundless. Now I could relax and enjoy motherhood.

However, panic set in soon after his birth.

Losing our firstborn son had shown me how precious and unpredictable life could be. Now that we had our beautiful healthy son, what if we were to lose him?

With me in the maternity ward and him in the nursery except for feeding times, how could I know he was still breathing? When I overheard two of the hospital staff talking about a recent cot death I became so distressed the doctor prescribed valium for me. I was breastfeeding, so I flushed the tablets down the toilet, determined not to take anything that might affect my baby. I knew all I needed was to go home with my son where I could keep him by my side and make sure he was safe.

Those first few days after we left the hospital, I refused to go to sleep unless my husband first promised to watch over our son. I woke our baby often to make sure he was still alive. I wouldn't leave him with anyone. When he began to crawl, then to walk, I shadowed him, a self-appointed guardian angel. I developed over-protectiveness to a fine art.

But as two healthy baby daughters arrived to join our strong, adventurous little boy, I realised I couldn't wrap my children in cotton wool to protect them from life. They hadn't come with any guarantees they'd be safe and well. I'd had a painful lesson in loss.

Now I had to learn about letting go, little by little as my children grew.

Nearly thirty years later, in a labour ward at the same hospital where I had given birth to our stillborn son, I briefly re-lived that shattering experience as my older daughter, her husband and I awaited the arrival of my first grandchild.

The labour had been long and unproductive. My daughter was exhausted and her baby was showing signs of distress, so she was transferred from the homebirth centre to the maternity section for medical intervention.

Suddenly the memories flooded back, all the sorrow and pain that I'd thought time had erased.

I was overwhelmed by fear that this child we'd been anticipating with such joy would not live to share our lives. The moments between my granddaughter's birth and her first cry seemed an eternity. Then the doctor pronounced her well and healthy and I began to breathe again.

A new life was beginning. I gave silent thanks for such a precious gift.

Teena Raffa-Mulligan is a reader, writer and daydream believer who is convinced there is magic in every day. She is a multi-published children's author of quirky, whimsical books full of warmth, gentle humour, hope and heart. When Teena is not sea gazing or sun dreaming, she likes nothing better than sharing her passion for storytelling with people of all ages and encouraging them to write their own stories.

Chapter 33

Facing Our Fears

by Zibby Owens

An hour ago, I asked my little guy to open the drapes.

'What if there's a man hiding behind there?' he asked. 'What if he's going to kill us? What if there are deadly fire ants who come to life and...'

'If there's a man behind there, we'll both be dead in two seconds anyway,' I said. 'Can we see if it's a nice day out first?'

'I can't.'

'You're watching too much YouTube.'

'Mom, being scared isn't from YouTube.'

'Come on–face your fears. You'll feel better for the rest of the day.'

He timidly opened one side and hopped back under the covers.

Facing your fears has been the theme of my summer–of the past six years of my life–epitomised by what happened in the lake during Camp Visiting Day.

My little guys went to a small sleepaway camp in Maine for two weeks. Interestingly, my son wasn't scared when he slept in the woods one night under a tarp that he and his friends made out of branches and garbage bags. A Hamptons bedroom, though: watch out.

Their camp's visiting day was an interactive experience in which all parents and siblings were supposed to take part in the activities including 'water toys', which featured two-story wobbling slides, climbable icebergs, and a trampoline connected to a Tarzan-like rope swing.

There was no getting out of it; my kids had talked about going in the lake on every call home. My daughter, it turns out, was waiting for me to go in so we could 'do it together' and hadn't been in the water the whole time except for a mandatory swim test. Was it the leeches or common sense? Who knows?

She'd been quite specific in her instructions: bring bathers and a cover up ('the Zara dress is too short, Mom; wear a long dress'), sandals and a change of clothes.

We got ready along with her older sister in her cabin, which smelled exactly how my cabin smelled when I went to sleepaway camp in the 1980s. What is that smell?! Rotted wood?

We walked down to the lake, our towels over our arms, sandals flopping.

'That's where the life jackets are,' my daughter said, when we reached the waterfront.

'Oh, I don't need a life jacket,' I said.

'No, Mom. You have to wear one.'

'I'm sure they're just for kids.'

'Mom, come on–you have to.'

I looked around and noticed a couple other dads with life-jackets on. *Damn it.* I searched on the rack for a dry lifejacket and grabbed a size large.

'Mom, that's too big,' she said.

'It's fine!'

My daughter walked over and lifted it up and down with both hands. 'It's going to be over your head.'

'It's fine! Don't worry!' I said.

Moments later, I was standing barefoot on a splinter-filled

walkway straight out of Peter Pan. Wendy walking the plank, I followed the kids down to the water, fully aware that my backside was on display for the rest of the camp. I tried to cover my butt–not even my butt, the area where my butt and legs become undulating mounds. Does that area even have a name?

I peered over the edge. *I can't f—ing do this*, I thought. But my daughter was also scared. Shouldn't I be showing her that we can face anything?! I had to do this! For her! For all the kids!

Nope; couldn't fake it.

'I'm ridiculously scared,' I said.

'Me too,' she said.

My little guy offered his hand. 'Let's go together, Mom,' he said.

I took a deep breath, bit my lip in anticipation, and, holding his hand, jumped in.

Three-two-one...SPLASH!

SCREAM.

'It's so cold!' I cried. 'Oh my God! It's so cold!' I bobbed in the water, my life jacket under my nose, screaming.

But I'd done it; I was in. And actually, it warmed up quickly. The lake was beautiful.

My little guy swam over to me.

'Now it's time for the slide, Mom!'

The slide was attached to what seemed to be a surfboard platform, which I could barely get onto from the water. (My arms were sore the next day.) With a little nudging from strangers, I climbed up and started scaling the wall, awkwardly finding the next rungs with my hands and feet.

Right as I approached the top, I froze – I was going to have to jump up a little. If I missed, I'd go hurtling down the slide face-first. If I fell the other way, I'd knock down the ten campers climbing up behind me. My little guy and older daughter were waiting for me at the top.

'Come on, Mom!' they urged.

I couldn't move; my legs were shaking and not just from the exertion. 'I can't do it!'

Campers cheered me on. My little guy held out his hand to help, but I refused to take him down with me.

'Well, I'm going,' my older daughter said, and went down the slide without me. Traitor.

'Me too,' my little guy said, preparing to slide.

'Do not leave me up here!' I screamed.

The eighteen-year-old blond lifeguard perched on the ledge was no help–he just stared at me. *Who was this middle-aged mom who couldn't even get to the top?* I'd like to note that I was the only mom who even *attempted* this.

Finally, a kind camper suggested I shimmy to the right to find better footing. Did I mention my ex-husband was also in the lake, and that my husband, Kyle, and my ex's new fiancé were dry and gorgeous on the dock, watching?

Quaking, I pushed up that extra bit to get to the top. Then once I actually sat down, it was time to slide.

'Push her!' someone yelled.

My heart pounded. 'Noooo!' Another deep breath; another bitten-lip and... 'AHHHH!'

I dug in my thighs and went down the slide which, devoid of water, basically became a burn machine. I couldn't even get all the way to the bottom. I came to a complete stop at the base, my feet hanging over the edge.

'This is the worst moment of my life!' I said before flopping into the water, hysterically laughing.

I still have an entire side of 'raft-burn' scabbing up. But I pushed through the worst moment–for the sake of the kids–and survived. Laughed. Made memories.

I'll skip the trauma of getting onto the trampoline, the fear of jumping onto the Tarzan rope, or how I was too afraid to jump off it so went catapulting back to the trampoline where all the campers ducked and took cover as I approached.

All my daughter remembered was that I did it. With her. Like I said I would. And she had a blast.

'I can't wait until we do this again next year,' she said, as we walked in our towels up the hill.

'You know, there are other camps…'

'Mo–om!' And she took my hand.

Facing your fears.

My drapes are still half-closed. But we're getting there.

Zibby Owens is the award-winning podcast host of *Moms Don't Have Time to Read Books* (www.momsdonthavetimetoreadbooks.com); founder of Zibby Books publishing house; and proud owner of Zibby's Bookshop, an independent bookstore in Santa Monica. An American author, her books include *Blank: A Novel*, *Bookends: A Memoir of Love, Loss, and Literature*, children's book *Princess Charming*, and two anthologies that she edited. She is the mother of four fabulous kids.

Chapter 34

The Moment I Knew (Again)
by Kylie Ladd

My husband Craig and I met–against all odds–at the Melbourne County Court on jury service, when I was only eighteen. We have been married now for almost thirty years. They have largely been good, rich, full decades, but anyone who has been together as long as we have knows that such longevity comes at a price.

The bright, shiny marriage we drove out of the dealership in 1995 has a lot of miles on the clock now, some visible scrapes, a few mismatching panels. One of the biggest is that I am a romantic, a feeler of big feels, a declarer of every possible emotion. My husband, in contrast, is the strong silent type, mostly silent. It has led to more than a few fights, me accusing him of not caring, his replying that love isn't–doesn't have to be–a song and dance.

Until this. Not long into Melbourne's first Covid-19 lockdown in 2020, Craig had a bike accident. We later determined that he had hit a stationary car, illegally parked in the bike lane, while descending a hill, head down, at around forty kilometres an hour.

Both his helmet and his bike cracked apart on impact, and he was thrown out of his toe clips and onto the road, where he was found by another cyclist as he regained consciousness. *He's not right*, the cyclist told me when I arrived at the scene. *I don't think anything's broken, but he's really repetitive.* I work as a neuropsychologist–someone who assesses brain damage–and immediately took Craig, against his protests, to our local hospital.

Yet when we arrived at A&E I wasn't allowed to accompany him inside. Covid protocols, I was told by a gowned and masked nurse. I should go home; they would call me. I started walking back to my car, but as I did my mobile rang. It was Craig, who must have relocated his phone in the back of his bike shorts.

'Chook!' he cried when I answered. 'What happened? I'm in hospital. Why aren't you with me?'

I explained that I had brought him there but hadn't been allowed in, due to pandemic restrictions. He'd had a bike accident, but the doctors would look after him and I'd be back to collect him as soon as I was allowed. He sounded mollified, and we hung up...but five minutes later he called again. This time he was crying.

'Chook! Where are you? Why aren't you with me?'

My stomach twisted. Crying. My husband never cried, not since 1995, twice: once when we were married and again eight months later when Carlton had won the premiership, a feat they haven't managed since. *A good year*, Craig had said at the time. Would he even remember that now, or ever again?

I repeated my explanation, wracked with guilt even though it hadn't been my choice to desert him. 'I wish you could be here Chook,' he said when I'd finished. 'I need you.'

He called twice more before I'd even arrived home; at least eight times before they finally took him to be scanned.

To my enormous relief, it came back clear, and Craig was discharged four hours later, wholly himself again. On the way home I mentioned that he'd rung me ten times. His eyes widened in surprise.

'Really? Are you sure?'

I held up my phone, every incoming call listed.

'Huh', he said, shaking his head. 'If you hadn't shown me that I wouldn't have believed you.'

I wouldn't have believed it either: Craig, in tears, sobbing that he needed me. Other than a short, and likely permanent, period of amnesia for the hour both before and after his crash he has made a full recovery. I am extremely grateful for that.

But I'm also grateful that he had the accident, given no lasting damage was done. Though it tore up his lycra, though his bike had to be put out for the hard rubbish collection, it fortified our marriage.

To see my stoic, silent husband with his defences down, to hear his need for me, has been restorative. Sometimes you need to be needed. Sometimes things have to be spoken out loud, not presumed, not taken for granted.

His accident, in a weird way, was a renewal of our vows. I wish all marriages, especially long ones, such moments of vulnerability, of defence-dropping, of being stripped right back to the bone. His accident may yet keep us going for another thirty years.

Kylie Ladd is an Australian novelist, psychologist and freelance writer. Her novels have been published in Australia and overseas and *The Way Back* has been optioned for film. She co-edited and co-authored two non-fiction books, and her essays and articles have been published in *The Age* and *Sydney Morning Herald*, *Griffith Review*, *Meanjin*, *O Magazine*, *Good Medicine*, *Kill Your Darlings* and *Readers Digest*, amongst others.

Chapter 35

How to Mend a Broken Heart
by Rachael Robertson

This story begins with a broken heart. My broken heart. My vulnerable broken heart shattered into a million tiny little pieces. Obviously, a broken heart is the analogy of great pain. Your heart doesn't actually break. Thank goodness. It's a saying. A term we humans use to express deep hurt. *You broke my heart.* Oof. Nothing hurts quite like the concept of having your heart broken or breaking someone else's.

The heart itself is quite amazing. It beats around one hundred thousand times a day. It quite literally keeps you alive, without even having to consciously think about it for even a fleeting moment. It pumps about six litres of blood around the body every single day. Each day, the heart creates enough energy to drive a truck over thirty kilometres. In a lifetime, that is like driving to the moon and back. It just keeps on ticking away, no matter what you do. Oh, you want to go for a run? Okay, it will tick a little faster. Need to sleep? Sure, it'll calm it down and tick a little less. The heart is quite frankly, amazing.

Heartbreak, not so much. Some scientists believe that heartache can, in fact, manifest physically. You can feel physical pain after enduring excruciating hurt. I personally know this to be true. For me, this happened while ten weeks pregnant.

My husband Scott and I had been trying for a baby for two years. Two years of every position and angle under the sun. That was the fun part. Two years of disappointment when my dreaded period arrived every month. The not so fun part. Two years of everyone around us managing to get pregnant. Two years of tracking and recording. Two years of feeling a slightly sorer breast or a random cramp and hoping it was *it*. Two years of post after post on social media of a black and white sonogram image of a new baby growing alongside a sparkly pregnancy announcement. *OMG. We are so shocked to find out...* or *All our hopes and dreams have come true.*

What about my hopes and dreams? Two years of wondering why not us? As we surpassed the two-year mark of trying, and we started to ask each other the difficult questions about fertility and other parenting options. Then, somewhat astoundingly, we turned out to be *that couple*. You know the ones. The couple that is about to embark on fertility treatment, but miraculously find out they had, in fact, conceived naturally. A late period, a gut feeling and a positive pregnancy test.

We were pregnant. We were ecstatic. Happy beyond measure. We couldn't wait to have our own little baby in our own little arms in our own little home that our own little love had created.

From the first wee on the pregnancy stick to the first appointment with our obstetrician, I tried my absolute best. I did it all. I did everything I possibly could to give my baby the best start in life. I ate well. Mostly organic, because seriously, who can afford all organic? I made sure I had iron. Folic acid. Calcium. Handfuls of spinach in smoothies every morning. I took prenatal vitamins. The expensive ones. And fish oil. And vitamin D. I walked every day. Swam. I had naps when I was tired. I cut out sugar. Meditated. Did not touch alcohol. I bought pregnancy books and read them. I downloaded all the right apps and tracked my baby's growth from a poppy seed to a prune. I joined Pilates. Did deep breathing. I booked appointments with all the right people. An obstetrician, GP, dentist, facialist, masseuse. I drank heaps of water. I did every possible thing I could to give my baby the absolute best start in life, and it wasn't enough.

I wasn't enough.

As we sat in the obstetrician's office, with what should have been a ten-week-old fetus, my heart beating out of my chest, mostly from excitement, I looked across at Scott and felt nothing but love. I was completely and utterly ignorant about what was to come. We met a bubbly, energetic midwife first who went through the logistics. Where to book our hospital stay. What vitamins I should be taking. When I needed to do more blood work (so much blood). What food to avoid (all the good stuff). I felt like I had finally joined the club. The parenthood club. After meeting the midwife, we returned to the waiting room.

Scott and I snuck a shy glance at each other, speaking the unspoken love language between us. *I am so excited.* My eyes fluttered, smile on my face. My heart finally slowing down to a reasonable beat. *Me too.*

'Rachael, come on in,' said our extremely elegant obstetrician. She looked like she had just stepped out of a *Vogue* magazine, not medical scrubs. She asked me to lie on her bed, ready for the ultrasound. I eagerly watched the monitor as she put the cold jelly on the stomach, then the scanner. Quick glance at Scott, back at the machine. This was the moment we had been waiting for. We were going to see the baby we so desperately wanted.

She swirled it around, trying all different angles. Up and down, left to right. She was taking too long to find it. She does this multiple times a day, come on! What was taking so damn long? The look on her face said it all. Her smile transformed to a frown.

Nothing.

A small sac with a gaping black hole.

'I'm sorry,' she mustered.

Tears welled in my eyes. My heart suddenly started to pick up the pace. I couldn't believe this was happening to me. She apologised again, although I am not sure I know why. She didn't lose the baby. I did. She said this was all too common and that I would likely miscarry naturally. If I hadn't within two weeks, give her a call and she would perform a dilatation and curettage.

Apparently, the fetus had stopped growing at six weeks. I couldn't bear to look at Scott. His hopes and dreams of becoming a father just shattered into tiny little pieces, and it was my fault. The scientists were right, my broken heart manifesting physically. The tightening in my chest felt like it was about to implode. I felt an overwhelming sense of guilt. I was the failure. I was the problem. I was broken.

Heartbroken.

We had to walk back through the waiting room of women with big bulging bellies. Women who were successfully growing tiny little humans. Women who didn't have broken hearts. Women who had done so much better than me.

The obstetrician was right. I miscarried four days later. A sense of loss and acceptance came as blood poured out of me. Hormones coursing through my body made the grief easier to bear. Hormones of acceptance. Hormones of betrayal. Hormones of loss. Scott remained, as always, the most supportive and loving husband. He tried to console me, despite me being inconsolable. He continually told me the miscarriage was not my fault. I found him looking up medical articles online, trying to put logic to an otherwise illogical situation. He was trying to support me. To love me. To help me.

Miscarriage. An eleven-letter word that holds so much weight. So much angst. So much secrecy. You aren't supposed to talk about your miscarriage, didn't you know that? You are supposed to deal with the pain on your own. In private. Wallowing in self pity. It can't possibly interrupt your work or commitments. You daren't talk about it and oh my goodness, don't you dare post about it on social media. Don't you know social media is all about happiness? The good bits. Living your best life. Holidays and babies. Engagements and birthdays. Delicious food and nights out on the town. Not baby loss. Come on, you know this.

You can't talk about miscarriage in case it offends someone. Or upsets someone who is pregnant. Or speaks truth to the torture you have experienced. Or someone else has experienced. You deal with it on your own. Cry into a pillow if you need to. But don't cry too loud in case you wake the neighbours. They can't possibly know what you're going through. This is why you wait until twelve weeks to announce you're pregnant at all. The risk of miscarriage decreases. Do not mention your pregnancy to a single person until then, okay? Go through the hardest trimester on your own. You have to, because you daren't mention the M word.

Miscarriage. An eleven-letter word that is all too common for many of us. Miscarriage. Something that happens to twenty percent of pregnant women.

The next few months were awful. I cried all the time. I felt jealous of new mums, then anger and then confusion as to why this was happening to me. But time is magical. Time heals. As the days, and weeks, and months passed, I started to feel like myself again. I was crying less. I started to stop wallowing in self-pity. I realised that perhaps, the miscarriage wasn't my fault after all. I didn't feel resentment every time I saw a baby. I started to feel ready to take matters into my own hands. I started to feel ready to begin fertility treatment.

I booked an appointment with the fertility specialist and started treatment almost immediately. A plethora of blood tests, medication, scans, and more blood tests were undertaken. Lots of waiting in waiting rooms. The pathology clinic, the fertility clinic, the ultrasound clinic. The waiting room of a fertility clinic is one of the most dire of all the waiting rooms. Women, of all different shapes and sizes, different ages and ethnicities, different stages and different treatment plans all sitting in this same waiting room. Waiting to do blood samples, waiting to see the doctor, but mostly waiting to become mothers. Most of the women aimlessly scroll their phones. Probably looking at pregnancy announcements from high school acquaintances, or work colleagues, or family friends. All yearning for the same thing.

After three months of treatment, daily needles, too many blood tests, internal ultrasounds, and the dreaded two-week wait, I got the phone call. THE phone call.

'Hi Rachael, it's Claire from the fertility clinic. Your HCG levels today were 435. Congratulations. You're pregnant.'

PREGNANT!

Complete disbelief. Complete happiness. Complete anxiety.

I felt overwhelmed with joy, my heart ticking that little bit faster. Such a surreal and unique feeling. I didn't feel any different, and yet my whole world and my whole body was about to change.

The fertility clinic tracked my levels for the first two months and then it was handballed to the obstetrician. They knew I was nervous, so additional appointments were made. No matter what I did, or how well the baby was growing, I was still nervous. Miscarriage does that to you. You never truly embrace the pregnancy glow. The passing months were filled with trepidation. Filled with anxiety. Filled with worry. Snippets of excitement were interrupted with an overwhelming feeling that a miscarriage would occur again. I was positively paranoid that I would lose this little baby that I so desperately wanted.

As I neared the forty-week mark, I started to believe that maybe, just maybe, this baby would enter the world and make me a mother. One day before the due date, as I walked down the hallway to make my way to the coffee machine, my waters broke. Not the dramatic cinematic experience you see in the movies, just a slight gush and then a continual to trickle all day long. Scott and I made our way to the hospital. We were relaxed and ready. A round of antibiotics, an induction and seven hours later, I had my baby in my arms.

A little girl. 2.87 kilos. Fifty centimetres long. The paediatrician described her as cool, calm and collected. The sweetest little bundle I could have ever dreamed of.

This story began with a broken heart. My broken heart. It ends with a heart overflowing and bursting with an unwavering sense of love. A love that is incomparable to anything or to anyone that I have ever loved before. A love that burns so deeply into my whole sense of being.

A broken heart can be mended. Mended with time and with kindness. Mended with love and understanding. Mended with determination and drive. My broken heart was well and truly mended by a little girl, who makes my heart speed up a little bit faster every time I look at her. Miscarriage is awful, but it is not the fault of the woman. Sometimes things just happen, and that's okay. Just keep on going until you get what your heart so desperately needs.

Rachael Robertson is an author, illustrator and primary school art teacher based in Perth/Boorlo, Australia. She has been writing for as long as she can remember. Her first book, *My Amazing Animal Alphabet Alliteration Book* is illustrated in collage. Rachael's first book as an illustrator, *What Is It?*, explores the beauty of creating. She writes about matters of the heart, and loves to use painted-paper collage and experiment with multiple media.

Chapter 36

Maurice

by Helen Auld

'Maurice Gibson is a monster!'

Nora slapped the dinner tray down on the counter. She was close to tears, but she would not cry in front of the others. Instead, she bit her bottom lip. Hard. Until it throbbed. Then she exhaled, cleared her throat and looked at Maureen.

'Can you *pleeease* answer his bell next time? He's different with you.'

'What do you mean, different?' asked Maureen. 'I treat him the same as anyone else.'

'Yes, I know. You're not scared of him.'

Maureen scoffed. 'Course not. What happened?'

'He yelled at me, then told me to shove that tray up my *arse!*'

The other nurses shrieked with laughter. They delighted in every story involving Maurice Gibson. There was a new one every day, and they never got tired of them.

Nora's face was a mortified red and her hands were shaky. She felt as if she'd never get the hang of this. Never learn how to be blasé in the face of his criticism the way most of the others were. She'd thought them hard hearted at first. Now she could see it was a survival strategy.

'You'll have to grow a thicker skin,' said Maureen. 'Anyway, he'll change his tune when he's hungry.'

Nora thought back to the day they'd brought Maurice in on the ambulance gurney, fresh from the rehab unit down the road. The paramedic had been grim.

'You've gotta live one 'ere, girls!' he'd said. 'Glad it won't be me lookin' after 'im.'

They'd all laughed. How bad could he be?

Maurice, at first, didn't look much different from the other residents. Frail, sure. But many of the others were too. His medical report said he'd suffered a catastrophic stroke. Everyone agreed he was lucky to be alive. The entire right side of his body was paralysed, and three months of rehab had achieved nothing. That meant he could no longer walk and could barely feed himself. He needed two nurses and a lifting machine to go to the toilet. A bed bath for washing. The right side of his face was droopy, and the stubble near the corner of his mouth was forever shiny with a slick of drool. He could still speak, though, a fact she had thought was a blessing the day she met him.

On closer inspection, she saw he was actually frailer than most. Gaunt, to be honest. His spine was a series of sharp protrusions down his pale thin back, and each rib was visible beneath his papery skin. His good arm, while thin, looked fairly normal, but the bad arm was perpetually bent at the elbow. It was tucked up into itself, like the wing of a Sunday roast chicken. His hand, at the end of that chicken arm, was purplish and swollen, the fingers unmoving. You had to be very careful how you lifted and moved it during the dressing and undressing. Too quick or sharp and he cried out in pain.

She'd helped Maureen get him settled that first day. They'd stood together on the far side of the bed and pulled him off the gurney while the paramedic pushed. Once he was safely in, they'd washed him and helped him change into pyjamas. They'd handled him so gently, sponging his face and chest with the warm soapy water. Carefully applying moisturiser to his dry skin. He was limp and mute, apart from an expletive when they'd moved his chicken arm. He didn't respond to Nora's chatty friendliness or her attempt at humour. There was just–nothing.

The paramedic must be wrong. Maurice Gibson couldn't hurt a fly.

Nora tried to make him feel welcome, the way she did with all the new ones. When she'd first started nursing, an older woman had advised her to always smile because it made people feel better. Especially people in bad situations. Nora felt this was important, and she'd taken the advice to heart. She smiled warmly at everyone, an expression that spread across her face as easy as butter. But no matter how much she smiled at Maurice, he never smiled back. Not that day, and not in the days that followed. He remained sullen and sour, as if he'd been sucking lemons all his life.

Nora remembered feeling sorry for him. That feeling didn't last.

After a couple of days, when Maurice had settled in, he started speaking. And the things that came out of his mouth were not pleasant. He would yell and swear, call them 'stupid' and 'hopeless'. He was irritable, impatient and impossible to look after. He refused to bathe, threw his meal trays across the room if he didn't like the look of the food, spat on the floor, tore his incontinence pads off and soiled the sheets on purpose. He even hit out if you got too close to his sore arm on a bad day. His room had to be kept completely dark and he'd paid extra for the installation of thick blackout curtains. He said the overhead light was too harsh on his eyes, and he only allowed it to be switched on when he wanted his pad or sheets changed, so the nurses could see what they were doing.

All the other bed bound people were washed every morning and had their incontinence pads changed at least three times a day, but not Maurice. With him, it was once a day if you were lucky. If something upset him more than normal, he'd go several days before he'd allow anyone to attend to him. One time, when Maureen was on holidays, he let it stretch out for a week. His room reeked by the end of it. Every day, the nurse in charge would try to reason with him. She'd tell him they had a duty of care towards him and he needed to let the girls do their jobs. But he wouldn't have a bar of it. His argument, apparently, was that he was paying good money to live there and he'd decide when and how things were done. He couldn't be swayed.

When Maureen came back, they told her what had been going on in her absence. She was horrified. She marched straight into his room and read him the riot act. Then an army of nurses (well, three of them anyway) got to work. Within twenty minutes he was bathed, shaved and sitting up in bed on fresh sheets and plumped pillows. The floor was mopped with a bucket of bleach and hot water and the heavy curtains pulled back. The window flung wide to allow the sunshine in and the fetid stench out.

From his position on the bed, Maurice surveyed the scene, shellshocked, but also with an air of smug satisfaction. Nora thought he might be secretly pleased, although whenever she glanced directly at him, he rewarded her with a thunderous scowl. For the rest of the day, he treated her with only mild annoyance instead of outright contempt, and she began to feel there might be hope.

Nora marvelled at Maureen's strange secret power over Maurice. He wasn't exactly civil to her, but he never yelled at her, and he did what she told him.

'How do you do it?'

'Do what?' asked Maureen, puzzled.

'How do you get Maurice to behave himself?'

'Just tell him how it is. Don't put up with his crap. Geez! You'll learn one day!'

From then on, Nora tried to be more assertive, but somehow she couldn't pull it off. She didn't have Maureen's strength of conviction, and Maurice remained steadily cantankerous whenever he spoke to her. Still, she reminded herself, she had to give him some leeway. Life had dealt him a harsh blow. His body wouldn't do what he needed it to any more. He'd lost his independence. He didn't want to be there. He was depressed. He was angry. He had every reason to be. She tried to make her peace with it.

Then one day he grabbed her by the wrist as she struggled to change his shirt. The shirt was too tight and made of stiff cheap material that had no give in it. His bad arm got stuck at an awkward angle and it hurt. She was trying to pull it back out to start again when he became livid.

'Stupid girl! What do you think you're doing?' he spat.

'I'm sorry, Maurice,' Nora whispered, the familiar fear of him rising in her chest.

'Stop fiddling about and leave me alone.'

'But you're only half dressed. We have to fix you up.'

Nora glanced across the bed at her work mate, a new girl who'd shrunk back as soon as Maurice lunged at Nora. She was no help. His good arm was surprisingly strong. He bent her wrist backwards and glared up at her.

'I said GET OUT!'

The other girl was already gone. He pushed Nora away. She dropped the shirt and clasped her aching wrist to her chest, shocked. Then she'd gone to find Maureen to help her finish dressing him. He wouldn't let anyone else in his room that day.

After that, something in her changed. The part of her that had been soft and open and eager became something else. Something reluctant and disengaged. Almost detached. Whenever his call bell rang, she made sure she was busy doing something else so one of the others had to answer it. Relief flooded her when she got away with it. Then she'd listen, with only a small pang of guilt, as the poor unfortunate bell answerer related the story of what Maurice had said or done this time.

Avoiding bells was really against her nature. The old Nora jumped as soon as she heard the tinny sound and saw the room number flash on the display board. A bell ringing was a signal that someone needed her help. Right away. Maybe it was a man having a seizure. Or a woman doubled over, unable to breathe, desperate for an oxygen cylinder. She'd shimmy down the corridor on high alert, only to find they just wanted a box of tissues, or help to get to the toilet. Nevertheless, like Pavlov's dog, she sprang into action immediately, every time. She prided herself on it.

Now, whenever she saw Maurice Gibson's number, her heart sank. God, what would he want? She knew that whatever she did for him, it wouldn't be good enough. Her care wouldn't *matter*, like it did to other people. She would just be a nuisance getting in his way at best, a target for his fury at worst. She still had to do her job, but her desire to help him had completely vanished.

The new Nora was tougher. Harder. Not such a *sucker*. She made sure her visits to his room were as brief as possible. No more attempts to make conversation or even smile. Just do what needed to be done, then get out. When he yelled at her, she pretended not to hear. Robot faced, she stopped reacting. After a while, she noticed he yelled a little less, and when he did yell at her, she didn't care so much. Looking after him became not pleasant, but bearable.

Then one day, Maurice fell out of bed.

Thinking about it later, she was never sure if it was an accident, or if he'd really been trying to harm himself. Maybe he thought that if he landed hard enough, in just the right way, his skull would split open, granting him a glorious release from his useless broken body.

If that was his plan, it didn't work.

Carrying his breakfast tray, she groped her way across the darkened room, hand outstretched to find the edge of the heavy curtain. He got angry, of course, if you just barged in and switched the light on. She'd learnt to wake him gently by opening the curtain a fraction before calling his name. This morning, the crack of light was just bright enough to reveal that the bed was empty, sheets rumpled and dangling floorward. The only sound she could hear was the ponderous ticking of Maurice's antique wooden clock. Startled, Nora put the tray down and bent to look under the bed. A rumpled man-sized shape lay motionless and twisted on the floor.

'Maurice?! Are you alright?'

There was no answer. She crossed to the light switch and flicked it on, not caring if he abused her for it. Maurice didn't even flinch. She could see his face clearly now, deathly pale with a wound above his left eyebrow, a pool of globby blood on the floor underneath. Nora's training kicked in and she smashed the emergency button with an urgent palm. Nurses from the other parts of the building would soon be running to help. There was a face washer hanging over the rail in the bathroom. She grabbed it then squatted beside him, pressing it against his wound.

'Can you hear me, Maurice? Are you alright?'

His eyes were closed but she could see his lips trembling as he breathed. He was alive. She touched his shoulder, carefully, to rouse him without moving him. He could have spinal damage. Although the worst had already pretty much happened to him, she didn't want him to lose the use of his good limbs as well.

'Maurice!'

He blinked and looked up at her, dazed.

'Sally?' he asked.

'No, it's me, Nora. You've fallen out of bed. They're coming, don't worry.'

She pulled the blanket down off the bed and covered him with it. She wanted to put a pillow under his bleeding head too, but knew she shouldn't. He was like an injured bird, lying there on the cold lino, helpless and mute in his private misery. His face was crumpled, the stubble on his chin coated in the familiar sticky drool. And all that blood. She wondered how long he'd been lying there. An hour? Two? He groaned and tried to lift his head, a pathetic movement that failed. He didn't have the strength.

For the first time, she saw him as he really was. Saw past his ugly rage to the pain that swallowed him up from the inside. To the defeated shadow he was beneath the surface. Maurice Gibson really couldn't hurt a fly. The hard part of her softened towards him, just slightly. She reached for his good hand. It was cold as ice. She knelt there holding it until the others arrived.

After he was cleaned up, bandaged and put back into bed, he slept deeply. Nora kept an eye on him all day. At the end of her shift, she went into his room to check on him again. She noticed with surprise that the curtains were open and the room was flooded with light. It was a golden afternoon. Maurice was awake and staring at the garden outside his window, transfixed.

'I'm sorry,' she said. 'I don't know who did that.'

She grasped the heavy fabric and began to drag it across to block the light out again.

'Stop! Leave it,' he said, in a croaky voice.

She took a step back, as if he'd slapped her.

'How are you feeling, Maurice?' she asked, tentatively.

There was no reply.

'I suppose they told you there's no broken bones or anything, so that's lucky. You won't have to go back to hospital.'

He looked at her for the first time since she'd entered the room. He seemed to be trying to decide who she was and why she was talking to him.

'Anyway, I just wanted to make sure you were okay. Is there anything you need? Have you got enough blankets? Would you like a drink?'

He still didn't speak. Well, really, what had she expected, a miracle?

'Alright then. Sing out if you think of anything.'

She turned to leave.

'Nora?'

'Yes, Maurice?'

'Aren't you supposed to be finished for the day?' he asked.

Her eyes grew wide. 'Yes. How did you know that?'

'I might be crippled but I'm not stupid.'

There was an uncomfortable silence before he spoke again. When he did, his voice was low and uncertain. Almost embarrassed.

'I realised today...I'm not ready to die just yet. Thank you for helping me.'

Nora's grin lit up her face like the sun coming out from behind a cloud. It was her old one. The one she used to spread around, easy as butter.

'No worries! Just doing my job.'

Maurice turned his head back towards the window, but not before she saw the corner of his mouth turn slightly upwards.

She went home that day feeling lighter. Lighter than she'd felt for about a hundred years.

Back in the dark ages, Helen Auld did a Bachelor of Arts and then worked in various fields totally unrelated to her studies. Her work has given her a wealth of life experiences which she now mines for Australian fictional stories like the one you've just read. She hopes you enjoyed it!

Chapter 37

Miss Tilly's Story

by AL Maze

The gumdrops mocked her. A colourful hard-boiled sweet that lay all quiet and demure on the table. Splashed in morning sun, their dulled surfaces refused to shine.

Tilly didn't care. She knew it was a trick. A clever ploy to get her to eat them but she would never do that. She'd promised him. Whoever *he* was. She tucked loose strands of honey blonde hair behind her ear.

'Hey!' she yelled to the guy in the white nurse's uniform sitting at the desk across the room. 'Hey you!'

Ben, the recreational room attendant, looked up and smiled. Getting up, he came to stand beside the pretty Miss Matilda McArthur.

At twenty-three, she was the youngest patient of The Parramatta Psychiatric Care Home for Women – a small private facility for those suffering from long-term mental illness.

'Miss Tilly, what can I do for you?'

The smell of antiseptic was strong in the pale green room. Scattered about were other chairs and tables. There weren't many patients there. They were full of quiet whispers or incoherent mumbles. Some sat and stared, others wandered aimlessly. If you screamed in this room, you were taken away.

Tilly ignored them. They were strange and she couldn't remember their names. She never remembered anyone's name, including her own. There was a lot she didn't remember.

'What colour's the sky?' Tilly asked.

Ben glanced out the high, arched window. Gardens and crisp green lawn rolled down to the bordering sandstone wall. The home had been built thirty years ago, in 1901, a grand old colonial on top of a high hill looking over Parramatta.

He smiled. 'It's blue, like your eyes.'

She pointed to the two piles of sweets. Ten in each pile, each sweet no larger than a fingernail. One pile was blood red, the other a dark blue.

'Which one is blue?'

He pointed to a pile. 'These, they're blue.'

'Blue? His eyes are blue, too.'

'Whose eyes?'

But her face was blank.

Sighing, he made his way back to his desk. The young lass was always coming out with strange things about someone they didn't know. A sure sign of the mentally ill.

Tilly's gaze turned to the strange markings on her arms. One wrist curled around on itself like a claw. She liked that wrist. It was bent like her mind. Scars ran all along both forearms. The skin was puckered, shiny smooth. She poked at one with a neatly trimmed fingernail, wondering how they got there.

'Tilly?' A nurse touched her shoulder. 'Your brother, Rick, is here to see you.' She motioned a couple over. 'Do you remember Rick and Elle? They were here a couple of days ago. They brought you the gumdrops.'

Matilda smiled blankly at them. 'What colour's the sky?'

'It's blue today,' the girl said as she sat down in the chair across the table.

'Which one's blue?'

Elle pointed to the same pile Ben had earlier. 'This one.'

Rick took the chair next to his wife and laid his black Fedora hat aside, exhaling heavily. Elle took her husband's hand in hers.

Tilly stared at their clasped hands. It was familiar, but she didn't know why. She knew someone else had held her hand like that once, but *who* and *when?*

'You two look very nice together. Were you born attached like that?'

Rick held in a laugh and even Elle had a hard time stifling a giggle. They knew that Tilly didn't take well to being laughed at.

Elle smiled patiently. 'Rick and I chose to be together. We're in love, and when two people are in love they like to be together. We got married yesterday.'

Tilly flinched. 'What colour's the sky?'

'It's blue,' Elle answered.

'Blue, like his eyes. His heart won't beat until I'm there.'

'Whose heart?' Elle asked, but Tilly just stared out of the window.

Rick's jaw tightened and he shook his head. 'I can't believe she still plays this game. She and John used to ask each other the colour of the sky all the time. Tilly?'

Tilly's nose wrinkled. She turned from the window where she'd been looking for the man in her dreams. The one they kept trying to tell her was dead. If he was dead, her heart would no longer beat. *Foolish people.*

'John is dead,' Rick stated. 'He died in that last robbery you and Dad pulled off.'

Scooping up the sweets in her good hand, she threw them at the funny man.

Rick jerked backwards. The sweets hit him in the chest and scattered; some struck Elle, but most fell to the floor with a clatter. 'Tilly! What did you do that for?'

Elle laughed as she picked up the sweets. 'I think you made her angry.'

Rick gave her a quizzical look as he removed the sweets from his clothes. 'How?'

'Well, she might not remember John or the fact that he's dead, but I think she still feels him.' Elle put the sweets on the table. 'It's like if you died, I'd always carry you in my heart, so maybe Tilly does too.'

Tilly stared at them, her hands folded neatly. 'What colour's the sky?'

'Blue,' Rick replied and dumped the rest of the sweets down. He pinched the bridge of his nose and closed his eyes as he counted to three. 'This is a waste of time. Let's go.'

'Blue,' Tilly repeated.

'Yeah, blue...Ben?' Rick motioned the room attendant over.

'Morning folks, how can I help?'

Rick took a folded cheque from the pocket of his double-breasted pinstripe suit. 'Do I give this to Matron to deposit?'

'My heart would not beat if he was dead,' Tilly interrupted.

Ben chuckled and patted her shoulder. 'I know.' He opened the cheque and let out a low whistle. 'Now that's a lot of zeros. I take it the case settled?'

Rick nodded and rubbed the back of his neck. 'Yeah, Tilly was exonerated from all charges due to her state of mind. The surgeon pleaded guilty and the judge ordered compensation be paid. But only part of that is from the surgeon – the rest is from the jewellery store.'

Ben's eyebrows rose. 'J. R. Dalgety and Sons?'

J.R. Dalgety and Sons were established in 1851 – an exclusive jewellery store catering to Sydney's elite.

'Yep. Old Mr. Dalgety has a niece Tilly's age. When he heard what happened during the robbery, the surgery going wrong and her becoming a resident here, he wanted to pay for her care. My sister is a very wealthy woman. Let's hope our greedy mother doesn't get her hands on it. She was in court when the judge awarded compensation.'

'Rick,' Elle murmured. 'I'm sure Evelyn wouldn't do that.'

Rick looked at her but said nothing. Elle turned away with a sigh.

Ben nodded. 'Well, I'm glad for Miss Tilly's sake and, don't worry, Matron will keep an eye on her.'

Tilly looked up at him. 'Who are you?'

'My name's Ben, Miss Tilly.' He winked at Rick and Elle. 'If it's any consolation, she's happy with her gumdrops.'

Rick sat up and patted down his pockets. From inside his jacket, he drew out a packet. 'I almost forgot. Here you go, Tills, these are for you.' He pressed the packet into her hand, holding it before leaning across and kissing her ear, whispering. 'You can't eat these, they're special.'

Giggling, she wiped her ear on her shoulder and tore the packet open, tipping it up. Ten green and four slightly larger cloudy sweets spilled out across the table. She clapped her hands, eye's shining. 'Lemonade.' She mixed them in with the blue and red ones.

Rick smiled, feeling some of the tension ease. He liked seeing his sister happy. 'Yes, Tills, Lemonade. The rarest of rare.' He leaned back in his chair. 'Dad always bought her gumdrops when she was little. Mum used to get so mad at him; she never liked sweets. Reckoned they spoiled a girl.'

Elle smiled. 'I haven't heard of Lemonade gumdrops, and these are so oddly shaped too. They look like coloured-glass rocks.'

Rick stared across the room at a resident. He watched her unpack feathers from a box, feel each one, put them back in the box and then start again. His knee bounced. 'That's what they look like after all the powdered sugar has been rubbed off. Tills plays with them so much she polishes them.'

'Like precious gems,' Elle laughed. 'I always thought gumdrops were round.'

Rick shrugged and ran a hand down the leg of his suit pants. 'Maybe they're trying a new shape.' He collected his hat. 'We should get going if we're going to make the train, love.'

Ben chuckled. 'So, the police never found the uncut gems they stole?'

Carl MacArthur, Tilly's father, had run a successful jewel heist gang for fifteen years. His daughter was amongst them.

'No. The stones were stolen in their natural state so they're easy to move. All you do is cut them and they've changed shape and form. If you get two or three smaller stones from the one you can split them up, which makes them impossible to identify. Dad excelled himself this time.'

'Wasn't Miss Tilly engaged to one of your dad's gang?' Ben asked.

Rick swallowed and nodded. 'Yeah, John. Dad's right-hand man. Dad was supposed to retire after the last heist and let John and Tilly take over.' He snorted softly. 'I remember the day I brought John home from university. Tills told me straight up she was going to marry him. I asked her how she knew, and she replied, *my heart knows.*'

He thought of his father lying dead in the alley behind the store. Three bullet wounds to his chest, John beside him. The police had gone, and he'd waited for the undertaker. Crouching down next to his father's body, he'd bowed his head to say goodbye. Something had scraped across the cobblestones. The bloodied hand pushed a dark pouch towards him. 'For Tilly.' John croaked, before drawing his last shuddering breath.

Rick could still feel that velvet pouch, heavy and rattling with the uncut gems inside. The soft fabric, sticky; the metallic scent of blood. For two years he'd kept them hidden and no one knew. He smiled to himself.

'With John around there was no keeping Tilly in school nor out of the thieving business. She quit at fourteen and joined the gang. Dad was furious but he could never say no to his Tilly. I was supposed to join too, but decided to continue with university.'

'What happened the night of the robbery, Rick?' Elle asked quietly. 'You've never told me.'

Rick let out a long sigh. 'Breaking into the store, Dad and John cracked the safe. Tilly went looking for her engagement ring, only she couldn't decide. John smashed the glass cases and told her to take them all. But then she cut her wrists and severed a tendon. That's why her wrist is curled. The surgeon never reattached it properly.

'John rang me and asked me to come get her. *Get her to a hospital quick*, he said. But when I left, I heard Mum on the phone talking to the police. She and Dad had argued earlier that night, and she was reporting the robbery. They'd been after Dad for years. The funny thing was Dad's heists were for her. Mum loves her fancy cars, furs, jewels, the lavish house, the best furniture money could buy. She wanted it all, so Dad stole for her.'

'I drove down to the store and warned them, then took Tilly to the hospital. When she was taken into surgery, I went back to see if they'd gotten away. As I got closer, I heard the gunshots. Dad and John were dead, the other three gang members escaped. They were caught a month later.'

Rick shrugged. 'You know the rest. The uncut stones were never found, and Tilly was given too much nitrous oxide when they operated, which caused the brain damage.'

Elle sniffed dabbing at her eyes with a handkerchief. 'That's so sad. She's so young.'

Rick patted her hand. 'I know, love.' He sighed and gave his sister an affectionate smile. 'Sometimes I wish there was more I could have done for her.'

He glanced at his watch. 'We'll need to hurry to make that train.'

Elle got to her feet, gently touching Tilly's shoulder. 'Tilly, we're going now.'

'Going?'

'We'll come back and see you next week.'

Rick donned his hat and stood. 'Don't eat all those gumdrops at once, Tills, they're the special ones.' He winked at her. He guided Elle around the tables and chairs. Some of the other patients stared.

'Rick?' Tilly's voice suddenly rang out loudly.

He whirled around and she was there behind him. They hadn't heard her approach.

She reached out and cradled his cheek. 'Thank you, and you did your best.' She kissed two fingers and placed them on his lips. 'Dad would be pleased.'

Before he could say or do anything, she walked back to her table and sat down, once more staring out of the window.

Tilly's days were simple and spent in blessed ignorance. In the morning, nurses helped her dress and gave her breakfast, then she'd sit at the table near the window in the large sunny room watching for the man in her dreams. The one who made her heart feel strange. The one who's name she couldn't remember.

Today she sat swirling the sweets around on the table, listening to them click together, smiling, humming a tune. It stopped when Ben appeared beside her, a grave look to his face.

'Miss Tilly, you have some visitors.'

She looked up at him. 'What colour's the sky?'

'It's blue, Miss Tilly, and you need to come with me to the conference room.'

Tilly's hand slammed down over her sweets. 'No, gumdrops!'

Ben picked up an empty packet from the floor. 'Let's put them in here, then you can take them with you.'

Tilly smiled as Ben scooped sweets into the packet. He was surprised they were warm, but not sticky. 'Here, Miss Tilly. What flavours are they?'

She snatched the packet from him, clasping it tight. 'Blueberry, raspberry, lemonade and lime.'

Ben shook his head; the girl didn't know where she was and yet she knew those Gumdrop flavours.

'What colour's the sky?'

'Blue,' Ben replied automatically, as he guided her from the room.

'Like his eyes.'

Ben led her from the recreational room and along a dim hallway lined with closed doors. Tilly knew many strange people lay behind the doors and she moved in closer to Ben, almost tripping on the back of his heels. It was icy cold and a faint cloying scent of evil wrapped around her. Distant screams, agonising howls, and rantings of the insane greeted Tilly's ears. She shivered. She wasn't familiar with this part of the hospital.

Reaching a set of green double doors, Ben unlocked one and led her through into the brightly lit foyer. They made their way past the brocade settee and paintings of nurses attending smiling patients, arriving in the doorway of the conference room. This was where a patient either left or began their stay at The Parramatta Psychiatric Care Home for Women.

Evelyn MacArthur stood in the wood-panelled room with its big table, dressed in the latest fashion of maroon suit and fur stole. A matching pillbox hat, complete with feathers and diamond pin, sat atop the blonde hair that matched her daughter's. Two diamond bracelets peeked from beneath her gloves. A cloud of the newly released Chanel No. 5 saturated the air.

Tilly stopped. Her heart raced and she clutched the packet of gumdrops tighter. As she tried to back away, Ben's grip on her arm halted her progress. Three sets of eyes stared at her, but only one pair made her tremble with the power of an earthquake. Small noises emitted from her lips.

'Matilda,' Matron stood and took Tilly's hand. 'Come and sit down.'

Tilly flinched. 'I don't like that name. Is that my name?'

'Yes, Matilda, it is.' Matron led her to a chair.

Tilly's jaw clenched and she stared at the weird lady dressed in blood. An image came to mind of her staked to the ground and left in the sun for the birds to eat.

'You're ugly,' Tilly sneered. 'He won't come now, so you need to die.'

'Matilda, that's enough.' Matron patted her hand.

'I'm sorry, Mrs MacArthur, she's not normally this difficult. We all thought she was having a good day.'

Evelyn gave a single nod. 'It's alright and it's Mrs Rawson now... Matilda, honey, I'm your mother and this is your new father, Joseph.' She indicated a dark-haired man with a pencil-thin moustache sitting silently beside her. 'We've come to take you home.'

'No. You don't know the colour of the sky.'

Evelyn's hand rose and played with the necklace at her throat. Her eyes narrowed. 'The colour of the sky?'

Tilly sat tall, pulling her shoulders back. 'Only he knows the colour of the sky.'

Evelyn gave her a quizzical look until her face hardened with recognition. 'Not this silly game again.' She leaned forward in her chair. 'John is dead, Matilda.' Her voice was cold. 'The police shot him.'

'No! You lie. I don't feel it *here*!' She slammed a fist against where her heart lay, spittle flying from her lips.

It wasn't empty. It wasn't. He was still there.

A memory caught. Her eyes blinked. 'You killed my father! Rick heard you on the phone to the police. You wanted us all dead.'

Evelyn blanched.

But as fast as the memory came it was gone and Tilly fell back against her chair. She gripped the gumdrops to her chest, knuckles white. 'What colour's the sky?'

'No, Matilda, the police killed your father, and John. Honestly, I don't know where you get this nonsense from.'

'What colour's the sky?' Tilly's voice rose.

'It's blue, Matilda.' Matron laid a hand on her arm. 'Mrs. Rawson, Matilda has irreversible brain damage, which unfortunately hinders her ability to think normally. That is why she is here.'

'She is here because my son put her here.'

'The doctors put her here, Mrs. Rawson, and you will need their permission to take her from our care.'

Evelyn snatched up a piece of paper that lay on the table in front of her. 'Good thing I have it then.' She handed the paper over with a flourish. 'And I also have Power of Attorney to handle Matilda's assets. All declared by reason of insanity.' She smirked.

Matron settled her glasses on her nose and perused both documents. Her heart sank. Evelyn Rawson was right; she had the doctor's permission and Power of Attorney. Everything was now out of her control. 'Very well then. However, considering how upset Matilda is, I'm going to recommend against her removal from this facility.'

Evelyn's jaw set. 'She is my daughter, and I will be taking her home. Please see to it that the paperwork is in order and that she will be ready to leave by ten tomorrow morning. A car will collect her then.'

The woman walked around the table and stopped beside Tilly, who shrunk back against the chair. 'And she's not to have any more sweets.' Evelyn swiped the packet of gumdrops from Tilly's hand.

Something dark boiled inside Tilly, burning hotter and hotter. Her nostrils flared and she screamed, launching herself at the strange woman. 'No! They're his!'

Evelyn fell backwards against a chair, knocking it over. Her heel caught. Tilly scrabbled for the packets of gumdrops as they tumbled to the floor. 'He won't come if they're gone!' She sunk her teeth into Evelyn's wrist.

Evelyn screamed and dropped the packet. Tilly pounced like a mouse on cake crumbs, scooping it up, before scrambling backwards into a corner. Drawing her knees up to her chest, she buried the sweets deep in her lap where no one could see them. She started to sob.

Joseph rushed to his wife's side. 'Darling? Darling, are you alright?' As he helped her up, the elegant hat hung down the back of her head, barely held by the pin.

'She bit me! That heathen bit me. What sort of place are you running here?' Evelyn ranted, snatching the handkerchief from Joseph's hand, and holding it to her bleeding wrist.

'I'm quite sure Matilda did not mean it, Mrs. Rawson. You must understand that with illnesses like these, patients can get a little violent, especially when threatened.'

Evelyn scoffed. 'I did *not* threaten her.'

She re-secured her hat and picked up a leather kidskin bag. 'Let's hope she is much better behaved tomorrow, or I will lock her up.'

Evelyn swept from the room, followed by Joseph.

'He's not dead,' Tilly whispered, rocking back and forth. 'I hold his heart.' She looked up. 'He can't die without his heart.' Strange water streamed down her cheeks, dripping from her chin, splashing the front of her dress.

'What colour's the sky? What colour's the sky?' Her voice was small and broken.

Eleven o'clock that night...

'It's time.'

'What's happened?'

'Evelyn has shown up and is taking Tilly away tomorrow morning. She also has Power of Attorney. The doctors have agreed to Tilly's release. She can't stay in the home a moment longer. Not unless I declare her insane and then she'll be locked up permanently.'

'Rick?'

'He's on his honeymoon.'

'The stones?'

'She has them. The court case settled last week, and she was cleared of all charges. It's safe now for both of you.'

'Thank God. I can't go a minute longer without her.'

There was a different feeling in the air the next day. It was dark and dismal. Two nurses were in her room, touching things. She didn't understand what they were doing or why, and she clutched the packet of gumdrops close once more. Something bad was coming and she didn't like it.

The recreation room was full. Rain poured down and the wind howled, so no one could go outside. It was noisy and the sound bounced through her head and upset her thoughts. Growing more restless by the minute, Tilly snapped and snarled at anyone who passed by. Already, three of the nurses had been tripped intentionally. To the staff, it was one of Miss Tilly's bad days.

Tired and cranky, Tilly screamed, 'I don't like it!' Two of the residents started to cry. Then a calmness came over her; her heart started to swell. *Look over there*, it said, *look over there*.

She turned; it was him. The man whose heart she held in her hands. The man who haunted her dreams. The one who wasn't dead. The one her heart had told her would come back. She couldn't remember his name, but that didn't stop her flying across the room like her feet had grown wings.

John held his arms out to her. She ran into them, and they closed about her tightly. 'Hello beautiful,' he whispered in her ear.

Matilda burst into tears. Mysterious water leaked from her eyes again! Strange sounds erupted from her throat, choking her breath, but he held her close. His voice was a sea of soothing whispers and warmth.

'You didn't forget me.'

'I could never forget you. Did you forget me?'

'Yes.'

John laughed. 'Best news I've heard all day.'

'What's colour's the sky?'

John looked at her. 'Aquamarine and I'm taking you home.' He wrapped his good arm around her.

His left shoulder and arm were useless, thanks to the bullet on the night of the robbery. He'd been lucky; the undertaker declared him dead–until he came to and sat up. Gave the poor guy the fright of his life.

Escaping the morgue, he'd fled to his sister's place. As Matron in charge at The Parramatta Psychiatric Care Home for Women, she'd nursed him back to health. When he'd fully recovered, they got Tilly moved from the state mental hospital into her care.

Tilly's heart soared. She'd trusted it and it hadn't let her down. She patted her pocket. 'I have the gumdrops and I didn't eat *one*.'

AL Maze is the pen name of an Australian writer who lives in Sydney with her husband, two older girls and a cheeky parrot who likes to laugh at her. She has been writing fiction since she was fifteen and has dabbled in sagas and romance. She is currently working her way through a military romance novel.

Chapter 38

Burn

by Carolyn Dunn

Filling in the sandy soil around the roots of the gangly banksia seedling, I sat back on my heels for a moment and admired the contrast of the young green leaves against the ash-covered soil of its new home. All that goodness released to the roots by the gentle licks of fire. The smoke wafted around me, and I looked over to the motley crew that had come together to shepherd the fire through the beautiful bush that covered most of our coastal club land. After a day working together, I'd trust these people with my life. What a precious day.

Picking up my rake, I returned to the fireground. Raking around the old logs now home to small marsupials and lizards, I smiled at the way I tended the earth. What had once felt like a beautiful piece of untouched banksia forest now felt like a garden I was tending for future generations. Gentle laughs and quiet conversations burbled all around, like water over stones. We were tired and covered in ash, but we were very much alive to our task and enthralled by the flames we monitored.

Beside me, Andy, our Indigenous coordinator, was quietly prodding his trainees to take care of the flames moving towards the base of the big blackbutt trunk in front of them.

'See the way it's starting to smoke above the line of fire? Just scrape away the bark there. That's it.'

Nick, the more confident of the three, rubbed away the flames at the base of the tree as the other two watched on.

'Alice, can you bring that rake over here? I think we could clear this patch away from the flames of that burrawang. That's it. No need to clear too much, just to stop it licking back over to the blackbutt trunk.'

His tone was like a father with his sleeping babies. Such gentle calmness. I took the rake over to where he was gesturing and began to pull back the leaves. Over the past year I'd come to cherish our encounters. The calmness he instilled in his cultural burn practice seemed to spill over into all of his interactions, leaving me feeling rejuvenated afterwards.

It had taken three years of planning and back and forth between the club committee, the local Elders and the fire service to get to this day. Peter, our diligent committee member had tirelessly worked at the conversation between the three parties, bringing together their different needs and quelling competing worries. Like Andy, he'd shown up to each meeting, smiling and curious and willing to meet the needs of others at least part way.

In the end they'd managed to reach agreement on the details, but it was the need for a date on which to plan their fire that had threatened to bring their hard work undone. The committee and fire service came to the slow realisation that what the Elders had tried to tell them all along had been true – the land would decide when the day to burn the patch had arrived, not the calendar.

And, finally, that day arrived.

We'd been at it for hours, but time had moved so quickly. Looking back over the day, one might imagine it had been organised down to the tiniest detail with all the planning culminating in exactly the burn we'd planned. 8am start, three fire grounds, done by five. But the shape of the burns and their number had changed as the conditions of the day changed, and the full effect of the fuel load on the ground was observed. As the fire interacted with the land, we moved along with it, curating as best we could.

For the Indigenous people who were overseeing this burn, I knew it was entirely different. Their measures for the day were set against observations that were ages old, a very different framing for planning and outcomes.

Until today, we had only lit small patches with Andy, where he could demonstrate the humid warmth of the soil as the fire passed over the vegetation above, and the way the insects and small lizards scurried out of its path. We had also spent time walking around with Andy learning about the different types of country on our property and the cycles of plant life and weather that dictated when and how to burn. He was so generous with his knowledge and humbly acknowledged at every point what the Elders had generously shared with him.

In contrast, our club's understanding used a different framework of observation and in some aspects, it was rudimentary. Finally coming together today, it felt like we'd moved to the next level, learning the next steps by watching and following the lead set by the actions of Andy and the Elders.

Strangely, my nervous excitement–building as we'd driven down to the burn at dawn–quickly dissipated once the fire was lit. I'd had no understanding of how slowly we'd walk beside the passage of the flames, how quietly the fire would burn. In place of my anticipation, a calm contemplation settled, and a trusted space for questions that bubbled up in me throughout the day.

Watching Andy with Les and Owen, the Elders, I noticed they'd spread out across the land they were walking through, quietly taking in aspects of note, and then at other points, coming together to quietly swap notes before returning to the fire ground and weaving back into the rest of the group. No loud orders, no stepping out of a plan, just *being* and *doing*.

Les and Owen had visited with us once for an introduction to cultural burns, and it was there that I'd first witnessed the quiet respect they engendered from everyone, from the young trainee

Indigenous rangers, to the club and Rural Fire Service members alike. They'd welcomed our earnest questions with the perfect mix of information and light-hearted ribbing, humouring our need to learn and apply new skills. The simple lunch they'd brought to share was both unexpected and a lesson in collaboration beginning with simple gestures and open hearts. Curiously, they embodied the latest in management techniques without the bureaucratic lingo and colossal fees that often accompany the skillset.

The breeze slowly came up from the ocean below the headland as we moved through the day, as conversations ebbed and flowed. The final fireground contained hot burning burrawangs under oldman banksias and to our childlike surprise, the banksia cones lit up like Christmas candles as the hot flames passed beneath them. As the banksia cones brightly burned before dropping to the ground, the hot flames from a burrawang momentarily whipped into a crescendo and the air between me and the other side of the fireground began to ripple.

For a moment I was in a car hurtling up the side of a mountain, being stalked by the terrible roaring dragon lurking below. It was the day before New Year's Eve, two years ago, and I was leaving our coastal retreat with my family, as softly furled burnt fern fronds had begun to rain down on us from the mountains above. As we reached the top of the mountain and looked back over the chaos below, we noticed another dragon lurking above, a massive pyrocumulus cloud forming overhead.

The nightmare had slowly built throughout that summer, as dragons moved up and down the eastern and southern seaboards, slowly joining forces over an ever-increasing landmass. By the time we were smelling burnt animals on the evening easterly breezes, it had begun to feel like the end of days had truly come. Everyone I knew had stopped listening to the politicians and instead started daily monitoring the air quality in their homes and workplaces.

The firechiefs past and present became our saviours, talking us through the daily fire strategies, helping us to feel like someone was in charge, and putting voice to our collective outrage that our governments had no plans to turn this climate-induced disaster around for future generations, let alone to buy in the equipment required to have any hope of saving the precious forests and homes that were igniting all around. The realisation that we, the humans, were not in charge, and never had been, had come hard and fast to me and to everyone I held dear.

In the months after that summer finally ended, the drought and fire-ravaged country felt the cool trickling of rain. But I raged inside at my powerlessness to do anything about anything. Knowing others felt as I did provided no relief. Collectively our powerlessness was magnified in the echo chambers of the media, and my anger built.

It kept raining, and the trickles of water turned to floods as the torrents washed the dead trees and ash into the rivers and out to the sea. As fear of fire turned to fear of floods, we stopped measuring our air quality and, slowly, life kept going on and a sense of new normal descended.

But it was not the same world anymore. I could no longer look at a sunset and carelessly breathe in its beauty. Or feel an evening breeze without bracing myself for the smell of forest fire. Or listen to a magpie morning chorus without remembering the way the birds had taken refuge in my deciduous garden trees that summer, beaks open panting, all types sheltering together along the branches. Now I worried they might not live through next summer's crisis.

The images receded as the fanning flames of the burrawang died down, and I was back on the edge of the fire ground again. I caught Andy's eye momentarily and sensed he had seen into my moment of fear. He gently smiled at me before touching a lighted piece of bracken to the last unburnt corner of the patch.

Andy had spoken of how the Elders called the ground we were on Healing Country; that this was where their people came to heal and talk and nourish themselves and those around them. Watching the last flames from the burrawang build before slowly dying down, I felt something like sadness that the fire was almost out, and the day almost over. For a moment, I couldn't quite pinpoint why. This burn had been such a success, and the beginning of what we hoped would be many more as we worked our way across the large property.

I stood with my sadness, curious about its cause, and I realised I'd witnessed the power of fire as a healing tool. I wanted to unleash it now, across the country into every corner of darkness. It was a tool we needed to sit with for a while, get its measure, and fit it into the fabric of what we were making on this beautiful piece of land.

Today had opened up a space to ask and learn and watch and feel and trust. Together we'd worked and moved with something that wasn't ours to control, rather to gently shape and bend with as it moved around us.

How liberating not to control. After that summer of no control, I would have guessed the last thing I wanted was to make room for the thing that I worried might be the end of us. But, just in that moment, it seemed exactly what we needed.

Carolyn Dunn is an Australian writer with a professional background in public health and education policy. She and her partner live in Canberra and share three kids and one grandchild. Her writing is inspired by her love of people, exploring landscapes, cooking delicious food, gardening and reading.

Chapter 39

This Too Shall Pass

by Trisha Helbers

2007

Who was it that coined the term 'bittersweet'? Whoever it was, they weren't talking about chocolate. They were talking about love. About the exquisite agony of complete, all-consuming love. Love so overwhelming that it fuses conflicting emotions: bliss with grief, joy with sorrow.

They were describing the state of my heart since you were born. Since I became a mother.

I thought my heart was full of love before you came. I have felt, have known, have given and received, abundant love – all kinds of love. But this? This bright, joyous, watchful anxiety... This arms-out-wide-encircle-the-world warmth; shut-us-away-keep-us-safe fear...This heart-and-head-feel-my-way uncertain sureness...This filling me, draining me, teaching me, tiring me, opening-me-up and smalling-me-down...All this in the blue of your eyes, the flutter of your pulse, the tight grip of your little fist on my index finger...

When a friend tells me now that they are expecting a baby, my heart both leaps and lurches for them. Yes, they may anticipate the nights of broken sleep, the changes to their career, the new demands on their budget and the toys that will litter their floor. They might lather themselves in cocoa-butter as they anticipate stretchmarks, tears, veins and stitches. And, as I did, they might imagine changes taking place, deep inside, as they learn to respond to and fulfil another, utterly dependent, person's needs.

But until they look into the eyes of their own newborn baby, they will not imagine the massive tear that will simultaneously halve and double them. Bliss and grief, joy and sorrow: every emotion forever with a shadow; every feeling borne as a conjoined twin.

They will learn that time becomes a cheat, the clock and the calendar no longer keeping pace. Minutes stretch and bulge, fat and full–crammed with small things that take forever. Long nights follow long days of long hours. But whole months are suddenly spent and gone. Past. And these hands that listened through my skin to your secret stirrings are now steadying you as you stand.

I look at your fat little knees, the only rough skin on your perfect, chubby, alabaster body. You have been slow to walk, crawling instead, fast and boisterous over our floor, wearing holes in your pants.

I drink in every detail of you: the tips of your eyelashes, the pores of your skin. Somewhere deep in my brain I know this little cherub on my lap will become a man. This soft down on your arms will turn coarse and manly. Your white skin will go brown. You'll get big, stinky, hairy feet. You'll play sport and get bruises and might chip a tooth or even break an arm. And that's as it should be.

You'll make friends and share secrets. You'll have arguments. And you'll fall in love. Your heart might get broken. You might get a tattoo. And you'll probably drive too fast, work too hard, travel too far…and that's all as it should be.

It's as it should be and it's impossible. Yes, I want it all for you. I want you to walk and run and fall and get up and bruise and heal and trust and try and laugh and grow and explore and learn and love. But, oh, I want you to stay exactly as you are, with your warm weight on my lap and the sweet softness of your hair against my lips forever and forever and forever.

Oh, sweet darling, stay just like this my darling Little Little and let me hold you to me and keep you small and safe.

I wash and fold and pack away your too-small clothes: 000s, 00s, 0s, 1s... I am bustling and busy, but I stop. Still. I hold your clothes against my face and breathe them in. Then I fold and gently pack away my Little Little baby. I fill your cupboards with new, size two clothes for my beautiful, big, strong toddler. My Little Big Boy.

You took six steps towards your dad last night and we, all three, laughed and clapped. Your plump little body is slimming and you can reach the kitchen benches. You say a new word each day–sometimes two. Ball, car, cheese, bikky, daddy... One day you'll say 'I love you, Mummy.' One day you'll say 'I've got to go now.'

And that's as it should be.

This too shall pass. My mantra makes the unbearable bearable. It makes the sweet bittersweet. And it compels me to linger. To hold each moment still, even as I let go to welcome the next.

And there it is, my Darling Little. I will celebrate every one of your precious achievements, big and small. I will carry you until you can walk. Then I will hold your hand to steady you, and be ready to catch you when you fall. I will brush off your knees and say 'uppaday' when you stumble, and I will hold you as tight as tight and dry your tears when you fall hard. Then I will steady you and help you to try again.

And one day, as I walk beside you, you will shrug my hand away and I will step a little to the side. I will be proud of my empty (ever-ready) hand as I watch you make your own way. You will grow taller and you will run and play and climb, as you must. Then I will walk behind you–and return, perhaps, to some of my own paths. And, one day, I will need to stand still in my doorway and be content to blow you kisses as you walk away.

And I will be full of joy for you. It will be a bittersweet day, as all my days are now. Now that I am a mother.

2023

I know it was me who wrote that, back in 2007. I know that you–you tall, handsome, blue-eyed, curly-haired man-boy–full of testosterone and teenage angst and humour and impatience and inexperience and concerns and confidence–were that darling chubby nugget of silky-skinned toddler that I attempted to freeze-dry, then, for my future self. Knowing you would grow on past each moment. Hoping you would make it through and that we would still be oh-so-close.

I know it was me. I know it was you.

I know I baked and decorated all those birthday cakes–wobbly racing cars and trains to start with, and later, as work pinched my time ever tighter, simple number cakes plastered in chocolate icing and lollies. I know I arranged all those birthday parties–the gym party for all the Reception kids. The one with the hired giant bouncy castle that swallowed our whole backyard. The bowling one. And the everyone-in-the-family-with-winter-birthdays parties with shared crockpots and warm, noisy laughter; you and your cousins and the neighbours' kids playing endless loops of chasey though our passage with two successive dogs barking with crazy joy.

I know I sat with all those teachers discussing your progress–darling Rosie, terrible Ms M, gorgeous Miss Hammond (who came to see you shine this year in your Year 11 play, because you were always her favourite and she is our angel). I know I attended all those sports days, assemblies and end-of-year concerts. I know those tea-towels and windcheaters printed with fat-bodied stick figures with wonky eyes and crooked birds' legs–always with one grossly swollen foot–were drawn by you and your classmates as you progressed through primary school.

I know you're on your fifth basketball tunic now, and that the first one came down to your knees, as they always do on the littlies. I was there when you first grabbed that giant orange ball with your small hands and triumphantly dribbled it to the impossibly high hoop at the wrong end of the court. I remember meeting your eyes, and shooting you a shruggy little winky oops. I am here now, every Saturday, as you skilfully steal and weave and dodge and intercept and shoot–and point and nod, sending your teammates secret signals. I'm with you, afterwards in the car, as you dissect the game and explain all the ways in which the team needs to lift.

I saw your Dad hold you high to put the star on the Christmas tree. I saw you drag the step ladder over to reach up and do it yourself. I'll see you, this year, drop it to its top from your own lofty height.

I saw your face, alive with wonder and excitement, when I first turned your baby capsule around to face the front of the car, and you could see, for the first time, where we were going. I see your face, now, as we fit the L plates and you take the wheel, complaining and frustrated that so many of your mates already have their Ps. I'll see you, all too soon, waving as you drive away on your own.

I see myself, at your age, already snogging boys at parties. Are you already snogging girls?

I watched the Wiggles documentary last week. On my own on a quiet Saturday night–you off at a party, your Dad living in another house now. I almost drowned in my own nostalgia. There you were again–that toddler with fists full of Hot Wheels cars, who first named the primary colours as 'An-a-nee', 'Muwway', 'Eff', 'Geg', 'Dor-a-tee', 'Wags-tha-dog' and 'Henry'.

I know that was me. I know that was you. I know all those years have passed (minute-by-minute, day-by-day, week-by-week) as they should, as I knew they would. But, my darling, how are we here already? Already? Already!

Yes, you have big hairy stinky feet now. Stinky socks. Stinky shoes. A stinky room. No tattoos yet. So many bumps and bruises. Teeth intact. Heart already wounded. Proceeding now with romantic caution. (Probably not snogging girls, because, for you, it won't happen until the right girl, in the right moment. Darling you.)

And me? Yes, I have stepped to the side. Back to some old paths, and forging new ones. I'm planning my first holiday that may not include you–because holidays with just mum? Yeah-nah-prob'ly-not. Because you're almost eighteen and you're gaming in your room with the door shut and firing off texts and talking through your headphones to your mates. (Too much casual swearing, but still with sudden fits of giggles that waft through the gap under the door and lift my heart.)

I watched every episode of *Stranger Things* (spiders and bent limbs and distorted clocks and creepy music just before bedtime every night for weeks) at your request–your generous invitation. Just to sit and share those hours with you.

I'm proud of all you're achieving, of all the glimpses you let me see of you on your path with your friends and your interests and talents and choices. I'm watching you go. Helping you go.

I'm so grateful that it's all happened, and that you and I still laugh so easily together. That, despite the endless negotiations over homework and housework and the odd-slammed door, you still lurk behind my pantry door to scare me, mischievous, just so we can share a giggling fit. That we still play surprise attack with rolled up sock balls. That you still hug me, and let me hug you (one-millionth of the number of times in a single day that I want to hug you). Yep, I'm that mum, but I hold back, because, you know–I read the room.

Here I am, somehow, at the tail-end of 2023.

Time is still a cheat. (How *are* we here, already? Already!) My feelings are still drenched in sunlight and shadow. Double-edged, over-analysed, raw and carefully contained.

I still want it all for you–the best of the full magic catastrophe of living a good life. Be brave, Kiddo. Be careful. *Oh–stay safe! Stay here.* But go. Grow. Be. As you should. As you must.

This *too*. This *too* shall pass.

You laugh at me. At how I tear up in movies. Teasing me with your stinky-boy-affection.

You won't know, Kiddo. You can't. Not yet. You won't feel all the bittersweet, hot-teared anguish and heart-bursting joyful beauty of it all until it happens to you. Until you become a father.

Until then, or until whatever else you become, I'm here. Was. Am. Will be.

The time-traveller: Back and forth I go, to then and now and beyond. Riding these endless and finite loops of moments and minutes and memories with you.

Your cheerleader. Your pain-in-the-bum nagger. Your friend. Your mother.

Trisha Helbers was first published at age eight – a poem in the *Sunday Mail's Possum Pages*. In Year 7, she co-edited her school's quarterly magazine, setting the course (via a stint in children's libraries) towards journalism, feature writing and editing. When she's not writing corporate guff, or out walking and dancing, she's plotting the best-sellers that will make her millions and allow her to write more of her own stuff.

Chapter 40

Out on a Limb

by Mary Howley

'Any chocolates worth eating?' Dad is in the back seat, rummaging through a paper bag.

Mum is in the front of the rental truck, sitting next to me. Her words float over her shoulder, 'The best ones are gone.'

The rain has been falling steadily since we left the freeway. We're driving along the slopes and bends towards my new home; a country town in the Queensland hinterland which has a population of 2,530. It's going to inflate to 2,533 once I move in with my two children.

The town has one claim to fame, the double-decker vanilla slice. It features two squares of custard, each square as thick as a mattress, sandwiched between a crunchy wafer, concocted from free-range ingredients and baked in an artisan bakery. It was the lure of sampling this tasty morsel that brought me and my children here, one weekend. We drove through the town and ended up at a sloping 'For Sale' sign on the front paddock of this chicken farm.

Peppy, my Border Collie, is sleeping next to Dad. His grizzly snores are snuffled by the hailstones hitting the side windows, sounding like handfuls of rice thrown against glass. Mum says something, but her words are drowned out by the rumble of the truck and the swish of the wipers.

'What did you say, Mum

'Are you excited about the move, Libby? This new enterprise of yours.'

My mouth falls into a crooked smile. Ever since I purchased the thirty hectares of land with a depilated three-bedroom weatherboard home, Mum has been talking about me as if I'm an entrepreneur bravely venturing into uncharted territory. I'm just taking a risk and hoping it pays off.

'Ask me if I'm excited when the farm is operational, the kids are settled into their new school, and I've renovated the house. Right now, I feel like I'm on the edge of a cliff about to jump with my eyes half open.'

Mum laughs quietly. 'Your Grandpa Mick used to say it should be mandatory that every human take a risk in life; go out on a limb. He used to say it's character building.'

'Character building?' I shake my head. 'Well, I've had enough character building. Don't need anymore.'

My hands are desperately gripping the steering wheel as the truck's tyres slide over the mud and debris on the road. The wipers are barely keeping up with the water gushing down in front of us. A slap of water hits the windscreen and I slam on the brakes as we hit a downward slope of bitumen. 'The tyres on this damn truck must be bald as.' I mumble to myself, but it's loud enough for Dad to lean forward from the back seat.

'Just take it easy, Libby. This road is bloody narrow. We'll be in strife if a bus comes from the opposite direction.'

Despite the simmering anxiety in my stomach, I snuffle a laugh. That's Dad for you. He always tries to say something comforting during stressful circumstances, but his comments never fail to pile on layers of distress to an already dire situation.

Mum rolls her eyes so dramatically they could orbit the sun. She turns to glare at Dad. 'Ray, please. Libby's got this.'

We drive in silence for the next kilometre. The rain eventually stops, and my heart leaps with anticipation as the sky clears to reveal a canvas of blue. I wind down my window and inhale the fresh air. A flicker of hope and positivity ignites within me. The paddocks of lush green grass roll out in front of us, and I imagine my girls, the hens, fossicking and scratching the ground for worms, underneath a canopy of sunshine.

'Have the previous owners left you enough chicken feed to get you through today?' I can feel Dad's concern hovering like a dark shadow from where he sits in the back seat.

Since I purchased the farm, he's had a long list of questions for me. I know that he's worried that I'll sink all of my money into this, and then go bust, but I've incorporated all of my experience from the corporate world into this egg farm. I've spent hours plotting graphs for profit goals, conjuring marketing plans, and targeting budget estimates in the hope that all of that, accompanied by back-breaking work, will make this a successful venture.

'Don't worry Dad, it's all sorted.'

That's my stock standard answer to his barrage of questions. In reality, I've heard enough stories to know that the climate, nature and luck are the true elements that will determine my success or failure. Farming is subject to so many things that can't be controlled.

As we wind into the gravel driveway, Mum points out a rainbow arching over the sky. 'Now that's a good omen, Libby.'

We spend the next two hours moving my furniture from the truck into the house. The French provincial style of furniture sat comfortably in our house on the Gold Coast, but here it looks like the debutante who turned up to a Bachelor and Spinsters Ball dressed in a white formal gown, when everyone else is wearing checked shirts, jeans and RM Williams boots.

The house feels smaller once the furniture has filled every corner. Mum senses my misgivings and puts an arm around my shoulders. 'Cosy,' she says reassuringly.

We saunter outside. Dad rolls up his sleeves. 'Isla and Spencer are going to love this.'

I sigh raggedly as I mull over how they will cope with our move from the city to the country.

'They'll have to get used to the patchy internet out here.'

'Come on,' Mum says. 'The girls must be chomping at the bit to get outside.'

We walk to the barns, our feet sliding in the muddy ruts of the path. The hens have been inside since yesterday afternoon when the previous owners closed the barn doors for the final time. They've retired from this farm, moving to their new home in Rockhampton and left inexperienced me as the next custodian.

When we slide open the large wooden doors, the hens make a dash for the outside, clucking and complaining about being left inside for so long. I walk over to the laying boxes. I'm rewarded with eggs that are slightly warm, with the occasional coat of feathery-down on the speckled shells.

Peppy gambols around the perimeters of the land, his pink tongue lolling out of his mouth with excitement. I point to a flat area, close to the vegetable patch. 'You know how I promised Isla and Spencer a greenhouse for propagating their flower seeds, that's where I'll build it.'

I imagine the future–my teenage children realising their dream of owning a mail-order flower seed business, while I tend to my chickens. The last two years have been shadowed by grief and sadness, but I'm hoping that we'll find our happy places here.

There's a rumble in the distance and all three of us stop and listen. Dad walks out to the front of the property and me, Mum and Peppy all follow him. A semi-trailer pulls up at the front gate. We watch curiously as a dark-haired man with a bush-ranger beard steps out and strides towards us. 'I've got a delivery for Libby Prowse.'

I step forward. 'A delivery? Are you sure it's for me?'

The man stands tall and solid as the trunk of a grey gum. 'Well, this card might explain who it's from.'

I take the envelope from his outstretched hand. Mum's handwriting reads, Happy days for Isla and Spencer in their greenhouse, love from Pops and Nanna.

I wipe my eyes with the back of my hand, trying to suppress the torrent of emotions rising within me. 'Thanks, Mum and Dad. I don't know what to say.'

Mum puts her arm around my waist and Dad rests a hand on my shoulder.

The guy waits for a moment before he says, 'And where would you like me to leave your greenhouse?'

I point to the spot, and he gets back into the semi and drives it down the driveway. When he parks the truck, it takes all four of us to drag the massive, rectangular box to the flat spot that I've chosen.

'I'm going to start building it now,' I say with determination.

'I can help you,' the guy says. 'This was my last delivery for the day, and I've got nothing to go home to.'

'I'll make us coffee,' Mum says. She calls out to Peppy who follows her into the house.

'And I'll program your TV. That's more my domain,' Dad says rather sheepishly. 'Libby can build anything, but I can't even hammer a nail.'

When Mum and Dad walk into the house, the guy gives me a shy smile. 'I'm Craig by the way, and don't worry I've built a few of these. We'll have this together in no time.'

We start setting up the frame. Eventually, the jigsaw of pieces start to resemble a long rectangular building. Craig pulls out a flat carpentry pencil and a notebook from his shirt pocket. We plan shelves, work benches and storage boxes that will need to be built once Isla and Spencer get a feel for the inside layout.

'You just moved into the area?' Craig asks.

'Yeah. We've lived on the coast all our lives. Me and the kids have been dreaming of moving to the country and here we are.'

Craig raises his eyebrows, 'Wow! Big move. Brave of you.'

I fold my arms. 'Necessity, more like it. My husband went to work one day and never returned. He was a construction manager on a building site. He died when a steel girder fell on top of him.'

Craig flinches. 'Ah shit! I'm so sorry.'

'Hey, it's not your fault. Shit happens. It happened two years ago, so it's time for us to tuck our grief deep in our hearts and get on with living. Stuart would have wanted us to be happy.'

We stand together, a pocket of silence between us. I focus on a brown bantam chicken preening herself. 'This is why I moved here with my children. Nature heals.' My words catch on my breath.

Craig stares at the mountains that stand like silent boulders, his hands are on his hips and his feet are slightly apart. He finally says, 'Hits you like a steam train when your life changes like that. Every now and again, it hits me, how it is…now.' He sighs. 'I lost my family five years ago. The old wiring in the house was over a hundred years old and it was next on our list of things to do. Saving up we were, doing one thing at a time when we could afford it, but we should have just done it.'

Craig kicks a small rock on the ground sending it skittering into the distance. 'The old wiring sparked a fire in the roof. I was working interstate at the time. Happened while my family was asleep. They had no hope. My wife and ten-year-old twin boys didn't survive.'

He makes a painful groan and keels over at the waist and I can't help placing a hand on his shoulder. Shock falls through me and my eyes prickle with tears as I search for something to say.

He reaches for his phone and scrolls to a photo. His large, calloused hands cradle his phone with gentleness, as if he's holding a bird with a broken wing. On his screen is an image of his wife and two boys. 'This was taken two days before the fire.' His words have a raw, painful edge to them.

'Craig, I'm sorry.' My hollow words tumble out, and I just want to hug this stranger, because I know how grief can tunnel through your heart, leaving you irreparably broken.

'But they're still with me, here.' He places the heel of his left palm on his chest. 'In the same way that your husband is with you. Our loved ones leave their memories anchored to our hearts.'

He puts his phone into his shirt pocket. 'Everything changed after that. I packed in my job as a CEO of a mining company and started my own business, building greenhouses and garden sheds. It was something I'd always dreamt of doing. Funny thing is, because I lost everything and everyone I'd lived for, I reached the conclusion that I had nothing more to lose if this business venture didn't work out. I live in a caravan park now and I just take life day by day. If I'm having a sad day, I go fishing. I try to be kind to myself; do you know what I mean?'

I make a series of affirming nods. 'I sure do.'

We keep working on the greenhouse and when it's fully built, Craig points to the dirt track from the garden to the greenhouse. 'A little curved concrete path would finish this off. I could help with that if you like.'

I stand up, rub my aching back and smile at him. 'I'd like that very much.' Then I put my hands to my mouth. 'Oh hell! Do I need a permit for this?'

Craig laughs. 'Out here, you can build a sports stadium without a permit, and no one would know.'

I chuckle with him. At least he can still find a way to laugh, despite the tragedy he's experienced.

I shift from one leg to another, my fingers poised in the belt loops of my jeans. 'My teenagers move in tomorrow. We're having a barbecue lunch on Sunday, our first one here, to christen this place. You're welcome to come.'

His face breaks out into a grin. 'Are you sure? I don't want to crash your christening.'

'Aaahhh, come along. My Dad can't hammer a nail, but he's king of the barbecue so bring an appetite.'

Craig's eyes crinkle with a smile.

'And I might enlist your handyman skills for a few other jobs around the house.'

'No problem. Happy to help.' He grins and waves as he drives away.

Sometime later, Mum and Dad are about to take the truck back to the depot. Mum kisses me on the cheek, 'We'll be back tomorrow, with Isla and Spencer.' I lean against her, grateful for their love and support.

That evening, I watch the sunset from the verandah at the back of the house. Peppy sits at my feet. He's worn out after helping me round up the chickens into the barns, safe from foxes and other predators. I think of my darling Stuart, as I stare up at the sky. He's the first star that lights up the sky every night. I think about Craig losing his wife and boys. Life can be horrendously cruel, but the world keeps spinning, day after day. My children gave me a reason to go on. I wonder what helped Craig to piece together the remains of his life.

I breathe in the fresh air and raise my arms, grateful for new beginnings.

Mary Howley is a graduate of the RMIT Associate Degree of Professional Writing and Editing. Her writing has been published online, in magazines and in several anthologies. Mary lives on an acre near Victoria's Yarra Valley, where she loves to walk amongst the fields and vineyards, devising plot twists and creating dilemmas for her characters.

Chapter 41

Honey

by Lisa Ireland

It's a warm November day and I'm standing outside the church in Lindenow.

The light reflected from the white weatherboards makes me blink. I squint and try to identify the figure standing on the church steps. Eventually, my eyes focus and I realise it's Michael Tanner, my childhood friend. Mick has been dead for nearly three years, but he seems so lifelike. I can't look away.

Early morning sounds of the ward loom on the periphery of my consciousness, but I block them out so I can stay with Mick a little longer. He extends a hand in greeting and I try to walk towards him but my feet are lead and the earth is like quicksand beneath them. I can see his mouth opening and closing but no matter how hard I concentrate, I can't make out a thing he's saying.

The church door slams shut and I wake with a start.

It's almost dawn and the morning shift is arriving. I can hear Trina laughing at the nurse's station just outside my door. *Please, God, not her today with her rough hands and raucous laugh; I'm not in the mood.* But it's Louise–my favourite–who breezes through the door.

'Morning, Frank, how was your night?'

I wrinkle my forehead and answer with my eyes.

She understands my reluctance to expend what little breath I have. 'Nightshift banging doors again, eh?' She gets on with the job silently then, checking my vitals efficiently and closing the door quietly behind her when she leaves.

The constant hum of my oxygen supply fills the room and shards of morning sunshine filter in under the battered hospital blind. My thoughts drift to the bees.

I spotted the hive on the roof of the hospital's other wing the day they wheeled me in here. You have to look hard, and it helps if you know what you're looking for. Me, I'm a honey man from way back. My Uncle Ray, God rest his soul, was an apiarist, and he ran the family business. When I was a boy he'd suit me up and we'd go check the hives together. There were six of us kids on the farm: my brother, my sister, and me, as well as Ray's three sons. Out of us all, I was the only one who never got stung. Once, my brother had to go to the hospital after a worker bee got him on the eyelid. Normie looked like he'd gone three rounds in the ring with Muhammad Ali. It was even worse than the shiners we used to cop from our dad. Allergic, the doctor said.

But not me.

Mum said I was an old-fashioned bee-charmer. Uncle Ray said it was because I followed his rules. I reckon it was because I had no fear.

Our lives changed for the better once Uncle Ray took us in. Mum called him her 'Ray of sunshine' and as corny as that was, I think he liked it. He came for us on a hot December night not long after my tenth birthday. My old man was gone. Cleared out the moment Mum yelled at him that her big brother was on his way. At the farm, Aunty Gwen welcomed us with lemon cordial and a fresh batch of honey joys.

Ray left the farm to me. 'You're the only one who loves the bees as much as me, Frankie,' he said before he died.

Of course, some of the cousins didn't see it that way and they contested the will. In the end I had to borrow money to buy them out, but it was worth every cent I paid. Those bees have given me liquid gold. And I think old Ray would be proud as Punch if he knew that *Ray of Sunshine Honey* is in supermarkets all across the country now.

I close my eyes again and try to visualise the farm. I always said they'd take me out of the homestead in a box, but instead I've ended up here, hooked up to a plethora of machines. Evelyn tried her best, I know she did, but it was too hard to manage all this at home, even with paid help. 'I'm scared, Frank,' she confessed after one particularly bad night.

And that was that.

As sleep envelops me I find myself back at the church. Maggie Ferguson is there, first girl I ever kissed. She takes me by the hand and we walk towards the church steps. Maggie died over a decade ago. I remember because Evelyn got her knickers in a knot. 'Why would you want to go to an old flame's funeral, Frank? What will people think?'

I was never in love with Maggie, but I was fond of her. She was pretty in a wholesome sort of way. Sweet and undemanding. All she ever wanted was to settle down with a nice local fella and have a few kids. Sometimes I wonder if I should have married her.

Might have made life easier.

But the heart isn't interested in *easy*. Evelyn, a city girl with fancy clothes and an abundance of sass, was the only one for me. At first, my Evie wasn't cut out for country living, but she married me anyway and created a life to suit herself. Lord knows the locals didn't know what to make of her at first. Back then she was like a meteorite that had crashed into the centre of our sleepy town. These days she's the brilliant sun our community revolves around.

Maggie leads me into the church and I see Mick standing in the vestibule with his gums flapping, but no sound is coming out. I stare at him for a moment, trying to figure out what he is trying to say, but once again his message eludes me.

When the church door slams this time, I open my eyes and see my wife coming through the door.

Evelyn carries her grief around like a handbag. It seems she can pick it up and put it down at will. No matter how bad she feels for me, her life still goes on outside these four walls. Knowing this brings me resentment and comfort in equal parts.

'Hello, darling, did I wake you?' She doesn't wait for an answer. 'I know it's early but I just wanted to bring you some fresh pyjamas, because I know you're out of clean ones. I can't stay long. I've got that charity lunch today. We're raising money for the respiratory ward, remember?'

'Bees?' I whisper.

She forces a smile. 'I'll check.' She fumbles with the well-worn blind and as it retracts the morning sun streams in. Evelyn stands at the window, pretending to concentrate hard. 'There they are!'

After thirty-six years of marriage, I know when my wife is faking. I don't think she's ever seen the bees here; probably thinks they're a figment of my imagination.

She busies herself with little tasks, folding my pyjamas and collecting the dirty washing. She looks at me as little as possible.

I understand. Truly I do. It hurts me to look at her too. She's still beautiful and vibrant, full of life, while I'm a husk, clinging on to her like a limpet.

She wept like a child when the doctor first gave us the news. I rubbed her back and comforted her, telling her everything would be all right. 'But I'm nothing without you, Frank,' she sobbed. 'I can't bear the thought of you not being here.'

That was three years ago now, and my Evie's grown tougher in the interim. She's seen things and *done* things no wife should ever have to. And while she's never complained, I know it's changed the way she feels about me, the way she sees me. Christ, how could it not? We've become *carer* and *patient*, not husband and wife.

Evelyn would deny it, but I imagine it's hard to picture your partner as an object of desire once you've had to wipe their arse.

'Sorry, Frank, but I've got to go.' She bends to kiss me on the lips. Her familiar scent invades my nostrils and our eyes lock. 'I love you,' she whispers.

'How about a sponge bath?' I manage to wheeze out.

'Oh Frank!' She socks me playfully on the arm and grins as she pulls away. For a moment I see laughter, not pity, in her eyes.

Hours go by before the distinctive jangle of my daughter's jewellery alerts me that she is near. Lizzie's come home from some far flung place in Asia to spend time with me.

Before I die.

Of course, no one says that openly, but we all know why she's here.

There's a thread of restlessness in her that she just can't seem to quell. As a teenager she butted heads with Evelyn on an almost daily basis. Too much alike those two, although neither would admit it.

She comes to sit by me without uttering a word. Her hand reaches for mine, and as our fingers entwine I notice she has a small bee tattooed on her wrist. I run my thumb over it and cock a questioning eyebrow. 'Mum?'

She laughs. 'What do you think?'

A smile twitches at the corner of my mouth as I imagine Evelyn's horror.

Lizzie digs into that cavernous backpack of hers, pulls out a small pair of binoculars and presses them against her eyes. She walks to the window and stands there for a long time. Eventually, she turns to me and says, 'They're gone, Dad.'

Tears well in my eyes and begin to slide down my cheeks.

'It's okay,' she says. 'It's just like you told me when I was little. It's nature's way. A season for everything. It was time. We knew the bees wouldn't stay forever.'

There's a buoyant quality to her words. Each one lifts a weight from me. My lungs fill with the air I so desperately need and I feel light and euphoric, almost superhuman. 'Be kind to your mother,' I say and she nods.

'I'll do my best. I can't promise to be perfect, Dad, but I promise I'll be here.'

Mick's back again and this time he's shaking my hand. 'Hello, Frank.'

'Mick, I can hear you!'

'Follow me,' he says.

We walk down the church aisle, through the vestry and out the rear door.

Now the farm is spread out before me. I stand at the gate to appreciate the sight of the old homestead bathed in sunlight. I hear the crunch of gravel and look to the driveway to see a man and a woman walking towards me.

Uncle Ray reaches the gate and drags it open. 'Welcome home,' he says.

My mother holds out her hands and offers me a jar of honey.

Lisa Ireland is an Australian author of historical and contemporary fiction. Her novels include *The One and Only Dolly Jamieson, The Secret Life of Shirley Sullivan, The Art of Friendship* and *The Shape of Us*. Lisa has also written several rural romances, including the Australian bestseller, *Feels Like Home*. Her eighth novel, *The Studio Girls,* will be released in April 2024. Lisa lives in rural Victoria with her husband and dog, Lulu.

About the Editors

Anjanette Fennell is a literary agent, writing coach and podcaster who has been helping writers find their way to the page and publication for more than a decade. She happily reads more than she writes, but does let the muse take over now and again. Check out her writerly convos with authors at Writers Talking podcast.

Anne-marie Taplin is an Australian author, editor, copywriter and artist. Her gift book *Being Mummy* was published in 2007 by Wakefield Press and launched simultaneously with online platform, *Parenting Express*. Curated for more than a decade, Anne-marie published international creative writing about raising children. Her publishing history includes dozens of memoirs, short stories and feature articles across literary and trade outlets, from *MamaMia* to *Overland*. She is the devoted mama of two sons.

Megan Close Zavala is a book editor and writing coach based in the United States. A former literary agent, Megan has worked on well over a thousand script and book projects. She guides clients across the globe through all stages of their manuscript production, from first idea to last page, providing both editorial and mindset support. A lifelong bibliophile and wordsmith, nothing makes her happier than curling up with a good book.